CAMBRIDGE
HISTORY OF POLITICAL THOUGHT

——

The Dutch Revolt

CAMBRIDGE TEXTS IN THE
HISTORY OF POLITICAL THOUGHT

Series Editors:

RAYMOND GEUSS, *Professor of Political Science, Columbia University*
QUENTIN SKINNER, *Professor of Political Science in the University of Cambridge*

This series is intended to make available to students the most important texts required for an understanding of the history of political thought. The scholarship of the present generation has greatly expanded our sense of the range of authors indispensable for such an understanding, and the series will reflect those developments. It will also include a number of less well-known works, in particular those needed to establish the intellectual contexts that in turn help to make sense of the major texts. The principal aim, however, will be to produce new versions of the major texts themselves, based on the most up-to-date scholarship. The preference will always be for complete texts, and a special feature of the series will be to complement individual texts, within the compass of a single volume, with subsidiary contextual material. Each volume will contain an introduction on the historical identity and contemporary significance of the text concerned, as well as such student aids as notes for further reading and chronologies of the principal events in a thinker's life.

For a complete list of titles published in the series, please see end of book

The Dutch Revolt

EDITED AND TRANSLATED BY

MARTIN VAN GELDEREN

Assistant Professor, Department of History,
Technical University of Berlin

CAMBRIDGE
UNIVERSITY PRESS

CAMBRIDGE UNIVERSITY PRESS
Cambridge, New York, Melbourne, Madrid, Cape Town, Singapore, São Paulo

Cambridge University Press
The Edinburgh Building, Cambridge CB2 2RU, UK

Published in the United States of America by Cambridge University Press, New York

www.cambridge.org
Information on this title: www.cambridge.org/9780521391221

First published 1993
Reprinted 2001

A catalogue record for this publication is available from the British Library

Library of Congress Cataloguing in Publication data
Dutch revolt / edited and translated by Martyn van Gelderen.
p.   cm. – (Cambridge texts in the history of political
thought)
English translation of five texts originally published in the Low
Countries, 1570–1590. Cf. Pref.
Includes bibliographical references (p.) and index.
Contents: A defence and true declaration (1570) – Address and
opening (1576) – Brief discourse (1579) – Political education
(1582) – Short exposition (1587).
ISBN 0-521-39122-9 – ISBN 0-521-39809-6 (pbk.)
1. Netherlands – Politics and government – 1556–1648
I. Gelderen, Martin van.   II. Series.
DH185.D88   1992
949.2′03–dc20   92–3462 CIP

ISBN-13 978-0-521-39122-1 hardback
ISBN-10 0-521-39122-9 hardback

ISBN-13 978-0-521-39809-1 paperback
ISBN-10 0-521-39809-6 paperback

Transferred to digital printing 2006

Contents

Preface

This volume presents five texts which were published in the Low Countries between 1570 and 1590, during the crucial decades of what is nowadays labelled, with understatement, the 'Dutch Revolt'. From 1555 a series of revolutionary events led to the abjuration of Philip II by the States General of the Dutch provinces in 1581 and to the subsequent foundation of the 'Dutch Republic of the Seven United Provinces', one of the great powers of the seventeenth century.

Despite the general recognition that the rise of the Dutch Republic was of major political, cultural and economic importance for the course of European history, historians have tended to neglect the political thought of the Dutch Revolt. However, as more than 2,000 publications (published between 1555 and 1590) exemplify, the political debate of the Revolt was not only immense, but also comprehensive and, above all, passionate. The purpose of this volume is to make some of the most important texts of the Revolt available in a modern edition.

The first major issue which the protagonists of the Revolt had to confront was how to justify first the protest and resistance against the government of Philip II and eventually his abjuration by the States General. Closely related to the reflections on the limits of political obedience and the justice of political resistance was a fundamental debate on the true and desirable character of the Dutch political order. This quest for 'the best state of the commonwealth' and for good government focused on the problem of sovereignty, on the relationship between political and ecclesiastical authority and on the question of religious toleration.

Although other problems are not neglected, the main focus of the five texts in this volume is on the justice of political resistance and on the search for the optimal commonwealth. The texts have been selected because they not only exemplify the political ideas developed during the Dutch Revolt with regard to these issues, but are also amongst the most innovative treatises of the Revolt's political literature. Their ideological importance is discussed in the Introduction, which is an attempt to locate the following texts in the political and intellectual context of the Dutch Revolt. The introductory essay relies heavily on my monograph 'The Political Thought of the Dutch Revolt, 1550–1590', published by Cambridge University Press.

In their original version my translations of the sixteenth-century texts were a frail compromise between my knowledge of modern English and sixteenth-century Dutch and French. As such the translations have been revised and greatly improved by Simon Kuper, whom I should like to thank for his meticulous work.

I should also like to thank the editors of the 'Cambridge Texts in the History of Political Thought' and Richard Fisher from Cambridge University Press for their encouragement and patience. Finally I thank Raimund Schulz and Marie-Ange Delen for their assistance in retracting some of the more obscure references in the following texts.

Introduction

I

On a late October afternoon in 1555, the political elite of the Low Countries gathered in the Great Hall of the Ducal Palace in Brussels. The principal nobles, clergymen and representatives of the major towns in the Netherlands had come to bid farewell to Charles V. The Emperor, a native of Ghent, answered for his life and deeds and renounced an impressive number of titles in favour of his son Philip. It was a ceremony of both grandeur and disillusionment. For although Charles seemed a broken man, the very fact that his son inherited all titles covering the 'Seventeen Provinces of the Netherlands' as they were known – such as Duke of Brabant, Duke of Guelders, Count of Flanders, Count of Holland and Lord of Friesland – could be seen as the crown on the policy of centralization of the Burgundian–Habsburg dynasty in the Low Countries. After the formal unification of the Low Countries, which in 1549 had been declared 'one and unbreakable' by 'pragmatic sanction', Philip was the first, and, one should add, the last to govern the Low Countries as a whole.[1]

The new sovereign was probably the sole dissonant in the political theatre played out in Brussels on that October day. As Philip did not speak Dutch, Antoine Perrenot,[2] Bishop of Arras, had to answer for

---

[1] In this introduction words such as 'Dutch', 'Netherlands' and 'Low Countries' refer to the 'Seventeen Provinces' in the north-west of continental Europe, which included the present Benelux and French Flanders in the north-west of present-day France.
[2] For Perrenot see 'Biographical Notes'.

his lord. In a memorable speech he pointed out that it was natural for the prince to protect and uphold the liberty of the country.[3]

Perrenot, Lord of Granvelle, was an important figure in Philip's Dutch government, whose policy soon became increasingly unpopular. As usual, taxes were a major source of conflict. In an attempt to improve his catastrophic financial situation, and to make the provinces pay for their government, Philip virtually started his reign by proposing a series of new taxes. The proposal was vigorously opposed by the States of the core provinces Brabant, Flanders and Holland, and Philip was dragged into the quagmire of Dutch bargaining politics. The fact that Philip could not levy taxes without the States' consent was an important power resource for these provincial representative assemblies, who saw themselves as the main counterweight to central government. The States were of the opinion that important political decisions such as those concerning successions, financial policy, legal issues and foreign affairs should not be taken without their counsel and consent. The provincial States were united in the States General, which had been created by the Burgundian Dukes in the course of the fifteenth century to foster the idea of unity amongst the provinces, which in turn regarded the States General primarily as a useful instrument for increasing their influence on central policy. In negotiations, as Philip was to find out, their deputies never had full powers to act. The basic rule of the decision-making process was that provincial deputies could only grant what their principals, the estates far away in the provinces, had allowed. This not only made it almost impossible for the sovereign to exert the charismatic powers of his office, it also turned the negotiations into a time-consuming affair with great possibilities for creative obstructionism. Although eventually the States agreed to levy taxes, Philip interpreted their behaviour as an attempt to tilt the balance of power in favour of a sort of parliamentary government. When he left the Low Countries in 1559, Philip decided that the States General formed a grave threat to royal power and that, therefore, it should not be summoned again.

Soon, however, the king was to find out that there were other sources of opposition in the Low Countries. The 1559 papal bull 'Super universas' decreed a thorough reorganization of the rather outdated diocesan structure of the Catholic church in the Nether-

[3] *Oratione di Carlo V, Imperadore de Romani, da S. Ces. Maesta recitate nella dieta di Brussell* ... (Florence, 1556), fol. B.

lands. The plan aroused vigorous opposition. The noble members of the Council of State – the main governmental council of the Low Countries – had not been consulted at all. Moreover, the papal bull gave Philip II the right to appoint the bishops, who in most cases would acquire membership in the provincial States, thereby strengthening Philip's grip on the States. Granvelle, for example, who was appointed Archbishop of Malines, became a principal member of the important States of Brabant.

The conflict over ecclesiastical reorganization strongly contributed to a rupture between the leading nobles and Granvelle, who became part of the inner circle of the new Governess, Margaret of Parma,[4] and was soon regarded as the top policymaker in Brussels. As such he was, however wrongly, considered to be the evil genius behind the plan for ecclesiastical reorganization. In the eyes of noble members like Lamoraal, Count of Egmont, and William, Prince of Orange,[5] Granvelle was usurping power – their power. Egmont was a celebrated military commander, second only to the Duke of Alva in Philip II's forces. William of Nassau, the oldest son of a German Lutheran noble family, had inherited the principality of Orange together with numerous rich manors in Dutch provinces in 1544, which made him one of the principal nobles of the Netherlands.

These grandees had strong political ambitions, which since Philip's accession had been repeatedly thwarted. Within the Council of State, for example, the high nobles were continuously confronted with the overbearing presence and influence of professional bureaucrats such as Granvelle. The resulting struggle for power eventually ended with the withdrawal of Granvelle in 1564. The grandees revelled in the triumph. Philip II, however, had by no means accepted the policy demands of the high nobles. Above all, the crucial issue of the persecution of heretics remained unresolved.

The harsh policy of repression with regard to Protestant heretics, as favoured by Philip II, was highly controversial in the Low Countries and met with mounting opposition. In addition to the rising number of Protestants there was a large 'centre group' of people who, though themselves not Protestant, despised harsh persecution for legal, political and humanitarian reasons. The towns considered the growing activity of inquisitors an important threat to their autonomy

---

[4] For Margaret of Parma see 'Biographical Notes'.
[5] For Egmont and Orange see 'Biographical Notes'.

and privileges. Particularly the 'jus de non evocando', the right to be put on trial only by the court of Aldermen in one's own town, was threatened. Moreover, the severe persecution of heresy was regarded as an important threat to the cherished values of public order and civic unity. The towns also had economic reasons for opposing the inquisition, as its actions threatened commercial relations with unorthodox foreign merchants. Finally, in the circles of the town magistrates and the nobles many were appalled at the idea of executing people merely because they happened to have another version of the Christian faith.

Hopes for moderation, however, were crushed. On the one hand, Philip II insisted on his rigorous religious policy, as he informed the Dutch in his famous letters from the woods of Segovia, which were an outright rejection of the demands for moderation. On the other hand a process of gradual radicalization took place within the ranks of the Reformed Protestants. At around 1560 they had come into the open. During Easter 1562 the first public sermon was held in Flanders, followed by the first armed 'mass-meeting' at the churchyard of the Flemish village of Boeschepe in July 1562. Increasingly the arrests and executions of Protestants provoked demonstrations and riots, and successful attempts were made to free those who had been imprisoned. In the spring of 1566 large-scale hedge-preaching started; in August the Iconoclastic Fury, beginning in the Flemish 'Westkwartier', started to sweep over the Low Countries. The culmination of the radicalization process among Reformed Protestants was the decision in the autumn of 1566 at a synod in Antwerp to defend their religion with military means, a reaction to the withdrawal of far-reaching concessions the Governess had made under the pressure of the Iconoclastic Fury. Chances for a middle course were crushed and the grandees, wavering between upholding their moderate principles and supporting the Governess in restoring public order, were forced to make a choice. Eventually this led to a split. Whereas Egmont, Hoorne and many others swore a new oath of loyalty to the government, William of Orange decided to go into exile. He returned to his family in Dillenburg. The defeat of Protestant armies, the surrender of the besieged towns Tournai and Valenciennes to government troops, and the arrival of the Duke of Alva as the commander of a Spanish army, commissioned by Philip II to restore order, were devastating blows to both the Reformed Protestant cause and the pleas for moderation. Like Orange, many opted for exile.

The intellectual legacy of what can be seen as the first phase of the Dutch Revolt was an impressive number of political treatises, which protested against Philip's policy of religious persecution, demanded moderation and started to discuss the questions of the limits of obedience and the legitimacy of political resistance.

From the very beginning many of these treatises accused the government in Brussels of hurting the very liberty it was supposed to uphold. However, as Jacob van Wesembeeke amply explained in a number of political tracts published during the late 1560s, liberty was the political value *par excellence*. According to Wesembeeke the Dutch people in particular had esteemed and cherished liberty throughout the centuries, as became particularly manifest when attempts were made to take away the 'old liberty', 'the liberty of which they [the Dutch] with an exceptional and extremely powerful assiduity had always been very great lovers, supporters and advocates'.[6]

Wesembeeke and others emphasized the intrinsic connection between the liberty and the prosperity of the Netherlands, an idea that was familiar to town magistrates and had been used throughout the past centuries in debates with encroaching central institutions. In 1568 the *Complaint of the sorrowful land of the Netherlands*, for example, argued that 'Marchandise', 'Manufacture' and 'Negotiations' were the sisters of 'Liberté', who herself was said to be the daughter of the Netherlands.[7]

In the political literature of the Revolt it was argued that the political order had originally been created with the deliberate aim of protecting liberty. This goal should be achieved by means of a constitutional framework consisting of a set of fundamental laws, the privileges, rights, freedoms and old customs, and a number of institutions, in particular the States.

Dutch privileges consisted of a diversity of charters acquired or extorted by cities, guilds, crafts, clergy and nobility from imperial princes, vassals, dukes and counts, who had ruled the Netherlands during the late medieval period. Some of them dealt explicitly with

---

[6] J. van Wesembeeke, *De Beschriivinge van den geschiedenissen in der Religien saken toeghedragen in den Nederlanden* (1569), p. 12. For Wesembeeke see 'Biographical Notes'.
[7] *Complainte de la desolée terre du Pais Bas* (1568), p. 3.

the division of power between prince and subjects, as shown by the privileges of 1477 (granted, or rather negotiated, on the occasion of the unexpected death of Duke Charles the Bold on the battle fields of Nancy which had led to a grave political crisis) and the famous Joyous Entry of Brabant, a constitutional document to which, from 1356, every Duke of Brabant had to take a solemn oath on the occasion of his inauguration by the Brabant States.[8]

The 1477 privileges and the Joyous Entry had been principal vehicles for formulating political rights and duties. They offered the inhabitants protection against arbitrary and corrupt rule and sought to guarantee civic rights, especially with regard to the administration of justice. Both the Joyous Entry and the 1477 privileges contained a clause of disobedience which stated that if the prince violated the privileges, the subjects and, as the 1477 Grand Privilege added, 'each of them in particular', had the right to disobey him, to refuse him services until he had repaired his ways. Finally, privileges such as the Grand Privilege and the Joyous Entry contained articles which restricted central power and articulated claims to participation in the decision-making process on behalf of the provinces, towns and inhabitants of the Low Countries. Thus, the 1477 privileges sought to decentralize the administration of justice, to strengthen the grip of the provinces on central policy, to guarantee the respect of all privileges and to strengthen the position of the States General.

As such the privileges of 1477 were the expression of 'a conception of a federal state, dominated by the great cities'.[9] Throughout the fourteenth and fifteenth century the towns of Brabant and Flanders in particular sought to create a political order marked by a weak but efficient central government and dominated by cities which wanted to act as self-governing city-republics.[10]

The 1477 privileges and the Joyous Entry were amongst the principal means to achieve this ideal of self-governing independence.

---

[8] It was confirmed again in 1406, 1427, 1430, 1467, 1477, 1494, in 1515 (by Charles V) and in 1549 (by Philip II).
[9] W.P. Blockmans, 'La signification constitutionnelle des privilèges de Marie de Bourgogne (1477)', in W.P. Blockmans (ed.), *1477. Le privilège géneral et les privilèges régionaux de Marie de Bourgogne pour les Pays-Bas*, in the series 'Ancien Pays et Assemblées d'états', vol. 80 (Kortrijk-Heule, 1985), p. 516.
[10] See W.P. Blockmans, 'Alternatives to monarchical centralization: the great tradition of Revolt in Flanders and Brabant' in H.G. Koenigsberger (ed.), *Republiken und Republikanismus im Europa der frühen Neuzeit* (Munich, 1988), pp. 145-54.

Thus these charters were an important part of the late medieval legacy of constitutionalist and republican ideals in the Low Countries and in appealing to them the political literature of the Revolt placed itself firmly within a well-established tradition.

II

For Orange, Wesembeeke and their friends in exile, the political situation worsened rapidly. Alva, the 'Iron Duke' and Philip's new Governor, eliminated the remnants of opposition by means of a forceful new tribunal, soon called the 'blood council' as it executed more than a thousand people, including the counts of Egmont and Hoorne. Moreover an invasion led by William of Orange failed dismally due to lack of overt popular support, a disastrous shortage of funds and Alva's military superiority. The prince was forced to withdraw his forces from the Netherlands. Again in exile he renewed his efforts to set up a more effective resistance movement and to organize another military campaign for what was in his view the liberation of the Netherlands. Foreign aid was crucial to the success of such plans. Thus Orange sought to consolidate his contacts with French Huguenot leaders and with German princes. One of the attempts to enlist German support was a petition presented on 26 October 1570 to the Reichstag at Speyer, the *Libellus supplex Imperatoriae Maiestati*. The English translation, *A Defence and true Declaration of the things lately done in the lowe Countrey whereby may easily be seen to whom all the beginning and cause of the late troubles and calamities is to be imputed* – the first text in this volume – was published in 1571 by the office of John Daye in London.

Until recently it was assumed that the Reformed Protestant minister Petrus Dathenus was the author of the *Defence*.[11] New research, however, has argued that Marnix van St Aldegonde, a principal assistant and friend of William of Orange and a leading publicist of the Revolt, was the author of the petition.[12] The work was translated

---

[11] See, for example, Th. Ruys, *Petrus Dathenus* (Utrecht, 1919), pp. 265–7.
[12] See D. Nauta, 'Marnix auteur van de Libellus Supplex aan de rijksdag van Spiers (1570)', *Nederlands Archief voor Kerkgeschiedenis*, 55 (1975), pp. 151–70. Nauta's argument is based on a letter in which Marnix mentions that he has been asked to write a request to the German Reichstag, and on a comparison between the argument of Marnix's 1567 *Vraye narration et apologie* and the *Libellus supplex*. Of course, the striking similarity does not necessarily mean that Marnix was the author of the *Libellus supplex*.

by Elias Newcomen (1550–1614), perhaps at Cambridge where he was a student and later a fellow of Magdalene College.

The *Defence* offered both an account of the origins and causes of the troubles in the Netherlands and a defence of the Dutch exiles and their activities. It asserted that Europe was afflicted by the conspiracies of 'certain idle men', who under the cloak of religion tried as inquisitors to usurp civil government. For more than fifty years the inhabitants of the Netherlands had patiently endured the attempts to frustrate hope for liberty of religion and to introduce 'a far more grievous tyranny', which would deprive the Dutch 'of all the residue of their right and liberty'.[13] In fact it had been their goal to turn the country into a kingdom, to have it, as the *Defence* put it, 'reduced into one body, and made subject to one form of laws and jurisdiction and brought to the name and title of a kingdom'.[14]

With great eagerness the conspirators had sought to destroy the privileges of the Netherlands. They had 'espied' that the flourishing country was not only well defended militarily 'with strong towns and castles', but also with 'good laws and ordinances, and with large privileges, prerogatives, immunities and other liberties'.[15] In other words, the conspirators had acknowledged that the privileges were the fundamental laws of the country, whose purpose was to guarantee the country's liberty and thereby to protect and foster its prosperity.

The role of the conspirators, Granvelle being a principal exponent, was unravelled in detail in the *Defence*. Their main focus, it argued, was on the position of the States. Continuously, according to the treatise, they tried to undermine the authority of the States' assemblies, for in their view 'the ancient liberty of assembly of the estates in parliaments' was a serious threat to 'the power of the prince'.[16] The *Defence* pointed out that following the 'most ancient usage of their forefathers' and 'the promises and covenants of the princes themselves confirmed with their oaths', the prince had no authority to undertake any action that affected the liberty of the people and the authority of the laws without 'the will and assent of the estates of the whole country'.[17]

The petition follows and extends the language and arguments as set up by earlier treatises and although Marnix was undoubtedly one of the main publicists, his line of argument was by no means unique.

[13] *A Defence and true Declaration* . . . (London, 1571), p. xxiii.
[14] Ibid., fol. A7.   [15] Ibid., fol. A6.   [16] Ibid., fol. A7.   [17] Ibid.

Thus the importance of the States in the political order of the Netherlands was stressed as being 'the only stay and remedy of all mischief and public calamities'. In this conception of the political order the prince was primarily a guardian of right and law, who was subject to the authority of the States, by whom he was elected and admitted and without whose assent no important political decision could be taken. Therefore the *Defence* could assert that 'the princes have in all ages from time to time been subject to the power of the general Parliaments, have been elected by them and confirmed of them, without whose assent and authority they never would decree anything, and it is manifestly provided and established by the privileges of Brabant and the customs of Flanders that they never have authority to do it hereafter.[18] In underpinning the claim that the prince was bound by his contractual obligations, as laid down in the privileges, the treatise referred to the works of the fourteenth-century commentators Bartolus of Sassoferrato and Baldus de Ubaldis. In fact it was one of the first deliberate attempts to locate Dutch arguments within the broader European framework of Roman Law.

As the *Defence* pointed out, the attack on the authority of the States had been a leading theme in the protests against the policy of the conspirators. The treatise rejected the accusations that these protests had been unlawful, arguing that the Joyous Entry granted the inhabitants of Brabant a right of petition and referring to its clause of disobedience. The treatise admitted that in spite of their great patience and humbleness, ultimately the inhabitants, facing a most gruesome tyranny, had resorted to armed resistance and as such could be accused of rebellion. However, so the *Defence* argued, any accusation in this direction should take the horrors of the new tyranny into account. At this point the blame was put directly on the shoulders of Philip II. As the petition put it, 'let it be so that they [who had resorted to armed resistance] were rebels, is it lawful therefore for the king to violate his faithful promise, to pervert the laws both of God and man, and to pollute all things both holy and profane with this unaccustomed tyranny?'.[19]

The *Defence* was a powerful reformulation of views that had been articulated during the 1560s, claiming that the foundation of the Dutch political order was a trinity of liberty as the crucial political

[18] Ibid.
[19] Ibid., fol. G2.

value, privileges as the constitutional guarantees of liberty, and the States as the guardians of the privileges. Although the importance of religion was not played down and the *Defence* presented an urgent call for freedom of conscience and religion, armed resistance was primarily depicted as a defence of the liberty of the country and its inhabitants against the attempts to turn the Netherlands into a kingdom, depriving it of its privileges and freedom. In short, from this perspective the Dutch Revolt was above all a fight for liberty.

III

In 1572 the provinces of Holland and Zeeland unexpectedly and to a certain extent reluctantly became the centre of the Revolt. First, on 1 April 1572, Orange's 'naval forces', the pirate-like 'Sea Beggars' captured the town of Brill in Holland. Soon the Prince followed with a second invasion supported by Huguenot leaders and indeed the French crown. After the massacre of Huguenot leaders on Saint Bartholomew's eve French support fell away, and Alva was able to regain the military initiative. Eventually Orange was forced to withdraw to Holland, thinking he would find his grave in the province of water, dikes and towns. However, Spain's lack of money and mutinies by Spanish troops undermined the vigour of Alva's campaign. Moreover, the brutality of Spanish forces, showing little respect for the laws of medieval warfare with regard to the treatment of reconquered towns, encouraged Haarlem, Alkmaar and Leiden to mount a firm defence, which made it impossible for Alva to complete his 'reconquest'.

To settle their internal affairs and make arrangements for financing their defence, Holland and Zeeland embarked on a revolutionary political course, which led to the construction of a parliamentary regime, guided by the spirit and timeless energy of William of Orange, who had been acclaimed Stadholder.[20] Gradually the two provinces moved towards political independence, and in the autumn of 1575 the States of Holland started to discuss the possibility of renouncing Philip II.

A few months later, in March 1576, the political situation in the

---

[20] As provincial governor the Stadholder was traditionally the direct substitute of the sovereign, who appointed him. William of Orange had been appointed Stadholder of Holland in 1559 by Philip II; he lost the job in 1567.

Low Countries changed dramatically, due to the death of the Governor who had succeeded Alva in 1573, Don Luis de Requesens. Although officially the Council of State became in charge of the government of the provinces under Spanish control, a number of provincial States such as those of Flanders, Hainaut and above all Brabant exploited the moment and seized the political initiative to press for a settlement with Holland and Zeeland. The programme of what again can be seen as a 'centre group' demanded the withdrawal of all foreigners from the Netherlands, the return to the old way of governing with a prominent place for the States, and some concessions to the Protestants. The aim was to get rid of the mutinying and ravaging Spanish troops in particular and of Spanish officials in general, in order to reinstitute traditional Dutch self-governance.

It was in this situation that the *Address and Opening to make a good, blessed and general peace in the Netherlands* was written.[21] The purpose of the author was to persuade the States General to open negotiations with Holland and Zeeland, in order to re-establish peace, privileges and (therefore) prosperity. As a consequence the *Address* put full emphasis on the position of the States within the political order.

In outlining the Dutch political order the treatise made the revolutionary move of contending that the Netherlands never had been governed by way of monarchy but always 'with right and justice, through a republican or rational civic policy'.[22] In this republic, so it asserted, the prince, though present, was no more than 'a servant and professor of the rights [and] laws', who only became lord of the country after he had been accepted by the States. Being 'elected from the whole generality . . . to represent the entire corps', the States had the right and principal duty of protecting and upholding the liberties and privileges of the country and the common peace and unity with 'power and force' against anyone who tried to violate them, even if it was the lord of the country himself.

In supporting this claim the *Address* offered a detailed analysis of a long list of late medieval charters and alliances amongst the towns of Brabant. The main purpose was to make clear that at crucial historical

---

[21] As the treatise refers to the ongoing siege of Zierikzee, it must have been written between 5 March 1576 (the death of Requesens) and 2 July 1576 (the day Zierikzee surrendered).

[22] *Vertoog ende openinghe om een goede, salighe ende generale vrede te maken in dese Nederlanden* (1576), fol. A5.

moments the towns, those of Brabant in particular, had shaped the political order. In this way a powerful constitutional argument was made for the political power and, almost by implication, the right of resistance of the States.

However, the treatise did not only elaborate a constitutional argument for the States' power and right of resistance. It also went beyond previous formulations by offering a more general reflection on the nature of the political order which resulted in the conclusion that, as a general political principle, it was fundamentally mistaken to discard any right of resistance.

Princes, the *Address* asserted, 'ought to stand under the laws'. They had been established to govern in accordance with the laws and rights of the community, whose welfare was the supreme law of politics. The community, so the treatise emphasized with a classic formulation, 'was not created for the sake of the princes, but they for the sake of the community'.[23] Therefore if the prince forsook his duty and oath and sought to govern the country at will, it was 'better to fall into disgrace with a prince' who acted as a tyrant, than to 'spoil, against right and reason, his own Fatherland and to incur the curse of the oppressed community and the wrath of God'.[24] In the case of tyranny the higher cause of the common good simply commanded resistance.

In short, the *Address* not only offered a refined example of the constitutional argument that the Dutch political order was built on liberty, privileges and the States, but also defended the right of resistance on behalf of the States as a fundamental principle of the art of politics, whose principal aim was to serve the common good of the *res publica*. For these reasons the treatise should be regarded an important moment in the development of the political thought of the Dutch Revolt.

IV

On 8 November 1576 the Pacification of Ghent, the 'firm and unbreakable friendship and peace' amongst all Dutch provinces, was concluded. The provinces vowed to assist each other 'with counsel and deed, goods and blood' and, above all, to get rid of 'Spanish soldiers and other foreigners and strangers'. Once the foreigners

[23] Ibid., fol. C4.
[24] Ibid.

were expelled, the States General would get together to settle all remaining issues including the religious question. Meanwhile the Pacification suspended the edicts concerning the persecution of heretics, certifying that the exercise of the Roman Catholic religion would not be hindered.

The Pacification was not the 'firm and unbreakable peace' it claimed to be. The most pressing problems – the attitude towards the king and the religious question – remained unresolved, and different factions continued to pursue their contrasting programmes, especially in the southern provinces.

On the one hand a powerful group of southern high nobles and provincial Governors within the States General, under the leadership of the Duke of Aerschot,[25] wanted to ward off the rise to power of William of Orange and to preserve the ties with Philip II as much as possible. The group advocated a return to the system of *dominium politicum et regale*, as it had been under Charles V. The privileges were to be reasserted and the States should play a prominent role in the government of the country. In this view, Philip II was to remain sovereign over the Netherlands, although his sovereignty would be far from absolute. Concerning the religious question, this group probably wanted the Netherlands to remain as loyal to the Roman Catholic church as possible.

On the other hand, thanks to the so-called 'democratic policy'[26] of William of Orange, revolutionary committees were formed in the major towns of Brabant and Flanders, first in Brussels and subsequently in Antwerp and Ghent, which started to dominate town politics. All of them were staunch supporters of the Prince of Orange; many turned out to be radical Reformed Protestants. Ghent in particular embarked on a truly revolutionary course, leading to the formation of a Reformed republic, the 'Geneva of Flanders',[27] whose programme longed for the restoration of the town's glorious medieval

[25] For Aerschot see 'Biographical Notes'.
[26] The term comes from J. Decavele, 'De mislukking van Oranjes "democratische politiek" in Vlaanderen', *Bijdragen en Mededelingen betreffende de Geschiedenis der Nederlanden*, 99 (1984), pp. 626–50.
[27] For the history of the Ghent Republic see J. Decavele (ed.), *Het eind van een rebelse droom. Opstellen over het calvinistisch bewind te Gent (1577–1584) en de terugkeer van de stad onder de gehoorzaamheid van de koning van Spanje (17 september 1584)* (Ghent, 1984), and many articles by the same author.

past and the liberation of Flanders from Spanish tyranny and Catholicism.

Alexander Farnese of Parma, appointed Governor by Philip II in 1578, exploited the tensions within the States General with great political and military skill. He stimulated the *rapprochement* with Artois and Hainaut, sealed by the Union of Arras in which both provinces reaffirmed their loyalty to peace, king and church.

These developments were a major setback for William of Orange, who tried to keep the provinces unified with a political programme based on the principle of religious toleration. However even in Holland, Orange's policy of unity was not unequivocally followed. In 1578 the idea of forming a closer union between the northern provinces – an idea the Prince, if only for strategic reasons, had always promoted – was taken up not only by his brother John of Nassau, but also by a number of town magistrates in Holland and Utrecht, who concluded the Union of Utrecht on 23 January 1579. The Union of Utrecht has been of great importance for the history of the Dutch Republic as it became, in the words of the Dutch historian Boogman, 'the only legal foundation, the constitution, as it was termed, of the Republic of the north'.[28]

However, as the Union was mainly the work of a small vanguard from Holland, Zeeland, Utrecht, Guelders and Groningen, its immediate political significance was limited. At first Orange himself kept aloof from the Union as he was making a desperate final attempt to save unity amongst the provinces. Orange failed, and the Unions of Arras and Utrecht were symptomatic of the basic rupture that occurred in the Low Countries. The rupture became particularly evident during the last dramatic attempt to reconcile all parties – the peace negotiations at Cologne which started in May 1579 under the auspices of the German Emperor.

The articles proposed by the mediating party, the commissioners of the German Emperor, gave rise to strong debate. Essentially the peace proposals promised a return to the old state of government. Philip II was to respect the privileges and liberties of the country and to accept the Pacification of Ghent and the Eternal Edict, while the States were to make restitution of the proper authority and obedience to Philip. With regard to the religious issue the proposals contained

[28] J.C. Boogman, 'The Union of Utrecht: its genesis and consequences', in idem, *Van Spel tot Spelers. Verspreide Opstellen* (The Hague, 1982), p. 64.

some concessions to the Protestants, who were offered sanctuaries in Holland and Zeeland. In general, however, the maintenance of the Roman Catholic religion was emphasized.

The great majority of the treatises that commented on the peace proposals adopted a strongly negative attitude. One of them was the *Brief Discourse on the peace negotiations now taking place at Cologne*, the third text in this volume, which combined a strong condemnation of Philip II's policy and person with a staunch defence of the political authority of the States and their right of resistance.

The *Brief Discourse* refuted the very possibility of reconciliation with Philip, arguing that princes in general, and the Spanish king in particular, were full of injustice and could hardly be trusted. Philip's one and only goal, so the treatise claimed, was to deprive the Low Countries of their liberty, to bring them into eternal servitude. Thus, although the wording of the treatise was particularly strong, it basically reiterated the familiar claims that the States had only resorted to armed resistance in order to preserve liberty and that they were fully entitled to do so.

In legitimating the States' right of resistance, the *Brief Discourse* made a remarkable move. Although the privileges were still presented as an important part of the Dutch political system, in order to defend the right of resistance on behalf of the States the treatise did not turn to constitutional documents such as the Joyous Entry. Instead it pointed out that the political dependence of the prince on the States had important ramifications for the issue of sovereignty. Endorsing the revolutionary view that the States were the leading sovereign powers in the Netherlands, the treatise contended that the States had 'reserved the power to decide on all matters concerning the sovereignty to themselves'.

As leading sovereign powers, the principal duty of the States was to maintain the rights and liberties of the people. In doing so the States were entitled to take up arms against the prince. Indeed, the *Brief Discourse* not only argued that the States had the authority to resist a prince by force, but also asserted the States had the right to abjure and replace him.

In short, the *Brief Discourse* can be said to have brought the continual emphasis on the political authority of the States to its ultimate conclusion, by arguing that the States were indeed the leading sovereign powers within the Dutch political order. Moreover, as the treatise re-emphasized the representative character of the States, it can be said to entail a notion of popular sovereignty.

V

The Cologne peace negotiations were a complete failure. Beforehand the States had announced that if the negotiations failed, they would renounce Philip II and appoint another prince in his place. For strategic and pragmatic reasons the first choice was François de Valois, brother of the French king and Duke of Anjou.[29] In August 1580 a commission under the leadership of Marnix of St Aldegonde was sent to France to offer Anjou the lordship over the Netherlands. The negotiations were difficult. While Anjou demanded sovereignty, the Dutch deputies, arguing (rather beyond the truth) that the word did not exist in Dutch, insisted on the title of 'highest lord'. Other problems involved the right of free assembly for the States General and the clause of disobedience, which the Dutch proposed to include in the treaty, in line with constitutional traditions. Nonetheless on 19 September the treaty of Plessis-lès-Tours was signed. It reaffirmed the parliamentary form of government that had been developing in the Netherlands. The States retained their powerful position. They now expressly elected the lord of the country and had the right to renounce him in case of disloyalty. The logical consequence of the treaty with Anjou followed on 26 July 1581: with the Act of Abjuration the States General formally renounced Philip II.

One of the treatises to comment on the rightfulness of the abjuration was *Political Education*, published anonymously in Malines in 1582. Its treatment of the issue can be seen as a delicate synthesis of the 'final' position on this issue, as developed during the Dutch Revolt.

Referring to Seneca amongst others, *Political Education*, the fourth text in this volume, emphasized that the purpose of government (which was said to be an office and a matter of public service rather than an empire) solely 'consists in the welfare and prosperity of the community and subjects.[30] Princes, the treatise argued with elaborate

---

[29] For Anjou and his role in the Dutch Revolt see Mack P. Holt, *The Duke of Anjou and the Politique Struggle during the Wars of Religion* (Cambridge, 1986). For Anjou see also 'Biographical Notes'.
[30] *Politicq onderwijs* (Malines, 1582), fol. B3.

references to biblical and classical sources and to Cicero's *De Officiis* in particular, were 'instituted to do justice'. Recognizing that the prince was ordained by God and accepted by the people to serve the common good, *Political Education* made an important point of arguing that princes were subjected to the law.

According to the treatise, a prince, or any other public authority, who served his own 'profit' and 'unbridled passions' and who suppressed 'what is right with force and violence',[31] should be considered a tyrant. This claim was substantiated by a lengthy analysis of the most famous late medieval treatise on the subject, Bartolus' *De Tyranno*.[32] By confronting the criteria which Bartolus had set out for recognizing tyranny with the governmental practice of Philip II, *Political Education* arrived at the conclusion that the government of the King of Spain undoubtedly fitted Bartolus' definition of tyranny.

Boldly the treatise asserted that the 'pious and godly citizen and subject cannot have community with the tyrant', and paraphrasing Cicero it pointed out that 'as one should amputate a rotten limb for the conservation of the body', so the tyrant should be 'destroyed'.[33] Again *Political Education* made a point of situating its theory of resistance within a broader European intellectual context, referring not only to famous authors such as Bartolus and Aquinas, but also to a number of contemporary Spanish and Italian authors. For example, in citing Domingo de Soto, a Spanish neo-Thomist from the Salamanca school, the treatise maintained that if the tyrant was a 'legal prince' due to succession or election, he should not be killed by any 'private person'. In such cases only the States of the country 'and those who represent the subjects' had as 'public persons' the right and duty to resist and kill the tyrant. In this context *Political Education* explicitly espoused the argument of the preamble of the Act of Abjuration, concluding that, also in regard of specific Dutch contracts, it had been perfectly legitimate to abjure Philip II.

After the abjuration the States had ordered citizens to take an oath of loyalty to the new regime. The main purpose of *Political Education* was to show the rightfulness of this demand by means of articulating a view of citizenship along republican, Ciceronian lines, which

---

[31] Ibid., fol. B4.

[32] For a recent authoritative study and edition of *De Tyranno*, see Diego Quaglioni, *Politica e Diritto nel Trecento Italiano. Il 'De Tyranno' di Bartolo da Sassoferrato (1314–1357)* (Florence, 1983).   [33] *Politica onderwijs*, fol. B3.

emphasized the importance of civic virtue as the proper means for a dutiful patriot to attain true honour and perfect glory.

Like other treatises, *Political Education* argued that the main virtue needed was concord. With references to numerous classical examples, some of them derived from Livy, the treatise attempted to show that concord was 'the foundation of all republics, or states of government'. The leading motto, derived from Sallust and Seneca, was simple: 'Concord makes small commonwealths great, discord disrupts the greatest ones.'[34] In this respect the oath as required by the States General was presented, again on the basis of classical examples and authors, as the 'best bond' amongst men, and therefore the best means to promote concord in the United Provinces.

The argument of *Political Education* was certainly not exceptional; its defence of the abjuration and its emphasis on civic virtue were well within the mainstream of the Revolt's political thought. The treatise, however, was unique in its systematic attempt to connect every step of the argumentation with broader European intellectual traditions. As such, it indicates the intellectual sources at the disposal of what was probably a Dutch jurist writing in 1582.

VI

Anjou's adventure in the Low Countries was a disaster. Politically his appointment was highly controversial and militarily his efforts were rather futile. This was partly due to the fact that as a military commander the Duke was no match for Farnese. The principal reason however was Anjou's permanent financial disarray, mainly caused by the States General, which failed to fulfil its financial obligations. Suffering from a lack of food and a harsh winter, the Duke's army deteriorated. Desperately Anjou took the fateful decision to seize Antwerp. The 1583 'French Fury' became a catastrophe. The attack itself was a complete failure, and Anjou had to flee for his life.

The French policy, as propagated by Orange, had become a fiasco. It had strengthened neither the military position nor the political unity of the provinces. It had only contributed to further division and to the disarray of central government. When the prince was assassinated in Delft on 10 July 1584 his policy seemed doomed. Orange's last words

---

[4] See Sallust, *Bellum Jugurthinum*, 10.6 and Seneca, *Epistolae Morales*, Liber 14, letter 94, section 46.

'My God have pity on my soul and this poor people' bore testimony to the great confusion that afflicted the Low Countries.

This confusion was partly due to the successes of the Prince of Parma, Alexander Farnese. His 'Reconquista' was impressive, especially between 1582 and 1585. Flanders and Brabant were almost completely reconquered. Bruges and Ghent fell in 1584, Brussels and finally Antwerp in 1585. The immediate consequence for the southern provinces was a dramatic exodus to the north. About half of the population left Ghent; Antwerp lost about 38,000 people, more than a third of its population.

The Spanish reconquest alarmed Queen Elizabeth I of England, who had no interest in an overall dominance of Spain in the Netherlands. Although she declined the sovereignty offered to her by the United Provinces, Elizabeth did decide to intervene directly in the Revolt. The Treaty of Nonesuch, concluded three days after the fall of Antwerp, pledged military assistance by an English army for the right to put English garrisons in a number of Dutch towns. Moreover the States General appointed the Earl of Leicester as 'Governor and Captain General'.[35] Leicester was awarded broad powers. The States declared that the Earl should command 'completely and absolutely' on matters of war and would have 'full and absolute power in matters of policy and justice'. There can be little doubt that the Earl's supporters intended it this way. The States of Holland certainly did not. When Leicester started to behave like an absolute ruler, conflict with Holland was inevitable. It was a desperate fight for the Earl, who was no match for the political genius of John of Oldenbarnevelt, Holland's new leader.

Supporting Leicester, the English councillor Thomas Wilkes (one of the English members of the Council of State) strongly attacked the States of Holland in a 1587 *Remonstrance*. Wilkes questioned the States' claim to sovereignty. He argued that, 'by default of a legal Prince the sovereignty belongs with the community', and not with the States, who were but 'servants, ministers and deputies of the community'.[36] As Wilkes pointed out, the community continuously limited

---

[35] For Leicester see 'Biographical Notes'.

[36] Pieter Christiaansz. Bor, *Oorsprongk, begin en vervolgh der Nederlantsche oorlogen, beroerten en borgerlijke oneenigheden'*, vol. 2 (Amsterdam, 1679; originally published in 1595), p. 921. Part of Wilkes' *Remonstrance* has been translated by E.H. Kossmann and A.F. Mellink, *Texts concerning the Revolt of the Netherlands* (Cambridge, 1974), pp. 272–4.

the authority of the States, setting conditions to their functioning and decisions. Therefore, their authority was as different from sovereignty as 'heaven is different from hell', for, as Wilkes put it, 'sovereignty is not limited neither in power, nor in command, nor in time'. Neither did the States represent sovereignty, for such was precisely the role of the Governor-General, described 'as a dispositarius or guardian of sovereignty until it pleases the prince or the people to revoke it'.[37]

Wilkes' ideas were radical, and devastating in their political implications, as he argued that the States were mere delegates who acted on order and instruction. Combined with the notion, probably derived from Bodin, that it was the essence of sovereignty not to be limited, neither in power nor in time, this greatly reduced the importance of the States, whose claims to political dominance, let alone sovereignty, were subtly rejected. In Wilkes' conception sovereignty had returned into the hands of the community.

Holland recognized the necessity of responding and the town pensionary of Gouda, François Vranck, was asked to write a defence of the authority of the States, which became the 'Magna Carta' of the Dutch Republic.[38] It was later published, in a slightly revised version, as the *Short exposition of the right exercised from old times by the Knighthood, Nobles and Towns of Holland and Westvriesland for the maintenance of the liberties, rights, privileges and laudable customs of the country.*

Vranck pointed out that for 800 years Holland had been governed by Counts in close co-operation with the States of the country. The Counts had never taken major political decisions without 'the advice and consent of the nobles and towns of the country', for they simply had no power in their own right. They were completely dependent on the States. If a Count, having received his authority 'with the approval and consent of the inhabitants', acted against the 'liberty and welfare' and became a tyrant, the inhabitants could oppose him lawfully by means of the States, whose main task was to 'maintain the rights, freedoms and privileges of the country and to avert and resist all infraction'.[39]

Thus the political authority of the States was reaffirmed. As Vranck emphasized, this authority did 'not consist in the policy, authority or

[37] Ibid.
[38] References are to the declaration of the States, as printed in Bor, *Oorsprongk der Nederlantsche oorlogen*, ii pp. 921–4. For Vranck see 'Biographical Notes'.
[39] Ibid., p. 922.

power' of the '30 or 40 persons' who appeared at its meetings.[40] In order to be able to oppose tyrannical rule and abuse of princely authority, the inhabitants were divided into 'two estates', the nobles and towns. The towns were described as independent self-governing political entities, governed by a college of town councillors. According to Vranck the 'Colleges of Magistrates and Town Councils, together with the corporation of the Nobles', represented 'the whole state and the entire body of the inhabitants'.[41] The persons forming the States assembly were not 'the States in person or on their own authority', but the deputies of nobles and towns. Their representative work had to be seen in terms of delegation. A delegate, participating in the States, could only act 'in conformity with his instruction and commission'. Therefore 'Wilkes and everybody else' should understand that to argue that 'the sovereignty of the country is with the States', was not to refer to the individual delegates, but to 'their principals, whom they represent by virtue of their commission'.[42]

Thus Vranck accepted the notion of popular sovereignty and argued that the term 'popular' could only refer to the 'nobles and towns' of the country. Like Wilkes he interpreted the representative character of the States in terms of delegation, accepting that the States only acted on order and instruction of their 'principals'. This did not, however, diminish the importance of the States. For although sovereignty resided with the people, it was administered by their delegates, the States. Thus, developing a crucial distinction between the residence and the administration of sovereignty, Vranck was able to conclude 'that the sovereignty of the country is with the States in all matters.[43]

Of course, the dispute between Wilkes and Vranck focussed on the nature of sovereignty, of popular sovereignty in particular, and of representation. As such it touched the heart and soul of the political thought of the Dutch Revolt.

There has been some debate about the proper interpretation of

[40] Ibid.
[41] Ibid., p. 923.
[42] Ibid.
[43] Ibid. My analysis of Vranck's declaration is indebted to Pieter Geyl's 'An interpretation of Vrancken's Deduction of 1587 on the nature of the States of Holland's power' in Charles H. Carter (ed.), *From the Renaissance to the Counter-Reformation* (London, 1966), pp. 230–46, which stresses the lasting influence of Vranck's ideas of representation on Dutch political thought.

early modern notions of popular sovereignty, such as those developed by both Wilkes and Vranck. Essentially, what seems to be at stake is the proper meaning of the terms 'popular' and 'representation'.

It has been argued that the great sixteenth-century pleas for popular sovereignty, as formulated by the *Vindiciae contra tyrannos* and Johannes Althusius, were developed in connection with 'holistic' and corporatist notions of the community and as such followed late medieval political thought. Thus the term 'popular' was not meant to refer to 'a group of independent individuals, who somehow or other have united themselves together', but rather to 'the permanent social framework by which they are united'.[44] Sovereignty did not, as modern notions would hold, belong to a 'quantifiable collection of real living beings' but to 'a network of ancient institutions, of councils, parliaments, colleges and estates, and secondarily, those who have a place in them'.[45] Accordingly, when Althusius or authors such as Wilkes and Vranck referred to certain colleges, such as the States, in terms of representative institutions, this did not 'mean that these assemblies are appointed by the people to give expression to popular will'.[46] Rather it meant that such institutions more or less personified the people, embodying 'the social bond which unites people in society'.

However, late medieval notions of popular sovereignty were, in spite of holism, certainly not by definition incompatible with more individualistic notions of society,[47] and the Commentators and Decretalists employing holistic language themselves often recognized that the 'populus' was both a 'whole' and 'a plurality of human beings'.[48] Moreover, the Roman law maxim, 'that what touches all is to be approved by all', promoted the development of influential theories of government by (popular) consent, in which the position of the individual was, one way or the other, of great importance.

Representation, meanwhile, had been interpreted by a powerful tradition in late medieval political thought (exemplified by, amongst

[44] See E.H. Kossmann, 'Popular sovereignty at the beginning of the Dutch Ancien Régime', *The Low Countries History Yearbook*, 14 (1981), p. 4.
[45] Ibid.
[46] Ibid., p. 23.
[47] The point is made by Anthony Black, 'Society and the individual from the Middle Ages to Rousseau: Philosophy, jurisprudence and constitutional theory', *History of Political Thought*, 1 (1980), pp. 157–9.
[48] See, most recently, J.P. Canning, *The political thought of Baldus de Ubaldis* (Cambridge, 1987), pp. 185ff.

Introduction

others, Marsilius of Padua)[49] in terms of delegation. As is well known, the question, and the fundamental ambiguities involved – whether the delegate could be said to personify the community or corporation he represented – was addressed with particular vehemence by William of Ockham. Ockham's nominalist philosophy not only resulted in the view that, as he put it, 'the people is not an individual, it is an aggregate of individuals' but also led to the idea that, therefore, representation had to involve the 'individual delegation by members of the community'.[50]

With regard to the issues of popular sovereignty and representation, the political thought of the Dutch Revolt, as exemplified by the texts in this volume, can be said to reflect and to elaborate the riches of medieval political thought. Endorsing holistic notions, the 1576 *Address*, for example, argued that the States represented 'the entire corps', adding that they should do 'in its name what otherwise the generality should have done itself'. Moreover Vranck himself consistently described the town councils as colleges, representing 'the whole state and the entire body of the inhabitants'. More and more, however, representation was explicitly interpreted in terms of delegation, the States' members being delegates, who, as Vranck pointed out so amply and in close correspondence with political reality, could only act in virtue, and on the order and instruction of the 'corporation of the Nobles' and the 'colleges' of the town councils. Although this language is undoubtedly reminiscent of old 'holistic' traditions, some passages, for example in the *Brief Discourse*, indicate that the relation between the representatives of the people, the States, and the people was not always interpreted purely in holistic terms. In defending the States' demand for freedom of religion, the treatise argued that, as the States represented 'the whole people and all the inhabitants of the country', it was 'reasonable' for them to 'conform themselves to the dispositions and desires of the inhabitants in just and proper matters for the common good of the country'.[51]

Such formulations contain not only a conception of representation

---

[49] See, for example, Jeannine Quillet, 'Community, counsel and representation' in J.H. Burns (ed.), *The Cambridge History of Medieval Political Thought, c. 350–c. 1450* (Cambridge, 1988), pp. 554–72, and Brian Tierney, *Religion, law, and the growth of constitutional thought, 1150–1650* (Cambridge, 1982), pp. 26–7.
[50] Arthur P. Monahan, *Consent, coercion, and limit. The medieval origins of parliamentary democracy* (Leyden, 1987), pp. 239–49. See also Quillet, pp. 561–65.
[51] *Brief Discourse*, fol. B1.

– not in terms of personification, but in terms of delegation – but also at least some moves towards the articulation of the idea that the States were the delegates of the individual inhabitants of the country, to whose desires the States were to conform.

VII

After the failure of the Leicester experiment, the Dutch themselves finally took full control of their government. The States asserted their sovereign power, and more than ever the States General became the centre of their improving federal co-operation. Haphazardly the United Provinces had found their own way, and with increasing confidence they were becoming a Republic, steered by the able political leadership of Oldenbarnevelt and the military genius of Maurice of Nassau, a son of William of Orange.

The ideological foundation of the new Republic was formed by a heterogeneous pattern of ideas, based on the key concepts of liberty, privileges, States and popular sovereignty. Liberty was seen as the political value *par excellence*, the 'daughter of the Netherlands', the source of prosperity and justice; and the intrinsic connection between the liberty of the country and the personal liberty and welfare of the inhabitants was emphasized time and again.

The Revolt itself was essentially interpreted as the defence of liberty, threatened by the lust for power and the tyrannical ambitions of Philip II's government. The political order was said to have been deliberately created with the purpose of safeguarding liberty. It tried to achieve this goal by means of a constitutional framework consisting of a set of fundamental laws, the privileges, charters and customs of the provinces, and a number of crucial institutions such as the States, whose functioning and flourishing, it should be added, required acts of civic virtue at all levels of society.

In articulating these arguments Dutch treatises abounded in references to great constitutional documents and traditions of the late medieval period. Nonetheless, from the very beginning the political ideas of the protesting and rebelling Dutch moved beyond the ideological legacy of their constitutional past. The reaffirmation of the right of disobedience as contained in constitutional documents such as the Joyous Entry, soon evolved into the articulation of a political right of resistance, one that allowed the inhabitants to disobey and oppose by force a prince who violated the privileges, and, by means of their representatives, the States, to replace him with a regent. Moreover, in the ultimate defence of the abjuration, some treatises moved beyond the privileges, articulating a right of resistance in terms of a fundamental principle of politics.

Similar ideological developments are to be noted with regard to the position of the States, traditionally represented as the guardians of liberty.

From the beginning the States were interpreted as representative institutions, created to check and bridle the prince and to take the important political decisions. Gradually the position of the States changed: instead of being institutions for 'inferior magistrates' they became leading sovereign powers. The notion of popular sovereignty entailed by such formulations was elaborated during a fundamental debate amongst the proponents of the Revolt, which focussed on the political implications of the idea of popular sovereignty. In Vranck's interpretation the States were presented as the foundation of the country, essential to the common good. The States were entrusted with the administration of sovereignty, as delegates, who acted on order and instruction of their principals, the nobles and towns, which, in turn, represented the entire body of the inhabitants. As noted, by developing notions of representation in terms of delegation, a crucial distinction was made between the residence and administration of sovereignty.

In short, the initial reaffirmation of old constitutional traditions led, in continuous interaction with breaking political developments, to the proliferation of ideas which formed the ideological foundations of the Dutch Republic. In doing so, as the 1582 *Political Education* and the other treatises in this collection exemplify, Dutch authors were inspired both by the indigenous legacy of Dutch constitutionalism and civic consciousness and by the intellectual legacy of the late Middle Ages, Renaissance and Reformation.

Chronology

1555   *25 October* Charles V renounces his titles in the Netherlands in favour of his son Philip.

1559   *5 July* Philip II leaves the Netherlands; Margaret of Parma appointed Governess-General.

1559   Papal bull 'Super Universas' decrees reorganization of Catholic church in the Low Countries.

1562   *Easter* First public Reformed Protestant Sermon in Flanders.

1562   Formation of the noble 'League of the Great' under the leadership of William of Orange and Egmont, which heads the opposition against Granvelle.

1564   Withdrawal of Granvelle.

1566   *Spring* Beginning of large-scale hedge-preaching.

1566   *August–October* Iconoclastic Fury.

1566   *December* Defeat of Protestant armies at Wattrelos and Lannoy.

1567   Arrival of the Duke of Alva in the Netherlands, who is appointed Governor-General in December. William of Orange in exile.

1568   *5 June* Execution of Egmont and Hoorne in Brussels.

1568   *Summer* First military campaign of William of Orange.

1570   *26 October 1570 Libellus Supplex Imperatoriae Maiestati* presented to the German Reichstag.

1572   *1 April* Sea Beggars capture Brill in Holland.

1572 *Summer* Second military campaign of William of Orange.

1572 *July* William of Orange acclaimed Stadholder by the States of Holland.

1572 *23 August* Saint Bartholomew's Eve Massacre in France.

1572 *19 September* Fall of Mons marks beginning of Alva's reconquest.

1573 *12 July* Fall of Haarlem; *21 August–8 October* Siege of Alkmaar.

1573 *29 November* Alva replaced by Don Luis de Requesens.

1574 *3 October* By flooding surrounding lands, the besieged town of Leiden is relieved.

1575 *March–April* Peace negotiations at Breda.

1576 *5 March* Death of Requesens.

1576 *Spring* Publication of the *Address and Opening to make a good, blessed and general peace in the Netherlands*.

1576 *November* Pacification of Ghent. Philip II appoints Don Juan of Austria Governor-General

1578 Death of Don Juan; Alexander Farnese of Parma becomes Governor-General.

1579 *6 January* Union of Arras between Artois and Hainaut.

1579 *23 January* Union of Utrecht signed by representatives of Holland, Zeeland, the town of Utrecht, five knights from Guelders and the town of Zutphen, and the 'Ommelanden' of Groningen, later followed by Friesland, and the main parts of Brabant and Flanders.

1579 *May–December* Peace negotiations at Cologne.

1579 Publication of *Brief Discourse on the peace negotiations now taking place at Cologne*.

1580 *19 September* Treaty of Plessis-lès-Tours between the Duke of Anjou and the States-General.

1581 *26 July* With the Act of Abjuration the States General formally renounce Philip II.

1582 *January* Publication of *Political Education*.

1583 *17 January* 'French Fury' marks failure of the Anjou government.

1584 *10 July 1584* Assassination of William of Orange at Delft.

1584   Farnese reconquers Ypres, Bruges and Ghent.

1585   Fall of Brussels and, on *17 August*, of Antwerp.

1585   *20 August* Treaty of Nonesuch between England and the United Provinces.

1585   *November* Maurice of Nassau appointed Stadholder of Holland and Zeeland.

1586   *4 February* Earl of Leicester appointed Governor and Captain General.

1586   *February* Johan of Oldenbarnevelt appointed Advocate of Holland.

1587   *March Remonstrance* of Sir Thomas Wilkes.

1587   Publication of Vranck's *Short Exposition*.

1587   *December* Departure of Leicester.

1588   *Summer* Defeat of the Spanish Armada.

1590   *4 March* Maurice of Nassau recaptures Breda in Brabant; beginning of Dutch reconquest campaign.

Biographical notes

PHILIP OF CROY, DUKE OF AERSCHOT (1526–95) was a member of the influential Croy dynasty from Hainaut. He was the leader of a group of southern nobles which supported the 1576 Pacification of Ghent as a way to reach a political settlement for the Dutch troubles. Aerschot was also the principal member of the Dutch delegation during the 1579 Cologne peace negotiations. In spite of his official reconciliation with Philip II, Aerschot withdrew from politics and died in Venice in 1595.

FERNANDEZ ALVAREZ OF TOLEDO, DUKE OF ALVA (1507–82) played an important role in Spanish politics first under Charles V and above all under Philip II. In 1567 he was commissioned by Philip II to restore order in the Low Countries. Alva seemed to crush the remnants of the opposition with a regime which in Dutch history has become proverbial for its terror and tyranny, but in 1572 the Iron Duke did not succeed in suppressing the second wave of the Revolt. He returned to Spain in 1573. In 1580 he led the annexation of Portugal.

FRANÇOIS OF VALOIS, DUKE OF ANJOU AND ALENÇON (1556–84) was the fourth son of Henry II of France and Catharina de Medici. From 1573 Anjou, full of political ambitions, was involved in the Dutch troubles. He was proclaimed 'Defender of the liberty of the Netherlands' in 1578 and was appointed lord of the country by the States General in 1581, after the abjuration of Philip II. The Anjou experiment was a dismal failure; the Duke returned to France in 1583 after a desperate attempt to increase his authority in the so called

'French fury', a catastrophic attack by the Duke's forces on Antwerp. For a recent study on Anjou see Mack P. Holt, *The Duke of Anjou and the Politique Struggle during the Wars of Religion* (Cambridge, 1986).

BALDUS DE UBALDIS (*c.* 1327–1400) had been a pupil of Bartolus, among others. From 1351 he taught at Pisa, Florence, Perugia, Padua and Pavia. He was involved in Perugia's politics and served on diplomatic missions. He took Bartolus' place as Europe's principal legal expert and greatly contributed to late medieval political thought. For a recent study of Baldus see J.P. Canning, *The Political Thought of Baldus de Ubaldis* (Cambridge, 1987).

BARTOLUS OF SASSOFERRATO (1313/14–57) was an outstanding political philosopher and commentator on Roman law. He studied at Perugia and Bologna and taught at Pisa and in particular at Perugia, where he spent the last fourteen years of his life. Being one of the founding fathers of a theory which legitimated a sort of *de facto* sovereignty on behalf of the Italian city republics, Bartolus can be regarded as an inspirator of late medieval Republicanism.

DON JUAN OF AUSTRIA (1547–78) was a bastard son of Charles V and therefore a half-brother of Philip II. He was one of the great military leaders of his time, but his governorship over the Low Countries between 1576 and 1578 turned out to be disastrous.

LAMORAAL, COUNT OF EGMONT (1522–68) was one of the principal high nobles in the Low Countries. Appointed Stadholder of Flanders and Artois in 1559, he became one of the leaders of the 1562 'League of the Great' and the opposition against Granvelle. At the breakup of the League in 1566 Egmont decided to stay in the Low Countries. He was arrested by Alva and executed in 1568. The count was celebrated by Goethe in his play *Egmont*.

ALEXANDER FARNESE, PRINCE (FROM 1586 DUKE) OF PARMA (1545–92), was the son of Ottavia Farnese and Margaret of Parma. Farnese, appointed Governor of the Netherlands by Philip II in 1578, was both an able diplomat and general. Due to his famous 'reconquista' between 1579 and 1585 the Low Countries were split up into the northern Republic and the southern Spanish Netherlands. After 1585 Farnese's campaign had to give way to the preparations for the Armada. Farnese never regained momentum, and was later confronted with military defeats suffered against Maurice of Nassau.

ANTOINE PERRENOT, LORD OF GRANVELLE (1517–86), was an important civil servant to the Spanish crown. In 1560 he was appointed Archbishop of Malines. Granvelle, as the principal exponent of Philip II's policy, was withdrawn from the Low Countries in 1564, due to the opposition of the high nobles, but continued to play an important role in the Spanish government.

PHILIP OF MONTMORENCY, COUNT OF HOORNE (1518–68), was an important member of the 'League of the Great'. Like Egmont he was arrested by Alva in 1567 and executed in 1568.

ROBERT DUDLEY, EARL OF LEICESTER (1533–88), was a confidant of Queen Elizabeth I of England. In 1586 he was appointed Governor by the States General, and was awarded, at least in theory, broad powers. In the subsequent power struggle with Holland the Earl was no match for John of Oldenbarnevelt. Leicester returned to England in 1587.

MARNIX, PHILIP, LORD OF ST ALDEGONDE (1540–98) was a leading protagonist of the Dutch Revolt. As a trained humanist Marnix was one of the Revolt's most prolific authors, publishing both political and religious treatises. As a politician, Marnix, a confidant of William of Orange, fulfilled many missions both in the Low Countries and abroad. He is also the alleged author of the Dutch national anthem, the *Wilhelmus*, composed in 1570 as one of the 'Beggar songs'.

MAURICE OF NASSAU (1567–1625) was the son of William of Orange and his second wife, Anna of Saxony. After Maurice was appointed Stadholder of Holland and Zeeland in 1585, he became the military leader of the Republic. As such he was responsible for a revolutionary reorganization of the army, which brought the young Republic many victories. In spite of their early co-operation Maurice later became the main political opponent of Oldenbarnevelt. After the latter's arrest and execution Maurice was the main political figure in the Netherlands until his death in 1625.

JOHN OF OLDENBARNEVELT (1547–1619) emerged as Holland's political leader after he was appointed Advocate of the States of Holland in 1586. The political genius of Oldenbarnevelt was greatly responsible for the build-up of the Dutch Republic. In the final years of his life Oldenbarnevelt became deeply involved in the conflict between the Arminians and their opponents, the Counter-

Remonstrants or Gomarists. In 1617 Oldenbarnevelt was arrested at the order of Maurice of Nassau, by then his main opponent; he was executed in 1619.

WILLIAM OF NASSAU, PRINCE OF ORANGE (1533–84), the eldest son of a German Lutheran noble family, inherited the Principality of Orange in the south-east of France together with vast lands in the Low Countries in 1544. At the order of Charles V, William was brought to the court in Brussels to receive a proper Catholic education. In 1559 the prince was appointed Stadholder of Holland, Zeeland and Utrecht. He became the leading figure in the opposition to the central government and the only high noble to go into exile in 1566. In 1572 William was acclaimed Stadholder of Holland by the provincial States. He became the undisputed, but by no means uncontroversial, leader of the Dutch Revolt. The Prince, who was assassinated in 1584, is one of the seminal figures of Dutch history, and still known as the 'Father of the Fatherland'. Dame Veronica Wedgwood celebrated Orange in her biography *William the Silent* (London, 1944; reprint 1989).

MARGARET, DUCHESS OF PARMA (1522–86) was a bastard daughter of Charles V. She was appointed Governess of the Low Countries by Philip II in 1559. In 1567 Margaret left the Low Countries, and was replaced by Alva.

PHILIP II (1527–98) in 1555 inherited not only the Spanish throne but also a long list of titles which made him lord of the Netherlands. From the beginning his government aroused opposition. Philip left the Netherlands in 1559, never to return again. His attempts to strengthen the power of the central government in the Low Countries and his policy of religious persecution in particular were among the main causes of the Dutch Revolt, one of the manifold problems of his reign. Although Philip II was not the intransigent absolutist leader he is often held to be, at decisive moments he showed himself unwilling to make substantial compromises in the Low Countries. For a recent biography see Geoffrey Parker, *Philip II* (London, 1978).

VIGLIUS OF AYTTA OF ZWICHEM (1507–77) was an important humanist, who became a leading civil servant of the Spanish crown as president of both the Privy council and, since 1554, the Council of State. Until his death he played an important and frequently under-estimated political role during the Revolt.

Biographical notes

FRANÇOIS VRANCK (1555–1617) was town pensionary of Gouda
when he wrote the *Short Exposition* in 1587. Six years later Vranck, a
close political ally of Oldenbarnevelt, became a member of the High
Council, which had the aspiration of becoming the chief judicial
institution of the Republic.

JACOB VAN WESEMBEEKE (1524–c. 75) was appointed pensionary
of his native town Antwerp in 1556, and as the town's highest civil
servant he became one of Antwerp's leading politicians. The troubles
of 1566 were the beginning of a close co-operation with William of
Orange. As Wesembeeke went into exile, he became an important
counsellor and the chief propagandist of the opposition during the
late 1560s. His publications, often long and wary, were of great
importance for the development of the Revolt's political thought.

Bibliographical notes

The study of the political thought of the Dutch Revolt

The political thought of the Dutch Revolt has not been widely studied. Two older Dutch studies are A.C.J. de Vrankrijker, *De motiveering van onzen opstand* (Nijmegen/Utrecht, 1933; Repr. 1979) and P.A.M. Geurts, *De Nederlandse Opstand in de pamfletten 1566–1584* (Utrecht, 1983; reprint of the original 1956 edition). My own comprehensive monograph *The Political Thought of the Dutch Revolt 1555–1590* is published by Cambridge University Press.

The Dutch historian Kossmann has contributed to the study of the political thought of the Revolt with a number of influential articles. See the chapter 'Bodin, Althusius en Parker, of: over de moderniteit van de Nederlandse Opstand' in E.H. Kossmann, *Politieke theorie en geschiedenis. Verspreide opstellen en voordrachten* (Amsterdam, 1987), pp. 93–111 (originally published in 1958) and his 'Popular sovereignty at the beginning of the Dutch Ancien Régime' in *The Low Countries History Yearbook*, 14, (1981), pp. 1–28.

The Dutch historian Nicolette Mout has published a number of fine studies of the intellectual history of the Revolt. See for example her edition and study of the 1581 'Act of Abjuration': M.E.H.N. Mout, *Plakkaat van verlatinge 1581. Inleiding, transcriptie en vertaling in hedendaags Nederlands* (The Hague, 1979). Her most recent synthesis is 'Ideales Muster oder erfundene Eigenart. Republikanische Theorien während des niederländischen Aufstands' in H.G.

Koenigsberger (ed.), *Republiken und Republikanismus im Europa der frühen Neuzeit* (Munich, 1988), pp. 169–94.

This article offers a view of the development of Republican ideas during the Revolt. For my own position on this issue see Martin van Gelderen, 'Conceptions of liberty during the Dutch Revolt (1555–1590)' in *Parliaments, Estates and Representation*, vol. 9, part 2 (1989), pp. 137–53; 'The Machiavellian Moment and the Dutch Revolt: The rise of Neostoicism and Dutch Republicanism' in Gisela Bock, Quentin Skinner, Maurizio Viroli (eds.), *Machiavelli and Republicanism* (Cambridge, 1990), pp. 205–23; and *The Political Thought of the Dutch Revolt 1555–1590*, pp. 276–87.

For the wider discussion of seventeenth-century Dutch Republicanism, a number of studies by Kossmann and the historian Eco Haitsma Mulier are noteworthy. See Eco Haitsma Mulier, *The Myth of Venice and Dutch Republican Thought in the Seventeenth Century* (Assen, 1980); Eco Haitsma Mulier, 'The language of seventeenth-century Republicanism in the United Provinces: Dutch or European?', in Anthony Pagden (ed.), *The Languages of Political Theory in Early Modern Europe* (Cambridge, 1987), pp. 179–95; E.H. Kossmann, 'Dutch Republicanism' in *L'età dei lumi: Studi, storici sul settecento Europeo in onore di Franco Venturi*, vol. I (Naples, 1985), pp. 455–86 (also in: E.H. Kossmann, *Politieke theorie*, pp. 211–34).

A fascinating (and highly controversial) interpretation of early modern Dutch culture is offered by Simon Schama, *The Embarrassment of Riches. An Interpretation of Dutch Culture in the Golden Age* (London, 1987).

For recent contributions to the history of late medieval constitutional traditions in the Low Countries see P. Avonds, *Brabant tijdens de regering van Hertog Jan III (1312–1356): De grote politieke krisissen* (Brussels, 1984), and a number of studies by the Belgian historian Wim Blockmans. See Wim P. Blockmans, 'D'un contrat féodal à la souveraineté du peuple. Les précédents de la déchéanche du Philippe II dans les Pays Bas (1581)' in *Assemblee di Stati e istituzioni rappresentative nella storia del pensiero politico moderno* (Rimini, 1983), pp. 135–50; W. P. Blockmans (ed.), *1477. Le privilège général et les privilèges régionaux de Marie de Bourgogne pour les Pays-Bas*, in the series 'Ancien pays et assemblées d'états', LXXX (Kortrijk-Heule, 1985), and finally Wim P. Blockmans, 'Alternatives to monarchical centralization; the great tradition of Revolt in Flanders and Brabant' in H.G.

Koenigsberger (ed.). *Republiken und Republikanismus im Europa der frühen Neuzeit* (Munich, 1989), pp. 145–54.

Finally some studies are worth mentioning which deal with certain specific aspects of the political thought of the Dutch Revolt. For an important interpretation of Vranck's *Short Exposition* see Pieter Geyl, 'An interpretation of Vrancken's Deduction of 1587 on the nature of the States of Holland's power' in Charles H. Carter (ed.), *From the Renaissance to the Counter-Reformation* (London, 1966), pp. 230–46.

For studies dealing with the issue of religious toleration and the relationship between ecclesiastical and political authority see, for example, G. Güldner, *Das Toleranzproblem in den Niederlanden im Ausgang des 16. Jahrhunderts* (Hamburg/Lübeck, 1968); H.A. Enno van Gelder, *Getemperde Vrijheid* (Groningen, 1972); R.L. Jones, 'Reformed church and civil authorities in the United Provinces in the late sixteenth and early seventeenth centuries, as reflected in Dutch state and municipal archives', in *Journal of the Society of Archivists*, 4 (1970–3), pp. 109–23 and Martin van Gelderen, *The Political Thought of the Dutch Revolt, 1555–1559*, pp. 213–59.

The most significant contributor to the debates on toleration was Dirck Volckertsz. Coornhert. For recent interpretations of his work see H. Bonger, *Leven en werk van D. V. Coornhert* (Amsterdam, 1978) and a number of essays in *Dirck Volckertszoon Coornhert. Dwars maar recht* (Zutphen, 1989).

Justus Lipsius, one of the founding fathers of Neostoicism, published some of his main works during the Revolt, while working at the University of Leiden. Lipsius has been widely studied by the German historian Gerhard Oestreich. See Gerhard Oestreich, *Neostoicism and the Early Modern State* (Cambridge, 1982) and most recently (with an introduction by Nicolette Mout), Gerhard Oestreich, *Antiker Geist und moderner Staat bei Justus Lipsius* (Göttingen, 1989). For attempts to locate Lipsius' work within the context of the Dutch Revolt see Nicolette Mout, 'In het schip: Justus Lipsius en de Nederlandse Opstand tot 1591', in S. Groenveld, M.E.H.N. Mout and I. Schöffer (eds.), *Bestuurders en geleerden* (Amsterdam-/Dieren, 1985), pp. 55–64, and Martin van Gelderen, *The Machiavellian Moment and the Dutch Revolt: The rise of Neostoicism and Dutch Republicanism*.

For the European intellectual context of the political thought of the Dutch Revolt see J.W. Allen, *A History of Political Thought in the*

Sixteenth Century, revised edition (London, 1957); Gisela Bock, Quentin Skinner, Maurizio Viroli (eds.), *Machiavelli and Republicanism* (Cambridge, 1990); J.H. Burns (ed.), *The Cambridge History of Medieval Political Thought, c. 350–c. 1450* (Cambridge, 1988); Donald R. Kelley, *The Beginning of Ideology. Consciousness and Society in the French Reformation* (Cambridge, 1981); J.G.A. Pocock, *The Machiavellian Moment. Florentine Political Thought and the Atlantic Republican Tradition* (Princeton, 1975); Charles B. Schmitt, Quentin Skinner (eds.), *The Cambridge History of Renaissance Philosophy* (Cambridge, 1988); Quentin Skinner, *The Foundations of Modern Political Thought* vol. 1: *The Renaissance*, vol. 2: *The Age of Reformation* (Cambridge, 1978); Brian Tierney, *Religion, Law, and the Growth of Constitutional Thought, 1150–1650* (Cambridge, 1982).

In general, recent syntheses of early modern political thought have, however wrongly, regarded the political thought of the Dutch Revolt as an application of the Monarchomach theory of resistance, as developed by Huguenot authors. For correctives see de Vrankrijker, *De motiveering van onzen opstand* (Nijmegen/Utrecht, 1933) and van Gelderen. *The Political Thought of the Dutch Revolt 1555–1590*, pp. 269–76.

Recent works in English on the history of the Dutch revolt

In addition to J.L. Motley's classic *The Rise of the Dutch Republic* (various editions), two more recent syntheses of the history of the Dutch Revolt in the English language are Pieter Geyl, *The Revolt of the Netherlands, 1555–1609* (London, 1932; reprint 1988) and Geoffrey Parker, *The Dutch Revolt*, revised edition (Harmondsworth, 1985). Extracts from many documents concerning the Revolt have been published by E.H. Kossmann and A.F. Mellink in *Texts concerning the Revolt of the Netherlands* (Cambridge, 1974).

The historian Helmut Koenigsberger has contributed to a further understanding of the Revolt with a number of highly influential articles. His recent studies on the subject can be found in his *Politicians and Virtuosi: Essays in Early Modern History* (London, 1985).

The Dutch Reformation and its impact on the Revolt have been studied in great detail by the English historian Alastair Duke. His fine essays have been collected in *Reformation and Revolt in the Low*

Countries (London, 1990). Other recent studies on the Dutch Reformation in the English language include H.A. Enno van Gelder, *The two Reformations in the Sixteenth Century. A study of the religious aspects and consequences of Renaissance and Humanism* (The Hague, 1964); Phyllis Mack Crew, *Calvinist Preaching and Iconoclasm in the Netherlands 1544–1569* (Cambridge, 1978); W. Nijenhuis, 'Variants within Dutch Calvinism in the Sixteenth Century', in *The Low Countries History Yearbook*, 12 (The Hague, 1979), pp. 48–64 and C.A. Bangs, *Arminius. A Study in the Dutch Reformation*, second edition (Grand Rapids, Mich., 1985).

Many recent studies have focussed on more specific aspects of the Revolt. Noteworthy examples (in English) include: J.C. Boogman, 'The Union of Utrecht: Its genesis and consequences' in his *Van spel tot spelers. Verspreide opstellen* (The Hague, 1982), pp. 53–82; C.C. Hibben, *Gouda in Revolt. Particularism and Pacifism in the Revolt of the Netherlands 1572–1588* (Utrecht, 1983); Rients Reitsma, *Centrifugal and Centripetal Forces in the Early Dutch Republic. The States of Overijssel 1566–1600* (Amsterdam, 1982); James D. Tracy, *Holland under Habsburg Rule, 1506–1566. The formation of a body politic* (Berkeley/Los Angeles/Oxford, 1990); Guy Wells, *Antwerp and the Government of Philip II 1555–1567* (Ann Arbor, 1982).

Some attempts have been made to study the Dutch Revolt within the larger framework of the history of the Spanish empire. Noteworthy are M. J. Rodriguez-Salgado, *The Changing Face of Empire: Charles V, Philip II and Hapsburg Authority, 1551–1559* (Cambridge, 1988) and Paul David Lagomarsino, 'Court faction and the formulation of Spanish policy towards the Netherlands (1559–1567)', unpubl. PhD thesis, University of Cambridge, 1973.

Finally, recent biographies of the Revolt's main actors in English include Mack P. Holt, *The Duke of Anjou and the Politique Struggle during the Wars of Religion* (Cambridge, 1986; William S. Maltby, *Alba: A Biography of Fernandez Alvarez de Toledo, Third Duke of Alba, 1507–1582* (Berkeley/Los Angeles/London, 1983); Geoffrey Parker, *Philip II* (London, 1978); K. W. Swart, *William the Silent and the Revolt of the Netherlands* (London, 1978); C.V. Wedgwood, *William the Silent* (London, 1944; reprint 1989).

Note on the texts

The edition of *A Defence and true Declaration of the things lately done in the lowe Countrey whereby may easily be seen to whom all the beginning and cause of the late troubles and calamities is to be imputed* is a transcript of the edition as printed by John Daye, London, 1571. For the sake of clarity some minor adjustments have been made, and the spelling has been modernized. The 1571 English edition has been compared with the original *Libellus Supplex Imperatoriae Maiestati*, published in 1570. Differences between the original and the 1571 translation are noted. The edition is based on the copy of the *Defence* in the Royal Library at The Hague (code 1709–F-17).

The *Address and Opening to make a good, blessed and general peace in the Netherlands, and to bring them under the obedience of the king, in her old prosperity, bloom and welfare. By way of Supplication* is a translation of the *Vertoog ende Openinghe om een goede, salighe ende generale vrede te maken in dese Nederlanden, ende deselven onder de ghehoorsaemheyt des Conincx, in haere oude voorspoedicheyt, fleur ende welvaert te brenghen. By maniere van supplicatie*, 1576. For this edition the copy of this treatise in the Royal Library at Brussels (code II-59-252A) has been used.

The *Brief Discourse on the peace negotiations now taking place at Cologne between the King of Spain and the States of the Netherlands* is a translation of *Brief discours sur la negotiation de la paix, qui se tracte presentement à Coloigne entre le Roy d'Espaigne, & les Estats du Pays Bas*, (Leiden, 1579), and based on the copy in the Royal Library at The Hague (code Pamphlet 492). The same text was published in Ghent as the *Petit traicté servant d'instruction à messieurs les estatz et touts bons patriots, à fin qu'ils s'efforcent pour remectre le pais en repos par moyen d'une paix asseuree sans se laisser abuser des offres amiellees qui ne tendent que pour nous reduire soubz le ioug de pristine servitude*, 1579. Differences between both editions are noted.

The *Political Education* is the translation of *Politicq onderwijs*, published in Malines, 1582. For this edition the copy in the Royal Library at The Hague (code Pamphlet 581) has been used.

The *Short Exposition of the right exercised from all old times by the Knighthood, Nobles and Towns of Holland and Westvriesland for the maintenance of the liberties, rights, privileges and laudable customs of the country* is a translation of the original Deduction by the States of Holland in response to a *Remonstrance* by Sir Thomas Wilkes (see pp. xxvii–xxix) as published in Pieter Christiaansz. Bor, *Oorsprongk, begin en vervolgh der Nederlantsche oorlogen, beroerten en borgerlijke oneenigheden*, vol. 2 (Amsterdam, 1679) (originally published in 1595), pp. 921–4. A slightly revised version was published as the *Corte vertoninghe van het recht byden Ridderschap, Eedelen ende Steden van Hollandt ende Westvrieslant van allen ouden tijden in den voorschreven Lande gebruyckt tot behoudenisse vande vryheden, gherechticheden, Privilegien ende Loffelicke ghebruycken vanden selven Lande* (Rotterdam, 1587), of which I have used a copy in the Royal Library at The Hague (code Pamphlet 791). Differences between both versions are noted.

A DEFENCE
AND TRUE DECLARATION OF THE
THINGS LATELY DONE IN THE
LOW COUNTRY, WHEREBY MAY
EASILY BE SEEN TO WHOM ALL
THE BEGINNING AND CAUSE OF
THE LATE TROUBLES AND
CALAMITIES IS TO BE
IMPUTED.

AND THEREWITH ALSO THE SLANDERS
WHEREWITH THE ADVERSARIES DO BURDEN
THE CHURCHES OF THE LOW COUNTRY
ARE PLAINLY REFUTED.

PSALM 43.

GIVE SENTENCE WITH ME (O GOD) AND DEFEND
MY CAUSE AGAINST THE UNGODLY PEOPLE: O
DELIVER ME FROM THE DECEITFUL AND WICKED
MAN. FOR THOU ART THE GOD OF MY
STRENGTH.

AT LONDON
PRINTED BY JOHN DAYE
dwelling over Aldersgate.

With the grace and privilege of
Her Royal Majesty.

The Preface

My singular good Lord. The doings of Papists standing wholly, as
their religion does, upon falsehood and cruelty, taking to themselves
by use a licence of untrue speaking and working, plainly show what
faith is to be given to such as think themselves bound to keep no faith.
Such has always been their manner, not only in dissimulation and
practising before things be brought to pass, but also in shameless
lying and misreporting them after they be ended. For what else is to
be looked for of that unfaithful faith that is grounded wholly upon
falsehood and blasphemy, is pursued wholly with malice and treason,
is announced wholly by cruelty and tyranny, and having no respect of
prosperity beyond this life, has by confidence in man destroyed the
fear of God?

What marvel is it then if such kind of men, Monks, Friars, and
other parasites, having been writers of histories heretofore, have filled
the world with feigned miracles and with intolerable absurdities, to
flatter Popes and deceive the people, have slandered Emperors, Kings
and Princes, and as ordinarily laid up in their libraries false treatises
and chronicles to beguile posterity, as in their cosers forged evidences
with which they daily made to rob true owners of their inheritance. In
these falsities they so far proceeded, that their impudence fell, with
want of shame by use of lying, into so great imprudence as that
manifest contradictions and inconveniences convinced them [to
which] they then resorted to justify their untruths, seducing the world

3

with pretence of profitably deceiving men with godly error. Surely whose conscience can serve them to do murders, to tumble up kingdoms, and raise all kind of horrible and tragical examples, will not much stick to tell lies in excusing or reporting the doings of themselves, and their adversaries. For *Ex ijsdem sunt et nutriuntur mixta*, a sect patched up of lies, must be fed and maintained with the same. Much like it is to the doing of King Richard and Catesbie to blear the world's eyes with the proclamation of treason supposed to have been intended by the Lord Hastings and Shore's wife, and showing out his own withered army, after the example of Antonius Caracalla concerning his brother Geta, and such like.[1] So did that honest man Boner immediately upon the death of the excellent Martyr the Archbishop of Canterbury, openly cause to be published in Print a report of the Archbishop's death and his words before his death, directly contrary to that which was spoken, and all in favour of Popery. Thence came it that all foreign histories are at this day so stuffed with slander against our estates, people and Princes, especially since King Henry VIII resumed his lawful jurisdiction from usurping Popes. Our kings are villainously termed Tyrants, virtuous Queens and Ladies defamed, Nobility disgraced, Parliaments despised, the people reproachfully taunted, thieves, whoremongers, Sodomites, murderers and traitors sanctified, victories pinched, facts and successes falsely uttered, and that so plainly, even though living witnesses present and parties to the matters themselves are able truly to disprove them. And all this they do upon trust that though it be shameful for a while, yet their books will outlive men's persons and so at length deceive posterity: and so they think it reason now that other papists hereafter should enjoy the fruit of their falsehood at this time, as they have the fruit of other's Papist's falsehood heretofore. So does fabulous Jovius,[2] so does prating Paradine, so does the whole heap of Popish pamphleteers, without

---

[1] William Hastings (1430–83), the lover of King Edward IV's mistress Jane Shore, opposed the succession in 1483 of the Duke of Gloucester, the later Richard III. The story of this conflict, which ended with the execution of Hastings, was the topic of Shakespeare's *Richard III*.

  Marcus Aurelius Caracalla (188–217) was Roman Emperor from 211 until 217 and well known for his brutality. The rivalry with his younger brother Geta ended in the murder of Geta and his friends in 212.

[2] Perhaps Jovius refers to Paolo Giovio (1483–1552), also known as Paulus Jovius, a contemporary Roman Catholic historian, well known for his vivid portraits of famous men and for his history of Florence, published between 1550 and 1552.

reverence of Princes' estates or of other men's ears, of their own worn out honesty. This has made common liars to show advises of news from overseas, so freshly arrived that the very ink blotted when the letters were shown in Paul's, men surely worthy of their card cousin to hang on their backs to warn them, and F.cudgel better to advise them. This doing of theirs has, of late years, continually enforced noble Princes and good men to publish Apologies and to set forth books, to give true account of their facts against this poisonous kind of Parasites and rumour spreaders. This, my Lord, has caused the noble men and others of low Germany to publish in Supplication, by them exhibited to the Emperor, the Electors and other Princes assembled at Speyer, the report of their doings and sufferings, with request of good interpretation and charitable aid. Because the same contains a great deal of matter of good historical knowledge, and because the daily rumours of Papists do amplify evils to kindle uncharitableness against poor men, I have thought good to turn the same into English, and to set it out to the world to behold, without prejudicing the credit of any, but leaving every man to believe so far with them or against them, as evident truth and apparent proofs shall lead them. Only this by the way remembered, that the public ministers, ambassadors, messengers and agents for those against whom these do complain, have not stuck against common faith to be certifiers and avouchers of untruths and partners of treasons against our noble Queen, as in public arrangements and other open places and doings, beside secret knowledge, has lately appeared.

Having performed this work of translation for credit of truth, and for raising of good affections in just and indifferent persons, and for a good monument of knowledge to such as lack help of the Latin tongue, where, and in the Dutch tongue, it has been before printed, I thought it my duty to offer the same to your good Lordship. Whereunto many reasonable aspects have moved me.

First, your zeal to true religion, your virtuous governance of your household, therein, your noble and sincere administration of justice, without using the Queen's service to private malice and affections, and your severe looking to dangerous carriers of untrue rumours and seditious speeches in your country; all which virtues become a personage fit to receive a work intended for declaration of truth and confutation of slander. Beside that I, being sustained in study by your Lordship's liberality, do owe you that duty that under your name should pass to the world's commodity such fruits of learning as I have been able to yield, humbly praying your Lordship to accept the same, and most humbly beseeching God long to bless your Lordship and my good Lady, long in honour and prosperity to serve our most gracious Queen, who God long defend to His honour and the succour of His church, and comfort of her own conscience, in not omitting anything to the help of God's flock, and sure removal of God's enemies' dangerous practices, that as her present government ministers abundance of good fruits, so the times imminent and posterity may find no lack, but for her good provisions yield her eternal thankful memory, when God shall have received her as His faithful servant to eternal blessed kingdom.

Your Lord's most humble,
ELIAS NEWCOMEN.

The same tempest, most victorious Emperor and most notable Princes, which now almost a whole hundred years has troubled sundry parts of Europe, has now also at this time, by most cruel tyranny, forced us, being spoilt of our goods, chased out of our native countries, oppressed with the slander of our adversaries, and tossed with all kind of calamity, to flee as most humble suitors to your clemency for succour.

For we suppose there is no man ignorant, that long ago Spain, and since also little by little a great part of all Europe not only has flamed with inward contentions and tumults, but also has in manner been overwhelmed with most grievous storm of persecutions and tyranny. Whereby certain idle men, which, only in name and outward posture, professed a solitary life severed from all governance of commonwealths, and only addicted to the preaching of the word of God or quiet study of holy scriptures, have begun to creep into courts of Kings and Princes, and, covering their greedy affections with cloak of religion, to minister such counsels whereby they might, by their new devised means of Inquisition against heresy, draw to themselves from the civil magistrate the hearing and judgment of the controversies of greatest weight and importance. And so by little and little, they have attained not only by searching and inquiring to become Lords of every private person's goods, possessions, houses and most secret places, yea and their wives and children, but also to bring the magistrates and Princes themselves in subjection to their authority. In what places they perceived their desires to be hindered either by the ancient liberty of the people, or by the discretion of the Rulers and Princes, they straightaway charged such with forged slander of heresy and rebellion, and so grievously inflamed the hearts of Kings and Emperors against their subjects. And by this crafty means they have stirred up civil dissensions, tumults of communities, and often grievous wars, whereby they have brought most flourishing countries into great displeasure and hatred of all kings, princes and nations, and so drawn them to extreme calamity.

If any province in Europe has ever felt this, surely our country, namely that part of low Germany that is subject to the most mighty king of Spain, has and especially at this time to their great destruction most miserably suffered. For since that by the most false slanders and other corrupt crafty means of the Spanish Inquisitors, this country has, under pretence of heresy and impiety, been brought in grievous displeasure with the Emperor Charles the fifth of happy memory, and his son Philip, King of Spain and Lord of low Germany, and oppressed with most heinous Edicts about Religion procured by guile and slanderous reporting, and so has of their great truthfulness and obedience to their sovereign Lords now more than fifty years with incredible patience born the Inquisitors' most cruel yoke. Now finally after matters in other adjoining countries [were] well settled to peace and quietness, and the truth of the matter [was] commonly disclosed, [the country of low Germany has] hoped to find some release of so great calamity. It is now come to pass that the adversaries, being grieved to see them aspire to such liberty of religion as by this time flourished not only in Germany but also in France and many other places, have in strange manner and with most earnest endeavour travailed, not only to frustrate the hope of the inhabitants, but also, by bringing in a far more grievous tyranny, to pull from them all the residue of their right and liberty that they had remaining. And so to spoil such wealthy ones of their goods, and such noble and mighty ones of their lives, as they saw to be able to withstand their attempts.

Therefore adjoining to them the Bishop of Rome, and having obtained his Bull,[3] they did by sundry slanders and with extreme

---

[3] In 1559 the papal bull *Super Universas* announced a thorough reorganization of the diocesan structure of the Low Countries. The plan to create three new archdioceses,

importunity wrest from the King an Edict against all the Privileges of the country, against their laws, ordinances, and ancient liberties, namely, for the precise observing of the decrees of the Council of Trent,[4] and for bringing in of new Bishops, that should put in execution throughout the whole land a new form of Inquisition, far more cruel than the very Spanish Inquisition, which was first invented against Jews and Mohammedan Apostates; and so in short time should openly bring a most flourishing and free Province into the most dishonourable servitude of strangers, and those most villainous and abominable persons, to torment at their pleasure the most honest and best men, upon subornation of any infamous informer or most corrupt witness, with bonds, with racks, with gallows and with fire, to trust the wealthy out of their possessions, to subdue the magistrates themselves to their jurisdiction, and to make themselves Lords of all, and especially to destroy utterly and, with most exquisite torments, to murder and root up all those that refused to obey the Bishop of Rome's power, and would have their consciences subject to the only word of God contained in the books of the old and new Testament.

This matter giving just occasion to the Nobility that they exhibited Supplication for stay[5] thereof to the Duchess of Parma, Regent there for the King, and in the same [they] declared what calamity would thereof undoubtedly ensue: and likewise when the communities, having heretofore used their religion within their private houses, and seeing the same thereby subject to slanders and envy, did now by laying it open in public preachings and assemblies, to the indifferent judgment and examination of all good men, deliver it from false and cavillous reports: it came to pass that the adversaries hereupon took occasion by raising of sundry tumults most hatefully to incense the King against the whole people, as guilty of the most heinous crimes of heresy, rebellion, sedition and treason against God and the King. And where His Majesty was fully determined to come into the Low Country, and himself in person to hear the cause, and to end the whole matter according to right and equity, they, partly by subtle powerful means and very traitorous practices purposely devised for

with a total of eighteen bishoprics, was widely considered to be an attempt to strengthen Philip's grip on the Netherlands. See pp. x–xi.

[4] The Council of Trent (1545–63) was the Roman Catholic church's response to the Reformation. The Council took major decisions, which led to a spiritual renewal of the church – the Counter-Reformation.

[5] Deferment.

the destruction of the people of that country, and partly by the importunate labour and impudent greedy endeavour of certain persons, and partly also by advises and threats procured from foreign parties, even in manner against his will, brought him to this that, being grievously incensed against his subjects, suddenly altering his former purpose, he sent thither in his stead with most large Commission to hear the cause and dispose of the state of the commonwealth, the Duke of Alva,[6] a man, both a most assured minister of their Inquisition and for old grudges a most bitter enemy to the Princes and state of the low country.

He coloured his own malicious affections with the glorious pretence of zeal to restore the Roman Religion and to chastise rebels. It is incredible to tell how great and how outrageous cruelty he has everywhere executed upon the poor inhabitants of the low country, without respect or difference: by how many and how strange devises he has robbed all men's goods: how he has spoilt the whole Province of all their ornaments, disarmed them of their defences, deprived them of their liberties, and stripped them out of their laws and privileges: how every honest man he has condemned by private warrant without judicial order. Every the most innocent man's blood he has shed, every most virtuous person he has put to most vile shame, all laws of God and man he has violated, the bonds of marriage he has broken, the Sacrament of Baptism he has polluted, all order of charity and friendly society he has overthrown, finally no part of most extreme cruelty and such as never was heard of before has he omitted. And yet in the mean time, he did not cease to throw upon us the blame of his heinous facts, and by proclamations published and by infamous libels printed, openly to all princes and states to accuse us of most grievous crimes, for this only cause forsooth, that in fleeing we gave place to his fury, and by the help of God's protection we have escaped his sword, most thirsty of our blood.

All such things, for as much as almighty God has so determined that we should for a time be here afflicted by the tyranny of the wicked, we would have thought it best for us to pass over in silence and in patience, and to wait for the time which the great Judge has appointed, either for bringing our innocence to knowledge, or for opening the eyes and ears of our King to understand our unjust

---

[6] For the Duke of Alva, see 'Biographical Notes'.

misery and just complaint, were it not that we do plainly see that such our silence, especially in this so sacred and so full assembly of your majesty, most victorious Emperor, and of your Highnesses most noble Princes, might hereafter bring no small prejudice to us and our innocence before such to whom the truth shall not be sufficiently known. For by such means the son of God, Jesus Christ himself, and his doctrine which we profess according to his word, should become subject to the most heinous slanders of the adversaries, as if the professors thereof before the so reverent judgment seat of Christendom, before so upright and incorrupt judges, before this theatre so furnished with so great assembly of sundry nations, were by silent confession found guilty, not only of heresy and pestilent ungodly error, but also of shameful rebellion, of wicked sedition and disturbance of common peace.

Wherefore we have finally determined, that we can no longer with good peace of conscience keep silence. But for as much as we know that the order of these usual assemblies of the states of the sacred Empire have their chief respect to this end, that such as be oppressed by force and injury may here present their complaints as to the chief throne of Justice in Christendom: we thought it our duty to declare our whole estate to your majesty, most mighty Emperor and to your highnesses, most noble Princes, and to open unto you the very original fountains of this, our most grievous calamity, that if the mercy of God have decreed to make an end of our so great miseries, we may by your goodness and liberality begin to take breath again after this most heavy weight of oppression. If not, yet the cause being more thoroughly heard, we shall before indifferent judges deliver our innocence from the most unjust slanders of our adversaries. Whereby, if nothing else, yet this we shall obtain that from henceforth our religion and the profession of the Gospel shall not bear the infamy of so grievous crimes with them that heretofore being filled with the accusations of the adversaries have not understood the truth: and that Jesus Christ, the son of God, whose name we profess, shall not be wounded through us, and finally that we shall not, as enemies of public peace and quietness, be expelled from common society by foreign Princes and peoples, which is the chief thing our enemies do seek, but that, the whole truth being thoroughly understood, the whole origin of the mischief shall be justly laid upon them that, inflamed with their own greedy malice, do tumble up all things. And such good and innocent men, as they have by wrong and tyranny spoilt of their goods and can not yet bereave of their lives, they labour to oppress with most vile, slanderous reports to your majesty, O Emperor, and your highnesses, O noble Princes, that so they may draw you into the fellowship of their cruelty, and by your help they may either satisfy their unsatiable thirst with our blood, or glut the most bitter hatred that they have conceived against us with our destruction.

Which thing that they shall not obtain, your equity, truth and uprightness, and our innocence do assure us. In confidence whereof we prostrate us at your feet, we flee to your protection and mercy, and crave help of your religiousness,[7] justice and uprightness: and we most humbly beseech you that, preserving the justice of law, you will vouchsafe most mercifully to defend our miserable and afflicted innocence against the outrageous power and unbridled boldness of our enemies.

That you may understand how justly you may do it, and that you may clearly perceive in whom the fault of the whole mischief rests, we beseech your majesty, most invincible Emperor, and your highnesses, most noble Princes, that at leisure you will gently and diligently read this book annexed to this our supplication, wherein with the truth of the whole history, we declare our innocence to all men: and that with the same patience and equity of mind, that you use to receive the complaints of all miserable and innocent persons, it may please you also to understand our cause, and to your power deliver us out of these calamities. So shall you show yourselves worthy ministers to the sovereign king of kings and supreme judge, and shall stir up our hearts to be continual suitors to His grace and mercy for you.

[7] Devoutness.

A DEFENCE
AND TRUE DECLARATION OF THE
THINGS LATELY DONE IN THE
LOW COUNTRY,[8] WHEREBY MAY
EASILY BE SEEN TO WHOM ALL
THE BEGINNING AND CAUSE OF
THE LATE TROUBLES AND
CALAMITIES IS TO BE
ˌ IMPUTED.

AND THEREWITH ALSO THE SLANDERS
WHEREWITH THE ADVERSARIES DO BURDEN
THE CHURCHES OF THE LOW COUNTRY
ARE PLAINLY REFUTED.

PSALM 43:

GIVE SENTENCE WITH ME (O GOD) AND DEFEND
MY CAUSE AGAINST THE UNGODLY PEOPLE: O
DELIVER ME FROM THE DECEITFUL AND WICKED
MAN. FOR THOU ART THE GOD OF MY
STRENGTH.

AT LONDON
PRINTED BY JOHN DAYE
dwelling over Aldersgate.

IN THE YEAR 1571.

[8] Where the *Defence* speaks of the 'low country' or 'low Germany', the original *Libellus Supplex* uses or adds the name 'Belgium'.

It is now near a hundred years ago since the most noble Ferdinand and Isabel, King and Queen of Castile, having ended their great and long war against the Mohammedans, which had invaded, inhabited and troubled the kingdom of Spain by the space of almost 800 years, and having chased the said enemies out of all Spain and recovered the kingdom of Granada, gave their minds to establish religion, and to root out all the remnants of the wicked Mohammedan and Jewish sects. The charge hereof was committed to the Friars of Dominic's sect, who had wholly possessed the King's and Queen's hearts and ears with a great estimation of holiness and wisdom: and therewith were also given them full authority in all things that might seem requisite to so great a matter. They, supposing themselves to have so obtained a most commodious occasion to advance their own power and dignity, persuaded the King and Queen that for achieving thereof a most extreme and unmovable severity was necessary. And as though the dealing with religion did not pertain to the civil magistrate, but properly belonged to Friars who as it were by a peculiar name called themselves religious men, and to Priests, they said it was necessary that a new court of Inquisitors should be erected, to whom not only the hearing and determining of such matters, but also the whole judgment of all religion, whatsoever it were, should with full power be committed. The well meaning Princes, which only directed their intention, by any way howsoever it were, to advance the Christian faith, lightly gave credit to those whom they thought to excel other men in pureness of life and holiness, and therewith committed to those themselves that were the inventors thereof the whole power of the Inquisitor's office, to use according to their own discretion. Thereto was added the confirmation of pope Sixtus the fourth, then Bishop of Rome. For he laboured with all his endeavour and earnest affection not only to establish but also to advance and magnify the four orders of Friars then lately sprung up.

To which his purpose he saw the zeal of the King and Queen of Spain to be a very fit means. Wherefore by his authority, which then was at the greatest that ever it was since the world began, and by his Bull he confirmed and ratified this new judicial throne, and new kingdom of Inquisitors.[9] So this power, upheld both by the Royal and papal authority, in short time marvellously increased. And since there is no man, whom the right order of religion does not concern, by this pretence they easily got to themselves the jurisdiction and judgment over all men of all estates and degrees. And by this means within short while after, they began to be Lords over all men's goods, possessions, lives and consciences, until of unmeasurable power arose in them pride and covetousness, and consequently thereof grew the hatred of all men against them, so as now nobody thought them any longer tolerable. Therefore by the counsel and means of certain bishops and others of the clergy that were in great estimation and credit in Spain, which repined[10] to be subject to the dominion of the Friars, it was procured that by the king's authority the power of Inquisition was taken from the Dominicans and given to the clergy. And it was ordered that out of the bishops and other priests should be chosen the masters of the Inquisition, which should indeed use the travail and advise of the Dominicans, but yet should still reserve to themselves the sovereign power of the Inquisitor's office. These, either for that they had some fervent zeal of religion, or for that they cunningly cloaked their ambitious pride, partly with wonderful opinion of holiness, partly by the favour and power of Princes and men of great authority to whom they were joined in friendship, kinship or alliance, partly also by corrupt and secret devices, in short time advanced this their new raised empire to so great a height, that now they not only used dominion at their pleasure over the community, but also brought

---

[9] By the bull of 1 November 1478 Sixtus IV authorized the Catholic Monarchs to appoint Inquisitors, which meant the beginning of the famous Spanish Inquisition. In fact the pope had been reluctant to give his permission, as he favoured the introduction of the papal Inquisition in Spain. The first Inquisitors were appointed in 1480.

[10] Rejected.

into subjection to the Holy Inquisition all the liberty of all the people, and estates of the realm. They broke privileges and immunities, they abated the dignity of the Nobility, whom they call 'The grand council' without whose authority in time past nothing was decreed in Spain. Finally, under pretence of religion and service of God, they usurped to themselves sovereign power over the King himself, and over the majesty of the royal scepter. All noble men and persons of any credit whom they thought in any wise able to hinder their enterprises, they caused to be accused of heresy and cruelly killed them, or defaced them with most reproachful note of open shame, such as should remain upon all their posterity, and so made them infamous and of odious memory forever.

These devices, though to many men they seemed strange and intolerable, yet both because they were principally provided against the most hateful enemies of Spain and of Christian Religion, namely the Moors, Mohammedans and Jews, and also for that they bleared most men's eyes with the pretence of God's service and opinion of holiness, and finally for that they not a little availed to the enriching of the King's treasury, now greatly wasted with many wars, to whose use the one moitie[11] of the goods of all persons condemned was employed, they were daily more and more established by the earnest favours, authority and power of the most part of the mightiest persons and especially of the King and Queen themselves, until the Aragonese, who are the principal province of Spain both in right of ancient liberty, in nobility and largeness of dominion, openly resisted. They, when they nothing prevailed with king Ferdinand by humble and lowly petition, attempted by force and arms to keep out this pestilence from their country, for that they plainly saw that their liberty which they had received most large and incredible from their ancestors, and hitherto kept inviolate, should by this means be destroyed, and that [they] themselves and all theirs should be made subject to the most dishonourable tyranny of the clergy. But they prevailed not. For after many troubles, much destruction and bloodshed they were compelled mawgre[12] their wills and per force, as the residue of Spain did, to yield their necks to stoop under this yoke of Inquisition so that the same province, than which in time past there was none or more freedom, is now in such case as at this day there is

[11] Half.
[12] In spite of.

17

none to be found in more servitude and subjection. By terror of which example, and by great opinion of holiness which the Inquisitors had gotten by the good success in this case, it came to pass that they subdued all Spain unto them without any further resistance.

The enlarging of the Inquisitors' dominion.

But as the greedy desires of men are naturally unmeasurable and unsatiable, this lust of dominion could not long be contained within the bounds of Spain, though they be full large; but, still forsooth, with the same plausible pretence of establishing religion they bent their mind to enlarge their empire and promised themselves the rule of the whole world. For there is scarcely any country which in short space following they did not attempt to make subject to them, even by the same subtle means whereby they had daunted Spain. For they compelled both the chief part of Italy and many islands both of the Mediterranean and Ocean seas, and England itself (though not for long time) to yield their necks to this halter of Inquisition. Yea, they not only ranged over the uttermost Indians, and to the far distant lands severed from us by the huge stream of the Ocean, but also under pretence of ordering religion they spoilt the poor and simple inhabitants of those countries of all their goods and possessions, and of their wives, children and lives. Yea and cruelly like butchers tearing them with all kind of torments, they slew them by heaps, and brought them to such misery and wretched plight, that a great number of them chose rather to slay themselves, than to come under such cruel subjection of unnatural men. Yea not long ago they employed all their counsels and all their practices and left no way unassailed, to bring whole Germany in slavery under the same yoke. And so far with the authority and threatenings of the bishops of Rome they drove on the emperor Charles the fifth of famous memory even in manner against his will and long withholding himself, that the best and most noble princes he proclaimed traitors, and made most deadly war upon them as upon sworn enemies, and under the pretended cloak of rebellion armed the Protestant princes the one against the other.[13] He brought the free cities into most dishonourable slavery of Spanish soldiers, and made the majesty of the most noble and sacred empire subject to the lust and intolerable desires of most villainous persons. Which most cruel yoke, if partly the valiance of the German princes and partly the equity and gentle favour of the Emperor himself at length

[13] This is probably a reference to the Schmalkaldic war of 1546–7, in which the Emperor defeated a number of Protestant princes, united in the League of Schmalkalden.

perceiving the matter as truth was, had not shaken of or taken away, whole Germany might long have been in such case as now is that parcel thereof from whence are now most unjustly banished, and forced to sue for and plead, the cause of our afflicted country, oppressed not only with most grievous tyranny, but also with most unworthy slanders: and to protest before almighty God and all mankind that there is no other cause of our calamity but even the same which had nearly overwhelmed whole Germany, namely the greedy ambition of these men, that under pretence of establishing religion, labour to enlarge their dominion throughout the whole by right or wrong. And so much the more earnestly they endeavour to bring it into the low country of Germany, because it is by alliance of the princes, by the community of one king, and by ancient intercourse of merchandise and conversation somewhat nearly conjoined unto them. Therefore of long time they think that they may lawfully enforce upon us the Spanish laws and ordinances, Spanish manners and the Spanish yoke of inquisition, abrogating all our country laws, abolishing all memory of the German name, destroying our privileges and oppressing our liberty.

When they long since espied that the Country though it be not great, yet flourishes in wealth and power, and is so fenced against foreign force, not only with strong towns and castles, but also with good laws and ordinances, and with large privileges, prerogatives, immunities and other liberties, that so long as it has her own prince's favour, it is easily able to defend her ancient freedom. They have these many years evidently purposed and practised diverse ways to bring the inhabitants into suspicion and displeasure, both with the Emperor Charles the fifth and with King Philip his son, to accuse them for heretics and rebels, and so to persuade to have them esteemed as enemies and traitors. [So] that by this means, the country which for many respects they accounted most commodious for their purpose, might be spoilt of all right of liberty, subdued, and added to their dominion. Sometimes they pretended this colour, that the seignories were too many and too several, sometimes that in respect of the number of seignories, the laws, customs and ordinances were too diverse. Sometimes they alleged that the people were too wild and proud by reason of their privileges, immunities and liberties. Sometimes they brought the king into jealousy of the too great wealth and power of his subjects. Sometimes they informed that the inter-

The subtle means and devises of the Inquisitors.

course and traffic of foreign nations were suspicious. Finally, they left nothing untried that might [in] any way seem to serve to aggrieve his mind toward them. Principally they urged this one thing that the ancient liberty of assembly of the estates in parliaments that has continued in all ages greatly abates the power of the prince, for that there both by most ancient usage of their forefathers it was so provided, and by the promises and covenants of the princes themselves confirmed with their oaths it was so ordained, that the princes should not decree or do anything to the prejudice of the people's liberty or of the authority of their laws without the will and assent of the estates of the whole country; and that therefore they more regarded the acts of the Estates than the king's proclamations; that they esteemed the king not as a king but as some common Duke or Earl, or rather guardian of their right and laws, to govern the commonwealth not by his own authority, but after a proscribed form of laws and the ordinances of the estates; moreover that as it is in most free commonwealths, so they

Burgomasters yearly create of themselves magistrates, and burgomasters with sovereign power of negative voice; that strangers are debarred from bearing office in the commonwealth; and ecclesiastical men, by the laws and statutes of the land, are excluded from power of jurisdiction, and so the way stopped up for the prince's nearest and most faithful servants to attain any government. These and suchlike things (say they) in times past have often given occasion to the community proudly to disobey the commandment of their princes, yea, to burden their Lords and princes to laws and conditions. Yea, and if their Princes attempted anything against the usage and will of the estates, they have presumed to chasten them sometimes with penalties, sometimes with imprisonment, and sometimes with deposing them.

This appears These things (said they) are not to be suffered of Princes. Therefore
by the they long most earnestly travailed with Charles the Emperor, and with
Spaniard's Philip his son, that the whole country might be reduced into one body,
own history, and made subject to one form of laws and jurisdiction, and brought to
written by the name and title of a kingdom, and that, abrogating the power of
Alfons Uloa popular magistrates and laws, it might be governed with new laws by
and printed discretion as the Kingdoms of Sicily and Naples be, that have been
in Dutch at acquired by conquest. Wherein, when they saw that they laboured in
Dilling. For vain, both because the states of all the towns most stiffly withstood it,
there they and perhaps also for that the Emperor himself began to smell their
confess that sinister purposes and untrue meaning, they deferred the matter to a
this was their
purpose to
reduce the

more commodious season, and this yet by the way with their importunate slanderous cavilling they obtained, that afterward he would never in any wise suffer the solemn parliaments or general assemblies of the estates of all the provinces to be kept as it had been used in his progenitor's times and that he placed in governance Ecclesiastical men and such, as not only by the law of God, the civil and canon laws, but also by the ancient customs of the country, and·by sundry decrees of the Dukes of Burgundy were excluded from judicial office and from bearing civil rule in the commonwealth. *whole country to a kingdom like Sicily and Naples.*

Finally to make themselves in easier way to that dominion that they had conceived, under pretence of establishing religion, they with importunity procured such rigorousness of edicts against those that professed the doctrine of the Gospel, as never any country, never any city, never any commonwealth had seen before. For they had fully persuaded him, as is also contained in the express words of the edict, that Luther, whose doctrine those did follow, professed the Pelagian error,[14] set naught by all the holy fathers and doctors of the church, abolished all Magistrates, overthrew all civil governance and political order, stirred up the people to take armour, made them apt to murder, steal, waste and destroy with fire, and finally gave every one leave to live as he listed. *The occasion and manner of the Inquisition and the edicts in the low country.*

The very words of the Edict, dated at Worms the eighth of May 1521.

In the which Peter de Soto, a Spaniard, his confessor and one of the masters of the Spanish Inquisition, not of the meanest sort, furthered them very much. By the which persuasion they easily enforced the Emperor Charles, a prince otherwise by nature gentle and merciful, to decree and *a*without the assent of the estates to publish, and from time to time to renew most cruel Edicts, and such as seem rather to be written with blood, than with ink. Not that he meant to have them executed with extremity, but that he hoped by the terror of this unaccustomed cruelty to call the people's minds from the study of that religion, which he in conscience accounted wicked. Of the which his hope and meaning he gave no small proof in that *b*exposition of the Edicts, which he afterwards set out, wherein it was appointed, that the Magistrates should by all means possible somewhat mitigate the extreme and immoderate cruelty of the former edicts, but the good masters of the Spanish Inquisition soon by their craft and subtlety suppressed this exposition. And it came at length to that tyranny that *aThat the assent of the estates was not taken, it is manifest by the very words of the Edicts, by the which the estates, governors and magistrates of the provinces were commanded with most grievous punishments to establish those Edicts,*

---

[14] Pelagius, a fifth-century English cleric, rejected the idea of original sin.

21

and to see them executed, and it is declared that in the behalf of the Bishop of Rome they were made only by the artrement of the King.

[b]That exposition was made and sealed in the year 1550, the month of September

they did not only execute the full rigour of the Edicts, but they observed also a new kind of Inquisition, not much unlike to the Inquisition of Spain, that thereby they might attain unto the full authority of that office and function, which they had long before obtained of the bishops of Rome. Therefore in the year of our Lord God 1550, when the King of Spain was authorized in Belgium,[15] with great and importunate suits they obtained an Edict concerning their Inquisition, whereby they usurped and took upon them so much authority, and power of the Citizens, and inhabitants of the whole province, as they thought sufficient for the subverting of the ancient liberties, and for the disannulling of all their accustomed privileges. But the senators and the estates of Brabant with long and earnest suit first stopped this their wicked enterprise, and afterwards the most noble princess Mary of famous memory, Queen of Hungary,[16] with great faith, singular piety and with no less wisdom suppressed it. For both when the Emperor Charles was at the Councils held at Augusta,[17] she went to him, and obtained that the cruelty of the Edicts should be somewhat mitigated, and that the whole name and purpose of the Inquisition should be omitted. And also many times after she stoutly set herself against the deceitful dealings, and rash attempts of the Inquisitors and divines, insomuch that at the length by their letters sent to Spain, she was accused of heresy before the Emperor. But she always bent her whole intent and purpose to keep the people of Belgium in the Emperor's good grace and favour, and to her power, to take away all the envy and hatred wherewith they were oppressed of their adversaries. With the which, her most merciful and wise design she so faithfully joined the hearts of the subjects towards their prince, that they for her sake thought no burden to be refused, in so much that in many things they did most willingly prefer her gracious favour and good will before the right of their ancient liberties, granted by the laws and statutes of their progenitors. For in all restraints, tasks, tributes or levies they showed themselves at the first commandment

---

[15] After the 1549 Pragmatic Sanction (see Introduction, p. ix) Philip toured the Low Countries; in each provincial capital he was sworn in and acknowledged as heir apparent.

[16] Mary of Hungary (1505–58), sister of Charles V and widow of the King of Hungary, served as governor of the Low Countries from 1531 until 1555. On the whole she faithfully supported her brother's religious policy, in spite of her own convictions, which have been termed Erasmian.

[17] Augsburg.

so obedient, that the princes could desire nothing, which was not delivered them with full consent of all their good wills, and that with speed. So that almost for the space of ten years, they gladly maintained that great, doubtful and most dangerous war, which was made against the most mighty kings of France; and they most willingly bestowed the greatest part of the charges thereof, the which by common books of account may be proved to surmount the sum of eleven thousand million of Florins. Neither did they give at any time so much as a small suspicion of rebellion.

Although in the mean time nevertheless these good masters of the Inquisition (while Charles reigned by the coloured show of the aforesaid Edicts and 'in the beginning of King Philip's reign by the grant of a new Edict bearing with it the King's authority, which they purchased by their subtle wills and crafty persuasions) raged most furiously in most parts of Belgium, but especially in Flanders, Hainaut, Artois, Tournai and Insule[18] and in many places in Holland, robbing, spoiling and most butcherly murdering the people with furious violence and extreme tyranny. ᵈFrom the which they abstained, lest that their deceit and subtlety being detected, this aforesaid commandment, wrested out by craft, should by the king's new letters patents be called in again. Neither yet were they without their friends in the Court, which being daily conversant with the king, always cloaked and covered their cruelty and insatiable avarice with the veil of godly Religion. At the length the King, having ended his war against the Frenchmen, prepared to take his journey into Spain;[19] his subjects for their singular obedience and their most faithful redeems in all affairs, thought they might justly hope· for some release from their other burdens but chiefly and especially they persuaded themselves that they should have the yoke of the Inquisition taken from their shoulders. But the king was so far from satisfying their expectation, that he did not only not remit or mitigate the cruelty used to them before, but also increased and augmented the tyranny, even as though their peace and other matters had been for none other cause concluded, but that they might the freer spoil poor men of their goods and most cruelly torment their conscienceᵉ. For at that time especially the Inquisitors by their old accustomed deceits and by the feigned show

ᶜIn the year 1555, December 1.

ᵈIn the year 1556, January 17.

ᵉThis may be proved by the letters and patents sent to the Cities in the year 1559, in August.

---

[18] 'Insule' probably refers to the islands comprising the province of Zeeland.
[19] The 1559 peace of Le Cateau Cambresis meant the end of a series of wars between the Valois and the Habsburg dynasty. Philip II left the Netherlands in the same year.

of setting forward religion, obtained of the king new letters patents to all princes and magistrates of every City, by the which the rigorousness of the former Edicts was not only openly confirmed, but also by the grant of many things contrary to the right, and privileges of their ancient liberties very much increased. With these letters the Inquisitors being armed after the King's departure, spoilt the poor people, being clean beggared before, of the remnants of their riches. They deprived cities and towns of their privileges, they most cruelly murdered the chief of the Citizens, having first spoilt them of their goods, destroying some with the burden of chains and long imprisonment, some by most cruel torments, some by the gallows, some by sword, some by fire, burying some quick, and drowning others. Yea, and that before their cause was pleaded, and many times at midnight, contrary to the accustomed manner of executing justice.

A new creation of bishops.

And that nothing should be wanting unto them whereby they might bring in this their holy Inquisition, to the utter abandoning and subverting the liberties and privileges of the whole provinces, and commit the chief authority to strangers, yea, to those only which were Priests and church men, contrary to all the orders and decrees of the former princes, and contrary to the king's covenant confirmed by oath; whereby they might challenge unto themselves not only full power and jurisdiction of all matters, but also the sovereign authority over all men's goods, riches, wives, children, yea over their lives also, and might captivate and make subject unto themselves the full power of the magistrates, and set the same forth to open zeal at their pleasure, they began with a new policy the old web of their Inquisition, which they had compassed in their minds, but not as yet thoroughly finished. /For when all the king's nobles and counsellors were departed from him, they persuaded him that it was necessary for the maintenance of the catholic religion to appoint new bishops, which should be the Inquisitors of faith. The charge hereof was committed to Sonninus,[20] a divine of Louvain. He going to Rome, with great diligence brought his matter to pass in a short time, as he desired. He divided the provinces as he was commanded by

/Not long before the King's departure, only Granvelle and Viglius, and three or four more knowing thereof.

[20] Franciscus Sonnius (1507–76) became professor of theology at Louvain University in 1543. In 1549 he was appointed Inquisitor of Holland, Zeeland and a number of northern provinces. Sonnius, who had participated in the Council of Trent, was one of the founding fathers of the plan to restructure the diocesan organization in the Netherlands, as a result of which he himself became the first bishop of Bois-le-Duc in 1560.

Granvelle[21] in the which he did not leave the power and jurisdiction of the [g]princes of the empire untouched, so far was he from letting the other bishops and nobles to escape. He [h]made certain men bishops, which had spent their whole study and travail, all of their lifetime in the administration of civil affairs, whereof [i]some of them, for their wit and learning were accompted as fools, and others for their unchaste life and odious crimes were famous with most noble infamy. He assigned unto Granvelle the archbishopric of Malines with the Abbey of Afflighem, the richest and most wealthy of all Belgium, that is to say, he gave him the sovereign authority of all things. He appointed to Viglius[22] the bishopric of Ghent, but to himself he reserved the bishopric of Bois-le-Duc, and adjoined thereunto many of the most wealthiest Abbeys, the which were evident signs and tokens of the eminent calamities, and public bondage. He imparted to the rest as their office and charge required,[j] but to every one he obtained licence to appoint new prebends in his cathedral Church, they which should be bound always to serve and help the bishop in his Inquisition throughout his Diocese, whereof two of them were always Inquisitors by office, the rest should seize upon the goods, confiscate, and serve for proctors to accuse the guilty. And every magistrate was bound to aid everyone of these with his full power and force. It was lawful for strangers to attain to these bishoprics, under which pretence the whole province might easily, and in short time be made subject to the Spaniards, inventors and masters of this Inquisition.

And thus this stranger and upstart Granvelle, born of a base degree and most obscure parentage, with that slavish sect of the Spanish Inquisitors, does [k]contrary to the whole liberty of the people, contrary to the laws of the City, contrary to the privileges of the province granted and confirmed by the king's oath, contrary to all former promises, contrary to all rights and customs of our progenitors, contrary to the making of laws, the foundations of old Abbeys, the jurisdiction of bishoprics, the privileges and immunities of towns, by force thrust upon the provinces of Belgium this new creation of bishops. He goes about, partly with flattering promises, partly with fearful threats to induce many cities and magistrates to apply themselves to his censure and judgment; and to some Cities he caused bishops to be given them will they nill they. The rest of the Cities, a

[g]Such as the bishops of Liège, Namur, Cambrai and Maastricht.

[h]As Granvelle, Viglius, Chancellor Niger.

[i]This may be proved by the public testimony of the provinces, by the bishops's sermons and by all their doings.

[j]This is proved by the Cardinal's decree made at Rome by the Pope's commandment.

[k]For by all the laws and privileges of Brabant and their other provinces, all ecclesiastical persons were excluded from all functions of judgment and jurisdiction, and all strangers are removed from taking of

---

[21] For Granvelle see 'Biographical Notes'.
[22] For Viglius see 'Biographical Notes'.

offices, and authority; and the divisions of bishoprics and Abbeys are before appointed, and the accustomed manner of giving judgment for ever ratified, and all power is denied to the princes to change anything therein without the assent of the estates.

¹February 27, 1562.

ᵐMay 5, 1562.

ⁿOne was put up and subscribed unto on January 23, 1562, another on March 18, 1562, and another on March 23, 1562.

ᵒIn June 1562 they put up many Supplications.

great many in number, openly resisted, and thought that the innovation of all these things so manifestly contrary to the laws of all antiquities, and to their old and accustomed privileges was not to be suffered. Likewise many Abbeys, but especially in Brabant, because their Abbots being dead none was appointed to succeed, resisted and grievously complained to the rest of the bishops and the estates of Brabant of so great, and so manifest injury. But when they saw their doings to be in vain, because Granvelle withstood them with great force, they, taking unto them the rest of the estates, put up a Supplication unto their Governess for the abrogation of this disordered order of bishops. She denied her authority to reach so far, and referred the matter to the king. Therefore by and by they sent their Ambassadors to the King into Spain, which with humble petition should require, that His Majesty would not suffer their state and condition to be altered, contrary to their old accustomed privileges, and to the laws of their progenitors. But with ¹open denial they had the repulse. Not long after the estates of Brabant urged the governess again, and craved that their cause might be heard, and judgment given with equity.ᵐ But their suit was all in vain, for she answered that it did not belong unto her. The magistrate of Antwerp with ⁿmany bills, and diverse petitions went about to stay this innovation of things. He openly refused the bishops, and besides that ᵒsent Ambassadors into Spain to the king. They after much ado and long soliciting of the matter, obtained at the length ᵖlicence to be exempted from the bondage of the new Bishops. In the meantime, Granvelle never ceased by most subtle and crafty means, and that openly, to achieve and win unto himself the full power of governing the commonwealth, and covertly ᵠto remove from all authority the governess of Parma, as one not being expert enough on the Belgian affairs, to ʳordain and appoint Magistrates in every City at his pleasure, ˢto break off and disturb the great Senate, not long before appointed by the King, and was called the noble council, being the solemn assembly of the princes and governors of the whole province (which ᵗhe a little before had with false persuasions unto the King very much blemished, and made subject to the council and Senate house of Spain, as it were to their guide) to cut in pieces all their decrees and to rule and appoint all things alone, according to his own will and pleasure, and by a new form of indulgence (as they term them) to bring in the Spanish manner of distributing benefices, and offices, both Civil and

Ecclesiastical the which he abused according to his pleasure. He challenged the whole power of indulgences to himself, leaving notwithstanding some of them to Viglius.[23] By this means, when offices or benefices were vacant, he sometimes stayed[24] the gift of them for a long space, and sometimes again upon the first day of their vacancy he set them out to open sale, and sometimes he twice sold them. The price he divided openly with his brokers, and proctors. He accounted himself the Archbishop of Malines, the metropolitan not only of Brabant, but also of the whole province of Belgium. And when he had received from the Pope his Cardinal's hat, he disdained all princes in respect of himself. He mightily threatened those Cities, which refused to submit themselves to the Bishop's bondage. He openly boasted and said that the king could not maintain his honour, and authority in Belgium, without the Spanish power and foreign aid. He said it was altogether necessary that the king should be released by the bishop of Rome from his oath, wherewith he bound himself by covenant to maintain the privileges of his subjects, and that he should convert this his lawful inheritance into a province, making it captive which before was free, as if it had been won by force of arms, or conquered by battle, and not enjoyed by succession of ancient patrimony, and briefly that he should make them new laws, and invent some kind of new regiment for them like the captives taken in war. *u*He said moreover that it was necessary for the performance hereof that four or five of the noble men should lose their heads, in whose authority and careful prudence, the health and safety of the people, and the only hope of their liberties was thought to consist. To conclude, he, openly condemning the whole company of the primates and nobles and the Governess of Parma herself, behaving himself both as King and Bishop, by force and violence, made his friends and clients, some of them Bishops, and some of them Inquisitors.

*v*When as the Princes and noble men of the province saw no end of his madness, they thought it most expedient for themselves, and for the state of the whole commonwealth, wholly to withstand his rashness, perceiving indeed manifestly, that if by some means or other he were not stayed or repressed, the people (though most patient and loving

All Belgium can testify this.

ᵖDecember 20, 1562 and August 3, 1563.

qThis is known by the testimony of the Governess given in the assembly of the Nobles.

rThe deed itself proves it.

sThis is proven by the nobles' complaints, given to the king.

tThat was Granvelle his study.

uThis his saying was heard of many and signified to the nobles, and confirmed by the king's legate's letters.

vThe resistance of the noble men.

---

[23] It was no exception in the political literature of the Revolt to depict Viglius, one of the great humanists of his time, as a loyal disciple of Granvelle. In reality Viglius' political position was on the whole carefully balanced.

[24] Deferred.

subjects towards the king) could not long be retained in their duty of obedience. Neither yet did they attempt then anything by force or violence, or by any crafty and wicked enterprise, but they withstood him only by making humble supplication to the King, fully certifying his Majesty, that if those rigorous judgments were executed still, with such cruelty, and that worthy Citizens were oppressed with such great tyranny, in so great a corruption and common pollution of all estates, it was impossible to retain the people any longer in their accustomed duty, and faithful obedience, but that doubtless the public slaughter and common destruction of the whole province was with speed to be looked for, unless his prudence, foreseeing the mischief sought some remedy for it with all expedition. *"*Baron of Montigny, one of the order of the Golden Fleece,[25] was sent as ambassador for the performance hereof. But not long after he returned, not speeding of his purpose. And no marvel why, for in Spain all things were no less governed by the Inquisitor's authority, than they were ruled in Belgium by the Cardinal's will and pleasure.

"1562, the month of August.

But in the mean time, whilst the liberty of religion was appointed in France,[26] and published with full consent, the Cities of Belgium, bordering upon the Frenchmen, began openly in public assemblies, and common preachings to profess the religion of the Gospel,[27] which for the space of forty years before they [had] kept close in their private houses. Which things they did partly, because otherwise they saw they could not avoid the slanders and reproachful opprobrium, wherewith their private meetings and secret conferences were openly and commonly defamed amongst the people; and partly because they saw the daily increase of those which professed the gospel to be so great, that private houses could no longer contain them. So that it was necessary either to let the citizens, leaving their cities void of men, flee to their

[25] In 1562 Floris de Montmorency, Baron of Montigny (1527–70), was sent to Philip II by the Council of State with the task of explaining the position of the nobles with regard to Granvelle.

The Golden Fleece was the highest order of Knights in the Burgundian era. It was founded in 1430 by Philip the Good in an attempt to increase the integration of the high nobility of the Dutch provinces in the Burgundian political system.

[26] The edict of January 1562 gave French Protestants the right to hold public services outside the towns and to worship in private inside the towns. Following the refusal of the Paris Parlement to accept the edict and the massacre of a Protestant congregation in Vassy, the first major religious war broke out in the spring.

[27] The first public sermon of Dutch Reformed Protestants was held at Easter 1562 in Flanders.

old enemies the Frenchmen, or else to satisfy the earnest desire of the people in that one point, which in all other things was most obedient. But by and by the extreme tyranny of the Inquisition, and the barbarous cruelty of the punishments, somewhat repressed them, though (God be praised) it could not altogether extinguish them. The more openly they professed their faith, the more vehemently did Granvelle seek to increase the number of the new bishops, insomuch that contrary to the will of the nobles, he attempted to deprive the citizens of Antwerp of the king's benevolence towards them, whereby they obtained their liberty and were made free from that extreme bondage. He stirred so long in this matter, that there had been like to have been a great sedition, if Armenteros the Spaniard[28] had not been sent again to the king, by the consent and counsel of the governess and nobles, who plainly should certify the king that the people could not any longer be kept in subjection, and that the princes themselves would renounce their authority, and leave of the ruling of the commonwealth, unless it would please the king's majesty to pluck in the reins of this untamed Cardinal, to repress and withstand his unbridled madness, to deliver his poor subjects from the yoke of his tyranny, to make frustrate his purpose of new alterations, and finally indeed to confirm and establish his liberality and benefit, bestowed and granted to the Citizens of Antwerp.

This pitiful complaint so moved the king, that he showed himself very angry, and heavily displeased with Granvelle, and thereupon depriving him of all his authority, called him home presently from Belgium.[29] By his departure all the whole of low Germany breathed upon, as it were with a more pleasant and fresh air. It seemed somewhat to rest and comfort itself, until such time as those good bishops of Spain put the king in remembrance, and caused him (according to their pleasure) to lay the heavy yoke of the Inquisition upon the provinces of Belgium again; and to will the bishops to execute the cruelty of the Edicts; and that they should moreover diligently urge again the due reverence of the Council of Trent. The

The departure of Granvelle, 1564.

---

[28] Thomas de Armenteros was the private secretary of the Governess. On her instructions he went to Spain to persuade Philip II that the recall of Granvelle was necessary and desirable.

[29] In fact the withdrawal of Granvelle from the Dutch scene was a tactical concession. By withdrawing the symbol of his policy, Philip hoped to avoid more substantial concessions regarding the political position and power of the grandees and the policy of religious persecution.

Cardinal's ministers (which as his chief friends and succours Granvelle had left in great authority at his departure) set this matter abroach to the utmost of their power, and therewithal (according to that state of government which he left when he departed) they easily wrung into their own hands the whole rule and authority of the commonwealth. They governed three courts of councillors[30] at their pleasure. They spoilt the noble men of all their authority. Finally, they determined and appointed all things according to their lewd appetite even as though Granvelle himself were there present among them in authority: nothing less seeking to set up their Inquisition, and to establish their bishops, than they did before. They exercised all kind of cruelty against those that professed Christ's gospel, seeking to extirpate and root them out with the gallows, fire, and sword, in such sort, that at the same time at Antwerp, which is an Earldom of the holy Empire, besides an infinite number whom they destroyed, some by day, and some by night, most cruelly, openly and in the middle of the marketplace, they stroke one to the heart with a dagger as they were burning him under a Gibbet, because they saw that both the cruelty of the punishment, and the honesty and godliness of the man being well-known unto all men stirred up the people to pitiful complaint and bewailing of his case. There was also another man taken with him, whose pardon the noble Prince Elector of Palatinate (because he loved him for his honesty and because he was teacher and master of the school at Heidelberg) most earnestly sued for. But they, wicked tyrants, would not dismiss him, before he was almost consumed to death with a sickness taken with long imprisonment and by the filthy smell and savour thereof.

But to what purpose should I recite their extreme tyranny, wherewith they oppressed those cities in the which they might do what they listed, with more authority and less danger? Their boldness was so notable that in Cambrai, a City, by all ancient and undoubted right of the Emperors, without controversy, obeying his laws and statutes, they were not afraid to apprehend an honest and godly man, because he preferred up unto the Magistrate a bill of supplication in

---

[30] In 1531 Charles V had established three Collateral councils. The Council of State, the Council of Finances and the Privy Council were to govern the provinces next to the Governess. Set up to channel the power of the high nobility, they were soon dominated by the rise of professional bureaucrats, Granvelle and Viglius being outstanding examples.

the name of no less than a thousand Citizens, by whom he was chosen and appointed to execute that charge. Whose request was nothing else but that they might freely, and with the good leave of the Magistrate, retain the confession made at Augsburg, which they confess themselves to follow. Yet, notwithstanding they slew, were bold to apprehend him and, and within less than four hours after, to behead him, though he appealed from them to the Emperor's Majesty. Infinite is the number of such things, which they committed contrary to all order of law, equity or right. They caused every wise man with fear to look for some open rebellion of the people, or rather the utter subversion of the province, if there were not with speed some remedy taken. Therefore, at the length, in the name of the governess and the nobles *Egmont was sent unto the king with commission to declare unto His *1565 Majesty, that unless it would please him to stay the rash enterprises of certain men, to mitigate the severities of the Edicts, and utterly to abolish the Inquisition, he should look for the eminent destruction of the whole province. The king answered him very gently and promised to please his province of Belgium in any thing, they could reasonably request, so that in short space, they should have all things well ordered according to their heart's desire.[31] He likewise gave them in charge, that they should take counsel together, and devise some means whereby they might, without any hindrance to the Catholic Religion, prevent and withstand such eminent dangers, promising faithfully to allow, and confirm that which they should lawfully devise. For the speedy performance hereof, at the return of Egmont to Belgium, there was appointed a council of three Bishops, three Divines, three Canonical Lawyers, and three Civilians, to whom the whole charge of finding this good order was committed.

Not long after being moved thereto by the importunate suit of the Spanish Inquisitors and Bishops, and by the letters of Granvelle, but especially compelled by the fearful threats of the Pope's Legates, thundering out not only excommunication, but also eternal damnation, except he did by all manner of means, yea though it were to the utter subversion of the whole province of Belgium, establish, and set

---

[31] In fact Egmont's mission became the source of serious misunderstandings. Whilst the count, impressed by the majesty of his reception at the court in Spain, by the personal favours he received and by Philip's soothing words, believed that the king had basically accepted the nobles' demands, Philip was quite sure he had not made any substantial concession.

up the Inquisition, and cleanly root out the least relics of the new religion, he changed his mind, and utterly refused the order of government devised in Belgium, not because it did not appoint most grievous torments for the Gospellers, or because it was far different from the rigorousness of the former Edicts, but because it seemed *yThe king's* somewhat more remiss and merciful in certain points. *y*Lastly, by his *decree by the* letters[32] he straightly commanded that the Inquisition should be *which the* established and set up throughout all of Belgium, and that to the *tumults of* Inquisitors of every province, and the chief councillors thereof, *Belgium* should adjoin themselves, and aid, and help them, with their counsel *began.* and force to the utmost of their power, that all old Edicts should be *December* executed in every point, the Bishops should be committed and *1565.* installed in every City, the decrees of the Council of Trent should be published everywhere. And briefly that nothing should be omitted which served to the rooting out of those, which professed the Gospel. Moreover he very much blamed the Judges and Magistrates of every province, that they did not with more severity execute the pope's edicts and his decrees, attributing the cause of all heresies to their dissolute negligence and foolish pity.[33]

When these letters were received, contrary to all men's expectations, and were sent to the Magistrates of every province, and that the king's last will was openly known and published, great heaviness, great trouble of mind, finally great fear and terror came upon them all. The estates of Brabant put a bill to the governess, declaring that it neither could, nor ought to be brought to pass in that wise, in their province. Yet they could get no certain answer, but one very dark and doubtful; and that a great while after, the same was done of the Flemish, those of Namur, Guelders and of other provinces next adjoining, yea and then the Churchmen and Abbots.[34] To be brief, there was so great amazement and terror amongst all men, that they all of what degree or estate so ever they were of, feared their own

---

[32] The letters from the woods of Segovia, signed on 17 and 20 October 1565, were in fact a toned-down version of what the faction around the Duke of Alva had required. Nonetheless, in the Low Countries they were regarded as a blunt rejection of the proposals of the nobles and as a great blow to their authority and prestige.

[33] In fact town magistrates continuously frustrated the Inquisition's work. The town of Bruges was a famous example of such behaviour. In 1563 the town magistrate even officially forbade to assist the Inquisitor in Flanders, the notorious Petrus Titelmans.

[34] The Flemish and Brabant requests had been published by Van Wesembeeke in *De beschriivinge van den geschiedenissen in der Religien saken toeghedragen in den Nederlanden* (1569).

safety. They saw all their hope and confidence, which they were wont to put in their innocence and honest life, cleanly taken away. They saw it impossible for any man to escape the rash attempts, the troublesome cavils, and malicious slander of the wicked. For by this means, any man might convey into every good man's house, chamber, or chests, some of the forbidden books, of the which there was an innumerable company. And so cause them to be suspected, and accused of heresy. They also saw that no man could escape or avoid the tyranny of the Edicts, because by them not only they which were found guilty, but all their neighbours, friends, kinsmen and acquaintances were likewise punished by most horrible death, unless they of themselves would betray their most dear and familiar friends. To conclude they likewise saw, that if they should cease and leave off from their purpose, all hope of forgiveness to be taken away, and that for their great benefits, and good will, they should be rewarded not only with great and infamous ignominy, with bondage and troubles of conscience, but also with most extreme and cruel death. The which truly the barbarous cruelty of the Spanish Inquisition could never abide for they thus thought, and persuaded themselves, that if they, when for want of favour and authority they could scarce execute their office of Inquisition, did not omit any kind of cruelty, [they] would now become intolerable free men, inasmuch as that they have for their defence and safeguard the manifest and unmovable will of the king, the authority of the public edicts, the help and industry of Councillors, a great increase of new bishops, the glorious title of the Council of Trent, the power of the Magistrates, the violence, and force of the Sergeants and soldiers ready to defend them in the execution of their tyranny. And therefore every man was in most desperate fear. Neither did any persuade himself (except he were of the number of those Catchpoles and thieves) to avoid or put from his goods and substance, his wife and children, yea from his own head, so great calamity. If there were any, who for the great favour they were in, or for their great power and authority, might in this point have persuaded themselves security, as there were very few, yet because they plainly foresaw that this tyranny continued would cause some tumults or open rebellion, they feared no less than the rest did, the spoil of their goods and possessions, with loss of their lives. In this great astonishment of all men, and heaviness of the whole province, many of the chief and wealthiest merchants, who persuaded themselves that their matter was in handling and that the wicked were seeking for their throats, or rather, by their throats their golden coffers, bags and jewels, prepared to fly. It came to pass that many of the nobility being moved with the public danger, and their own peril, both because the continual complaints and murmurings of the people were daily brought unto them and because their houses and gorgeous palaces, being in the fields, were subject to the prey and spoil of every seditious tumult, thought it necessary with one consent to go unto the governess, and to make plain and open unto her, the miserable destruction and calamities which are incident and like to ensue to the king himself, to his loving subjects, to his Cities, and to his whole province, if this his Edict, should have its full force and power. Therefore when they had made a league or agreement amongst themselves as concerning this matter,[35] and had promised that every one of them (keeping their faith and loyalty inviolated) should seek to the utmost of their power the subversion, and overthrow of this Inquisition, and to cause the severity of the Edicts to be mitigated, [there] came together at Brussels the fifth of April very nearly three hundred nobles, and Brederode being their captain.[36] They put up unto the governess a bill of supplication, in the which they required no liberty for themselves, or the people, no alteration of Religion, neither did they by their authority take upon them to proscribe anything to the king's Majesty, but, briefly rehearsing the dangerous perils and miserable calamities which then hung over their heads, they most humbly desired that the office of the Inquisitors, so manifestly against the king's honour, and the safety of the country, might be taken away and abrogated. And that it would please the king and his council to devise some other Edict for the maintenance of Religion, to the which all the inhabitants of Belgium, of what state or condition so ever they were of, should be bound to obey, and that the execution of the Edicts might be so long stayed, till such time as that the nobles and estates of the country, after the manner of their ancestors, and according to the

*1566.
A coming
together of
the nobles. A
supplication.*

---

[35] In 1565 a group of nobles formed the so-called Compromise, whose purpose was, as its constitutive document put it, the eradication of the Inquisition. For a recent English edition of this document, see E.H. Kossmann and A.F. Mellink, *Texts concerning the Revolt of the Netherlands* (Cambridge, 1974), pp. 59–62.

[36] Count Hendrik van Brederode was one of the most outspoken and radical Protestant nobles. He became one of the leaders of the Compromise and led the famous march through Brussels on 5 April 1566. Brederode died in 1567. For the text of the *Petition*, see Kossmann and Mellink, *Texts*, pp. 62–5.

custom of all well ruled commonwealths, might come together to the establishing of them by the king's authority. Moreover they protested that if by the contempt and neglect of this their request, the commonwealth hereafter should fall into any danger, they themselves were, by any right, not to be accused for it. Since[37] they had satisfied their duty in forewarning the same, this humble suit of the nobility was accounted just and godly, not only of the rest of the nobles, but also of the governess herself, of all the Senate, and of the whole concourse of people, so that by their common consent and open suffrages the Governess agreed, and promised to the utmost of her power to get their request satisfied, and that she would send her Ambassadors to the king, who should declare the whole matter unto him, and bring to pass (if it were possible) that their request should be granted. And therewithal they appointed the Baron of Montigny and the Marquis of Bergen[38] to perform that legation, and in the meantime, she promised, that there should be a vacation and respite from the execution of the cruel Edicts, and from the bloody butchery of the Inquisition, which she would faithfully perform, commanding the same by her authority, set forth by writing. This changed all their sorrow and heavy cheer into an unspeakable gladness, and made them all to hope well. In so much that not only they which determined to fly before, did not only change their minds, but they which were gone already, took counsel how to come home again.

These matters sore troubled the Cardinal's substitutes, the masters of the Spanish Inquisition, and the whole company of the bishops and catchpoles, which had in their minds already devoured and swallowed up the goods and blood of the noblest and richest men in the country. And therefore they tried all manner of ways, how they might recover so rich a spoil, and so fat a prey, which was by this means by force plucked out from between their greedy jaws. They accused with most slanderous cavils the force of the noble men. They went about to prove that it should be taken for a manifest sign of a rebellion toward. They affirmed that the noble men sought only to raise a tumult, that

---

[37] Here the 1571 edition uses the word 'seyng', translating the Latin word 'cum'.

[38] Floris de Montmorency, Baron of Montigny (1527–70), a brother of the Count of Hoorne, had been appointed governor of Tournai in 1559. Jean de Glymes, Marquis of Bergen (1528–67) was Stadholder of Hainaut, a member of the Council of State and a Knight of the Golden Fleece. Both Montigny and Bergen were arrested after their arrival in Spain. Montigny was sentenced to death and executed in 1570. Bergen died, imprisoned, in 1567 and was posthumously convicted.

thereby they might rush in by force upon other men's goods, that they might pay their debts with other men's riches, so craftily attained, yea that they sought the death of all priests and sacrificers, and the subversion of churches and the overthrow of cities. They feigned much more, the which they so cunningly persuaded the Governess, that she left Brussels, the most ancient demesne and mansion of the Duke of Brabant, determined never to fly to any defected city. The which truly she would have done, if being persuaded by the noble men which well knew the state of the country, she had not comforted herself and plucked up her courage. But when they saw their manifold and shameful slander disproved by the deed itself, and by the modest behaviour of the noble men, to take no place, they marvellously cried out and inveighed before the Governess against the solemn and great assembly of the nobles, against their league and society which they had made. And when they saw that all this could little prevail against them, they beat most upon this one point, and they made this the chief cause of their accusation, that they [the nobles] manifestly showed themselves seditious rebels, when they required a free and lawful assembly of noble men, or grand parliament, to be summoned, affirming that nothing more diminishes the power and authority of a prince, than the solemn meeting of the estates, wherewith most mighty kings and princes have been compelled to yield to their order. And truly all men do know, that Granvelle and Viglius were wont often to say that the king above all things had need to take heed, lest the estates of the province be licensed to make assemblies and general meetings according to the accustomed manner of their Ancestors. The which kind of government Charles the fifth observed diligently, contrary to the customs of the former princes and dukes, whereby he determined all things according to his will and pleasure: and therefore he cleanly put down the general meetings and lawful assemblies of all the estates, held at their grand councils, and appointed all things to be done and determined after his and their arbitrament whom he would vouchsafe to take unto him.[39] They said the king should take the same order, if he would have his dignity maintained safely without appearing, and

Slander of the adversaries.

---

[39] In many political treatises of the Revolt, Charles V was presented as the virtuous example his son should have followed. The *Defence and True Declaration* broke new ground in arguing that arbitrary government had already commenced with the former Emperor.

that he should hate nothing so much as the very mention of those free assemblies. But when they perceived themselves to profit nothing by this means, because all of them with one voice did desire to have a parliament, and every man (unless he were without sense or reason) did easily perceive, the royal dignity could be maintained by nothing so well, as by these general and free assemblies. And they all knew that their care was for themselves and for their riches, and not for the defence of the king's honour. For at the time of the parliament, they should render by their accounts of the common treasury, what they had received and spent since the time they had been in their office. And then were the actions of extortions and of the robberies of the common treasury to be pleaded. They thought it therefore best covertly by guile and crafty means to work some sleight, whereby they might undermine the godly endeavour of the nobles and chief citizens whatsoever, and clearly keep back the appointment of these solemn councils. Therefore, subtly they persuaded the Governess that she should call the estates of every province separately, and that she should suffer none to be of the council, but such as she should choose and call thereunto. And therefore as they gave her counsel, she *In the year* caused most hasty and troublesome assemblies to be made of every *1566, in the* province separately by themselves, unto the which were summoned to *month of* appear only they which were chosen. But they whom to have been *May.* there it had been most requisite, and they which by ancient right, and of a long continuance were wont to be present, were now cleanly omitted. Many were commanded openly to depart, and many to keep silence. The time of deliberating the matter, and taking counsel with their friends, and with the rest of the estates of the province and governors of the people (as the most ancient and certain custom of such assemblies had ever before granted) is now from all of them indifferently taken away. Moreover [as to] the chief provinces of all Belgium, whose cause especially was then in handling, as Brabant, Holland, Friesland, Guelders, Zeeland and the countries of Limburg, [it] was made unlawful for any of them to come thither, and thus the manner of mitigating these Edicts were referred to a very small company. Whereof it is manifest that the greater part were suborned, and hired for that purpose, whose determination in outward show seemed to be much gentler, but in the right meaning and true understanding of it was crueller a great deal than the former Edicts. In this one point it seemed to be more merciful, because instead of burning of them, it appointed them to be trust up upon a gibbet or gallows, tormented with a rack and chains. And for the Inquisition substituted a visitation, it did not confiscate the goods of these which had fled, but it so fetched them, so circumvented them, that a very fool might easily perceive, they sought nothing else but a more privy entrance to their old prescriptions and accustomed cruelty, especially since the governess did manifestly write unto the governors, and chief Justices of every province, that as concerning the king's Edicts for religion they should well understand, that they ought nothing to remit or mitigate the severity of them, no not although she herself should command to the contrary. And hence the fury and madness of the Inquisitors did no less outrageously rob and spoil than they were wont to do, and that without punishment or prohibition, and inasmuch as that the Monks and preaching Friars did not only with most biting taunts and spiteful reproaches defame the chief and noble estates, animating and harnessing the rude people against those Princes which put up the bill of supplication, but also out of their pulpits by *This was openly heard in the churches at Antwerp and in many other places.* name openly accused them of disobedience, disloyalty and seditious treason, and threatened them that the king would utterly destroy them and put them to death. And to conclude, hence everyman perceived by most evident tokens, and since they had it proved by many men's letters, and talk, that they sought nothing else but, by some means to delude and deceive the people, that from them getting aid, they might execute their tyranny not only upon the community but even also upon the chief of the Princes whatsoever, as if they were their deadly enemies. At the length, notwithstanding when they had determined what should be done, they offered up to the estates of Brabant the manner of their government, but in all haste, not looking for any answer, they caused it to be published. But whilst those things were adoing, the professors of the Gospel which had thereto kept themselves in their private houses, upon hope, that at length their cause being heard and the slanderous cavils, wherewith they were defamed, fully answered, they should have liberty for their religion, which they were ready to defend with the word of God, in as ample sort granted them, as it was to the Frenchmen by their king and the whole assent of his noble estates; [the professors of the Gospel were now] perceiving their hope and expectation frustrated and themselves to be daily more and more slandered, and that there was no more hope left, either in the king's clemency or in the expectation for the parliament, of having their cause heard, much less of equal judgment. And yet notwithstanding all of them everywhere did not cease to call for the preaching of the gospel insomuch that the multitude could not be contained in any private houses. Many of them began in the uttermost borders of Flanders, where the tyranny of the Inquisition had most extremely persecuted them, and by and by in Brabant, in Holland, and also the rest of the provinces, to come together into the fields to the preaching of God's word, and openly to set forth their doctrine, [so] that at the length they might clear themselves from the slanderous cavils of their own adversaries, being their Judges, and that all men might know who they were, what number there was of them, and of what estimation or worship they were of. First they came to all assemblies without weapons.

But when their adversaries began openly to threaten unto them *The* most extreme cruelty, many of them got their weapons,[40] some a *adversaries'* sword, some a spear, some a club, as men use them when they *oppress the* prepare to take armour, but a very few brought daggers. But within a *Gospellers.* while after their number began to increase to many thousands of people. When the Cardinal's Viceregents perceived they could not be oppressed without open violence, because by reason of their great number, of their favour and power, and of the equity of their cause, of the honesty of their life, of the integrity of their actions, they were becoming marvellously strong. But especially when they [the Cardinalists] saw the most part of the nobility openly favouring their cause (whose desire for public peace, which they of late had showed forth in their bill of supplication, and all their actions were slandered very much with sundry slanderous cavils), they flew unto their crafts and guile. They by sundry and many ways deceived the nobility, which came together in a solemn assembly at St Truiden to take counsel for the safeguard of themselves, and for answering to the most reproachful cavils, and the avoidance of their violent rashness.[41] First, they [the Cardinalists] went about to persuade them [the

---

[40] The first armed Protestant mass meeting took place in July 1562 in the Flemish village of Boeschepe. In addition to the area of western Flanders, Antwerp and Tournai were main centres of Reformed Protestant activity. The great hedge-sermons first started in the spring of 1566, beginning again in Flanders but soon spreading to other parts of the provinces, including Holland, where, in fact, it meant the public breakthrough of Reformed Protestantism.

[41] In July 1566 the confederate nobles met at St Truiden, a town in the principality of Liege.

nobles] to become the open enemies of the public preaching, and to dispatch them by force of arms. But perceiving themselves to labour therein in vain, because many of the nobles resisted them, which were professors of that religion, they compassed their matter about another way, feigning themselves to require their help for to pacify the tumults of the people. Therefore propounding many commandments, they obtained that Ambassadors should be sent from among them unto the Governess of Parma, the which should determine upon all matters according to equity and right, as best should be thought for the profit of the commonwealth. The Ambassadors meaning simply, went with them unto Brussels.

This composition or determination began first at Brussels, the 24th, 25th and 26th of August 1566.

The governess desired them [to end] the tumults of the people with all their power, and to obey the king and his magistrates with all obedience, not once minding to take upon them armour, but leaving all fond and sinister suspicions, and to persuade themselves that the king would very well allow of their doings, and account it a full satisfaction of their duties. She likewise granted at their request that it shall be lawful for them to keep their public sermons in their accustomed places as they had done heretofore. It was solemnly also decreed on both parties, that by the authority of the magistrates there should be appointed common places in every city and town, wherein they might make their sermons, and freely without fear exercise their preachings, and that the professing of religion should be hurtful to none, so that he observed his duty in all other matters without invading of churches, or moving any tumults hereafter. They promised faithfully on both parties, but the Cardinal's men bound themselves by oath, and by their holy devotion, to be faithful in performing their promise. The Governess for her part, to make it more sure, called a council of the nobles, who likewise promised their fidelity in performing the same and she gave forth letters patents authorized with the king's broad seal. Not long after she, sending these letters to the governors and [2]Magistrates of every province, gave in commandment that this whole agreement should be promulgated, and that the whole commonwealth should be governed according to the contents thereof and afterwards by [a1]public Edicts she forbade that any man should reveal or speak evil of others for religion's sake, as she pronounced that all men of both religions were in the king's safe government and good protection.

[2]The proof hereof appears both by the copy of the letters patents and by the Edict of the Magistrates, first proclaimed and later

It happened in the meantime, while those things were a doing at

Brussels, that, first in West parts of Flanders,[b1] and afterwards in many other [c1]Cities almost at the same time Images, pictures, and altars were overthrown in the Churches, whether by craft of the adversaries, which even now sought all occasions to accuse the people that having some fair show, they might gather an army, or by the fond zeal of many, which thought they could not earnestly repent them of their sins unless they had overthrown the instruments of idolatry, it is as yet uncertain.[42] But this is most apparent that in many [d1]Cities the sacrificing Priests themselves began first to carry out of their Churches their most precious relics and vessels, that then boys and rascal people, following them, overthrew the rest, and in many Cities. It is known also that the bishops themselves and they which were the greatest adversaries of the Gospel, did by public [e1]authority overthrow the Images, pictures, and the rest of the ceremonies, and that by their authority and example, many good and godly Citizens did the same likewise, supposing this their doing to be commanded by the authority of the Magistrate.

But howsoever it came to pass, the Cardinal's officers and Inquisitors took a very fit occasion hereby to execute their purpose, for by and by they, in all haste gathering soldiers together, apprehended many of those, which overthrew the Images, and cast them into prison, and hung them. Neither could they by any questions or kinds of torments, enforce them to confess (the which thing they most greedily desired) that any of the Ministers of the Churches, or any of the confederate princes, which were at the aforesaid assembly, or any of the professors of the Gospel, were authors of this enterprise.[43] But rather they confessed all with one voice that (as it was most manifest by their preachings and endeavours wherewith they disallowed that enterprise) it was done contrary to all their wills, and not without their great grief and sorrow. Therefore the governess did not [f1]cease to see the former contract of governing the commonwealth executed,

published in print. The Edicts for ceasing from railing was proclaimed at Antwerp, the last of August 1566; at Brussels August 24; the Earl of Mansfelt being present. Free liberty of preaching came from the governess August 25.

[a1]*Another public Edict concerning railing and reviling to cease on both sides was proclaimed at Antwerp, September 3, at Brussels, September 6, and so afterwards in other cities.*

[b1]*The 11th, 12th, 13th of August 1566.*

[c1]*At Antwerp, August 20. At Breda, at Bois-le-Duc, 22 and 23. In Holland and Zeeland, 25, 26, etc.*

---

[42] The Iconoclastic Fury started on 10 August 1566 in the Flemish village of Steenvoorde. In the following weeks it spread to other parts of the provinces, reaching Holland on 25 August and Friesland on 6 September.

[43] The apologetic defence of the Iconoclastic Fury, as formulated in the *Defence and True Declaration*, gives a rather liberal interpretation of the events of 1566, belittling the involvement of the Reformed Protestants. In fact the Fury, in itself a hybrid movement, was triggered off by a sermon held by a radical minister, Sebastien Matte, and, especially in Flanders, iconoclasts sometimes acted under the direct leadership of ministers. Occasionally groups claimed to act at the explicit order of governmental authority.

The Dutch Revolt

[41]As in Antwerp, in Breda, in Brabant and in many places of Holland.

[c1]At Ghent in Flanders; at The Hague in Holland; at Lier in Brabant; Also at Malines this was done most certainly by the commandment of the Magistrates. August 25, 28, and other following days.

[f1]As appears by the form of the latter Edicts made and set forth touching the stay of reviling words and of churches granted, upon the former promise and convention between the governess and the people.

insomuch that she gave by public authority unto many of the nobles and of the confederate princes charge over cities, in the which they should set all things in order, according to the due prescript of the former decree; that they should assign places out for the building of Churches, and for the people's assembly to hear Sermons, and that they should with open protestation will all men to be secure and void from all fear and danger, and certainly to persuade themselves that the garrisons of soldiers should not damage them. With the which thing all the people began exceedingly to rejoice, and to lay apart all fear, as though out of a most boisterous tempest they were already arrived in a most quiet haven, and staying themselves upon the public promise thus made and taken and confirmed by writing. They began to build their churches, and freely and quietly to set forth their religion. But yet notwithstanding the furious madness of their adversaries was not pacified, although they had already punished the overthrowers of the Images with grievous punishments, and did see the innocence of these Churches most manifestly witnessed by their open confessions. But rather most proudly advancing themselves, as though they had got a just occasion to punish the rebels, and that they should not fear hereafter the nobility, the which manifestly showed themselves to be heavily displeased with the insolence of the Imagebreakers, they began by little and little but openly to increase the number of their garrisons, and to set them in their Cities, with this pretence only to withstand the insolence of the Imagebreakers. And thus they armed themselves, with all things necessary, until such time that they had brought their matters to as good effect as they desired, perceiving the people quietly to rest themselves upon the faithful promise of the nobility and governess, set forth in the king's name under his seal and letters patents, and that the noble men also were quiet, not once misdoubting that they should have been so wickedly and unfaithfully deceived, they began openly to show forth what their meaning was. For in such places where as they might be most bold, and in the which the magistrate was pliable unto their desire, first with new commandments, obscure and doubtful edicts and with scoffing interpretation, they began to disannul the authority of the published commandments as concerning the late contract; and in many places to delay from day to day the sealing of the writing of the public promise, and with sundry cavils to deceive the miserable citizens, and in many

42

places to put those magistrates, whose dealing they knew would be always with justice, out of their offices, and, contrary to the orders of the cities, in their rooms to substitute most wicked men, prompt and ready to all kind of impiety. And then, at the length (as though all hindrances had been taken away) they began with great insolence by force of arms to disturb the companies assembled at sermons, tauntingly to revile the ministers and citizens, to warn them with weapons, and lastly, with open tyranny, to oppress them, imprisoning many, hanging many, banishing many, and appointing new kinds of oaths, whereby men should bind them to the popish religion, contrary to the former decree, covenanted and established before, and to account those which denied to obey for enemies and traitors to the king's majesty. Moreover they rebaptized infants, which were baptized before.[44] They spoilt all the professors of the Gospel of their weapons and armour. They armed and stirred up the rest of the community against them, as against the enemies of the commonwealth. Neither only did the sacrificing priests or preachers, out of their pulpits, as it were with an open outcry stir up the people to take armour against them but also in many places the Magistrates themselves, which were appointed by the Cardinal's officers and Inquisitors, sounding alarm, gave open licence unto the sedition and tumult of the people against the miserable Gospellers, the which were then lately called 'Geusians', that is to say Beggars and rascals. And hereupon began the most doleful and late calamity of the noble province. For even then, first of all, was that famous city of the Valentians[45] besieged in enemy wise of his own familiar friends and citizens, because forsooth, they refused upon the sudden to receive within their walls the cruel soldiers in that number that was commanded them, that is to say, four bands of horsemen and five ensigns of footmen but took unto them a day to deliberate, in alleging many causes that it would not be commodious unto them to receive them, seeing they had as yet before their eyes, amongst their neighbours a most cruel and doleful pre-

---

[44] The alleged act of rebaptizing children is probably mentioned to put the Inquisitors on a par with the Anabaptists, who were generally held in very low esteem. The reversal in policy, as depicted here in rather strong terms, was in fact supported by the Governess, who at the end of 1566, after the troubling summer and autumn, felt strong enough to act against radical Protestant groups.

[45] The inhabitants of Valenciennes in Hainaut, who refused to open the gates of the town for government troops on 14 December 1566.

cedent of the soldiers' rashness. For not long before in the country and town of St Amand, next adjoining unto them, the very same (which were thrust in contrary to their laws and privileges and contrary to the fidelity of the promise before given) violently robbed and spoilt the poor miserable people that professed the Gospel, of all they had, insomuch that from the very young infants they pulled their hose from their legs, they deflowered by course one after another (after the most horrible example of the Beniauntes) the chaste matrons and virgins, and at length in most cruel wise set them to open sale. At the sound of the drum they put many to death, burning them little by little with small flames, and with their swords opened the wombs of matrons great with child. The remembrance of these horrible things justly terrified the Valentians. They humbly desired that they should not be compelled to receive within their walls and houses such kind of soldiers, unto whose avarice, lust, and cruelty, they perceived themselves, their lives, wives, children, and consciences, should be at length in most servile bondage, and since that for four years of space before they had paid of their own proper costs and charges, unto the garrisons of soldiers their wages, upon this condition, that they should never hereafter be vexed or burdened any more with soldiers. Neither yet did they did so manifestly refuse it, but that they did openly in most humble wise signify unto the governess, and to the rest of the primates and rulers of the province, that they were ready to receive the soldiers of what number soever, if they had a captain appointed them, for that they should not hinder the liberty of Religion, which they had granted and confirmed unto them not long before, by the Edict of the governess, by the authority of the king's letters patents, by the nobility's constant confirmation, and with assent of all the Magistrates. But they nothing at all prevailed, by this their modesty and equity of their cause, but forthwith they were openly proclaimed as traitors and rebels. The City was besieged, until that at the length when they (being persuaded thereto by the letters of the governess promising all kind of clemency) had yielded themselves unto the fidelity of the Noircarmians, which besieged them.[46] Many were struck with the sword, many were hanged, many were burnt, and an

---

[46] Philip of St Aldegonde, Lord of Noircarmes had, as a member of the Council of State, played an active role in the opposition to Granvelle. In 1566 however, he decidedly supported the Governess, leading the siege of both Valenciennes and Tournai.

infinite number of them by the insolence of the soldiers shot through with daggers. Neither was there anything pretermitted against them, the which the furious rage of the soldiers use to execute in the sacking and subverting of Cities.

Many being terrified with these horrible examples of cruelty, and perceiving themselves so deceived to be defended from the fury and rashness of the soldiers, neither by the public promise, agreements, covenants or oaths, nor by the king's majesty, edicts or patents; and perceiving their adversaries to attempt and put in practice all kind of hostility against them, with great power and warlike force, and that all the hope of remedy or help was clean taken away, for their adversaries now accounted them not only as heretics, but also as seditious rebels, as perturbers of the common of the quiet, overthrowers of churches and traitors to the king's majesty; and although they, by most manifest proofs, and by the open confession of those, which were guilty, had proved their innocence, and had of their own accord offered themselves to be tried by the censures of equal judges, they understood nevertheless that they were accused unto the king of these most horrible crimes. They thought it best therefore to betake themselves to prayer, to vows, to tears and supplications, hoping by their humble suit and just purgation to pacify the anger of the king, vehemently built against them, by the false cavils of their adversaries. They therefore put up a bill of supplication whereby they might request the king's clemency testifying their own innocence and the slanderous accusations of their adversaries, and especially clear themselves of the destruction of the Churches, proving themselves to be in no fault, and that no suspicion of rebellion can justly be gathered upon them, most humbly protesting also their fidelity, obedience and due reverence to be always ready until the king's majesty in what things soever. Thus much [they were] only craving at the king's hands that they may have free liberty granted them, to profess their religion, which they make subject only to the trial of the word of God, and that they may not have their consciences grieved or burdened with any kind of authority. For the which benefit, in token of their thankfulness and for due proof of their faithful obedience to his majesty, besides their ordinary gifts, their accustomed tributes and all their other burdens, they promised to pay unto the king's Exchequer three million Florins within a certain time, and that they will disturb or destroy no churches, but they will put the same in good surety for the same, that they will diligently and carefully show forth their obedience, fidelity and due reverence in all points.[47]

November 1566.

All the cities well near gave up to their Magistrates a bill of supplication, most humbly desiring to show forth their diligence and fidelity towards their poor and miserable Citizens in the furthering thereof.

December.

They did moreover earnestly request the same thing of the governess and nobles; and because they would try all manner of means, whereby they might make manifest to all the world their true fidelity towards their king, they sent also their letters and Ambassadors to many of the princes of Germany, whom they judged altogether not to abhor from their religion, most earnestly desiring them that they would vouchsafe to entreat the king to be merciful to their innocence, and if there were any place free from the false accusations of their adversaries, and left unto the king's majesty for equity and mercy, that they would with their humble suit deliver them from their heavy calamity, hanging over their heads. But when they perceived that all these things did little prevail, and that their adversaries were more kindled and cruel against them, interpreting all things into the worst part, as though by the great sum of money offered, they had boastfully advanced their riches and power, and that they went about to threaten the king's majesty, minding to abuse the princes of Germany, for to disturb and withstand his will and pleasure; and seeing also no place to be left for their purgation or humble supplication before their Magistrates, that their ears, their eyes, thoughts and cogitations were made subject to the accusations of their adversaries, they did at the length with most doleful lamentation complain unto Brederode and other of the nobles (the which by the commandment of the Governess had promised their faith and fidelity to the performance of the former contract) that they were so unjustly and unfaithfully dealt with, contrary to their public promise, to their covenants granted and performed by oath, and they entreated them to perform that which they so faithfully promised by

February 8, 1567.

the commandment of the Governess, and also the nobles. Brederode, in the name of the other princes, sending his letters to the governess, desired licence to speak with her. But having the repulse, he sent unto

---

[47] The *Three Million Request* was a joint initiative of Reformed Protestants and Lutherans, whose stronghold was the Lutheran community of Antwerp. It has been a matter of debate whether the offer was sincere; it has been argued that it was a shrewd cover-up to raise money for armed resistance.

her the complaints of the people adding therewith a bill of supplication of the nobles, whereby they complained of so great and open injury, and requested therewith, that they might perform their promise of defending the late agreement which they had so solemnly vowed unto the people, that no man be damaged or hurt for his religion, or for the administration thereof, that the promised liberty of religion be granted, and that the soldiers gathered contrary to their former promise and oath, should be discharged and dismissed. And lastly that the commonwealth should be governed according to equity and right and to the covenants whereunto they were sworn. She in her answer made *February 16.* many doubts, and sought the fallacy of words, saying that there was nothing granted as concerning the administration of religion, but only licence given for their preachings and sermons, but as for baptizing children and the Lord's supper, there was no mention made; adding therefore that the people had first broken their covenants. Briefly she manifestly declared that she would no longer be bound unto these covenants, but (for she perceived herself to be of greater force) that she would govern all things after her own arbitrariness. And therewithal [she] signified that Brederode, and the rest of the nobles (which put up that bill of supplication) were the authors of the sedition and therefore that she accounted them as rebels and traitors to the king's majesty and as enemies of the country; and that the king would execute just and condign punishment upon them as guilty of those heinous crimes; and in the meantime she would use her authority, according as it should best please her.

These letters sent to Brederode, and the other confederate princes, it can not be told how greatly they were astonished, for they saw themselves most openly mocked and deceived, their fidelity promised by oath to the people nothing esteemed; themselves on the one part to be taken for rebellious traitors to the king's majesty, and on the other side for perjured persons, which with their vain promises had brought the people into a fool's paradise, and made them subject to the slaughter, and butchery fury of their adversaries: [they saw] their confirmed covenants, the king's name, seal, and letters patents to be of no force; their former agreement (by the which as by a bite they were drawn into the net) to be most manifestly deluded; and that they were so far from having licence to clear and purge themselves, that they might not be suffered once to entreat, or to make supplication for mercy; and that they were openly taken for enemies, environed about with soldiers, so that there was no place for them left whereby they might escape by flying.

They being thus at their wit's end, not knowing which way to take, were compelled at the length in all haste to muster their soldiers. Not that they meant to attempt anything as enemies, but that they might so long defend themselves from the violence, and injuries of their adversaries, until that they might either get equity for their cause or opportunity to fly. For if they would otherwise have invaded the king's Cities, there is no man so great a stranger, or ignorant of the matters done in Belgium, which does not know that many Cities, sending their Ambassadors, required their aid and desired that it might be lawful only by the grant and authority of Brederode, which was the captain of the confederate princes, to defend themselves by force of arms against the insolence and violence of their adversaries.[48] The Valentians required to have one of the nobility for their captain. Many other cities also being the chief ones amongst all the rest, both for their power and authority, and also for the number of their Citizens, made the same request. And many others also, if they had so desired, would have submitted themselves to their authority. And yet notwithstanding they granted not to any of them, so much as by their word to yield to that they required. Except unto the Buscoducentians[49] there was one granted, the which should defend the City in the king's name and of the confederate princes, against the insolence of the foreign soldiers and should make the nobility a way if it fortuned to be shut up. All the rest were refused, not because it was a hard matter for them to keep those cities, being already furnished with munitions of war, especially if the prince of Orange (whom now the adversaries most shamefully belie, calling him the author of the whole sedition) would but once have imagined so great an enterprise contrary to the will and the King and Governess, seeing that at his feet almost the whole province cast themselves down, with tears beseeching him to aid them against these violent thieves and murderers, and most perjured tyrants, and that they might commit themselves and all theirs

[48] After Brederode and other Reformed Protestants resorted to armed resistance, their armies were defeated in several battles. After Vianen, Brederode's home town in Holland, fell on 3 May 1567, the armed conflict was over; the Big Beggar, as he was called, fled to Germany where he died in February 1568.

[49] The inhabitants of Bois-le-Duc, one of the four capital towns of the core province of Brabant.

into his power and jurisdiction. He also might with a beck easily have retained in his power, not only Holland, Zeeland and the country of Truceland,[50] all which places he had in his government, being of themselves (as all men know) of ability to conquer the whole province, but also Antwerp, Malines, Bois-le-Duc, and many other of the chief cities. But that most godly Prince would not desire anything that should seem to impeach the king's authority. But he gave such godly counsels to the Governess, and to the other Cities, the which if they might have taken place, would have somewhat bridled the furious rage and covetous tyranny of the Spanish substitutes, and would have retained the whole province quietly and peacefully in their loyalty towards the king. But he could never be persuaded to take armour himself, or to give licence to the citizens to do the same.[51] The other confederate princes, as near as they could, obeyed his authority and followed his modesty, but that they were compelled many times by violence and necessity to take arms, not to invade or set upon any cities, or to do any violence, but only to withstand the violence, and to defend themselves from the insolence of their adversaries, and to make themselves a way to escape by force, if need should require.

And these things truly which we have reported, were only done before the Duke of Alva his coming, the which truly we have thought it necessary more largely to express, that all men may know how unjustly our adversaries are dealing with us. Although, at their lust and pleasure, they have governed all things and oppressed us eleven full years, with most extreme tyranny, and the which at length by their crafty and subtle devises, have stirred up such grievous tempests, that thereby they not only mancipated[52] and made bond ourselves, our wives and children, but have brought also the most flourishing province of Belgium into most doleful calamities and beastly servitude. They do not yet for all this cease to accuse us everywhere, unto all

The things done before the Duke of Alva his coming declare who were the authors of these tumults in Belgium.

---

[50] With the *Libellus Supplex* speaking of 'Transiselanum', this probably refers to William of Orange's possessions 'across the IJssel', such as the county of Buren and the towns Leerdam and IJsselstein.

[51] The attitude of the grandees, under the leadership of Orange and Egmont, was highly ambiguous. On the one hand they insisted on their policy of moderation and remained in touch with radical Protestants. On the other hand they were helping the Governess to restore order. When eventually forced to make a choice, the grandees split up. Most of them, including Egmont, took a new oath of loyalty. Orange refused and fled to his family in the German county of Nassau.

[52] Sold.

Princes and people of Europe, of most horrible crimes, and to lay the fault and occasions of all their covetous and mischievous doings upon our necks, complaining belike, because we would not with open bodies and stretched out throats, submit ourselves to their gloves and swords. They are grieved that we are safely escaped their hands, and that we have lost only our riches and possessions to be devoured of their greedy avarice, and that we have not committed our lifes, our wives and children, our souls and consciences to their lust, tyranny and impiety. Otherwise what is there that they can most especially lay

Of the confederacy of the nobles and of the supplication. against us, can they object unto us the confederate society of the princes? Let therefore the writings of the conspiracy be read; they truly (though we should hold our peace) would declare that they attempted nothing, did nothing, nor once thought upon any other thing but only whereby they might show forth their loyalty, fidelity and due obedience to their king, and only that they might, by the power and authority of the king withstand and suppress the cruelty, avarice and outrageous covetousness of many of the wicked. But if their letters, sealed and confirmed with their own hands and seals, be of no credit, yet let the effect of their doings be believed. For whilst all things were as yet in safety, what was it, which they went about? Did they not by supplication desire the king to disannul the unbridled power of the Inquisition, to mitigate the cruelty of the Edicts, and other Edicts for the ordering of Religion to be established by the king's authority and decree of the estates? But verily, here is the chief point of our adversaries' accusations; because, forsooth, they being free men, nobles, lovers of their country, and desirous of peace, faithfully addicted to the king's majesty, dared to be so bold by humble supplication to require that the Edicts, which were contrary to all equity, much impeaching the king's dignity, and disturbing the commonwealth, brought in by error and by false persuasion, should be made void, and that there might be some lawful assembly of the estates or Parliament[53] held for the good government of the commonwealth. Here we appeal to you (you most mighty Emperor of the Romans, and to you all the famous Princes of the Christian Religion) and by that only and immortal God, and by his son Jesus Christ, in whose name we plead our cause; we humbly desire you to give judgment in this point, whether we in this point so grievously offended, or

---

[53] The word 'Parliament' did not, of course, feature in the original Latin text, which spoke of the 'ordinum legitima comitia ad Rempublicam'. See *Libellus Supplex* (1570), fol. 58b.

rather whether they do not account our just and whole obedience of duty instead of great impiety. Truly when the king was authorized Duke of Brabant, he by solemn oath and faithful covenant promised that he would patiently suffer and most willingly hear all their complaints, requests or demands whatsoever, the which should be put up of the Bishops, Barons, Nobles, Cities or Towns subject unto him, either separately by themselves or jointly of them altogether, and as often as they would show forth their burdens or great oppression; [he promised] that it should be lawful for them to do it without any danger or offence, and without doubting that he would be angry therewith, and that he would never suffer any to be troubled for so doing. The which if it should chance to happen he promised to punish severely all those which may be found guilty of that offence. And at length, after many other things, he concluded that if he shall do or suffer to be done anything contrary to this oath and promise, he desired forthwith his subjects to be free from their oath and loyalty, until such time that he shall fully make them satisfaction in that point and in all other matters according to his promise.[54] Judge you therefore (you most renowned and puissant Princes) whether the nobles by putting up their supplication have justly deserved to have the king's so great and heavy displeasure against them and their poor Citizens and friends. Although who is so void of all sense and reason and so ignorant of the affairs of Princes, which does not know that it is most profitable for kings and princes that their subjects should move them by humble supplication to provide for the public weal, and that some ready and fit way should be taken for the good appointment and safe preservation of the common tranquillity.

Who is also ignorant that these free and solemn assemblies be not [only] used in all provinces and amongst all people, but also accounted as the only stay and remedy of all mischiefs and public calamities, and that no man has at any time heretofore gone about to hinder such solemn meetings but they which would rob and spoil the poor people of the right, of their liberties, of all their ancient laws and customs and freedom, of their privileges, and desired to rule all alone, according to their lewd lust and appetite, and by right or by wrong to execute

Of the nobles' request.

---

[54] This paragraph draws heavily upon the articles of the Joyous Entry of Brabant, on which Philip had taken an oath in 1549. The treatise not only refers to the right of petition as guaranteed by the Joyous Entry, but also explicitly and almost literally reiterates the charter's clause of disobedience.

tyranny upon their poor subject's souls and bodies. This truly is most manifest, that in Germany all the whole majesty and honour of their Empire is maintained by the due ordering of their solemn parliaments. Neither has there any wise man doubted but that in all the other provinces of all Europe all the safety of the people and the dignity of the prince has only been preserved by these general assemblies? But especially in low Germany. It is most manifest that the case so stands, for in it the princes have in all ages from time to time been subject to the power of the general Parliaments, have been elected by them, and confirmed of them, without whose assent and authority they never would decree anything, and it is manifestly provided and established by the privileges of Brabant[55] and the customs of Flanders, that they never have authority to do it hereafter. But as by their mutual assent and contract, they be in force of covenants agreed upon, and hereafter to be taken for their common[56] law of the country. It is of undoubted credit that the king can not violate or break them without the assent and consent of the other parties.

Admit it be so, the nobles have offended in this one point. Let it be accounted as wickedness unto them by humble supplication to show the way how the common destruction of their country might easily have been avoided. Wherein I pray you, did the poor community offend, or without crime have they deserved such great and accustomed cruelty? Unless you will say it was because they gave credit to the public Edicts published in the king's name, confirmed

---

[55] At this point the Latin original referred (in the margin) to articles 3, 18 and 25 of the Joyous Entry. See *Libellus Supplex* (1570), fol. 39. Article 3 of the Joyous Entry obliged the Duke of Brabant, first, not to wage war or to impose taxes without the advice and consent of the 'towns and country of Brabant', and second, never to hurt the rights, liberties and privileges of the country and its inhabitants. Article 18 limited the Duke's power in financial matters, pointing out that he could take no decisions concerning mintage issues without the 'consent of the common country'. Article 25 assured that someone who had hurt the country and its inhabitants, or had assisted their enemy, could not be pardoned without the consent of Brabant's estates.

[56] At this point the *Libellus Supplex* contained elaborate references to the works of famous late medieval Commentators. First, reference was made to Bartolus of Sassoferrato's comments on Ulpian's rule (Digest, Book 50, Title 6, Paragraph 2) that the conditions on which an office has been accepted must be respected, and to Bartolus' comments on Digest 50. 10. 5 and Digest 1. 1. 9, the famous *lex omnes populi*. Second, the *Libellus Supplex* referred to the work of the celebrated jurist Johannes Andreae (*c.* 1270–1348), and, finally, to a number of comments of Baldus de Ubaldis, for example on Digest 4. 3. 34 and Digest 1. 9. For Bartolus and Baldus see 'Biographical Notes'. The references were concluded with the sentence 'Ius autem gentium violari non posse, ne a Principe quidem indubitati iuris est'.

with his broad seal, and thought they might safely, without all fraud or deceit (having for their defence this licence granted by public promise) have recourse to the hearing of the Gospel preached. For whereas they do accuse the people of taking arms, against their king, of overthrowing of the images of Churches, of bringing a new Religion, their accusation is most vain and slanderous.

For as concerning their taking of armour, there was no man which *Of taking of* abused them against the king or his dignity, but truly before the public *armour.* promise and oath was neglected, before the king's Edicts (whereby the liberty of religion was granted) were violated, before the covenants agreed upon, and the league of their common tranquillity was broken, there was no man [who] went armed, except it were for defence of himself against the impudent violence of thieves and murderers, and the open threats of most wicked persons. And that also was when they went out of the Cities to the sermons. Some of them took a sword, some a staff, some a spear, very few [were] carrying daggers, even as one taking his journey into a far country arms himself to withstand the invasions of thieves and cut-throats. But afterwards, when in this point they were commanded to be secure, and that the governess had given in charge that [no one] should hurt or damage them, as long as they kept themselves quiet, by and by, they at the commandment of their Magistrates laid aside their weapons most willingly, committing themselves into them, to the laws of God and man, and to all their tuition and safeguard. But at length, when contrary to the promise made, and contrary both privileges, they perceived themselves to be overcome of the soldiers, the which had obtained full licence to destroy them (although they had committed themselves to the public faith) and with robberies, murders, wastings, rapes, adulteries, and all kind of wickedness, to rage against them, as if they were enemies and traitors, then at the length many of them began to defend themselves with gates and walls from the violent fury of their adversaries. Last of all, when they perceived neither public liberty, nor their wives' chastity, nor their consciences' tranquillity, nor their own lives safely defended from their violence by their gates and walls, many, we confess, took upon them armour, not against the king's majesty or any Magistrates, but rather that they might defend their liberty granted them by the king's Edict from the rashness of thieves and wicked soldiers. Neither was this done of all men, but of a very few, the which when they perceived no other hope to escape but only exile, and seeing the same also, by the wickedness of their adversaries to be shut up from them, they thought it best by force of arms to make themselves some way to escape by. The which truly if they had not done, and also if that the terror of Brederode's soldiers had not made their adversaries a little doubtful, doubtless not one of them from so great a slaughter had escaped safe from the greedy jaws of their adversaries. They can never prove that any other, or that these for any other cause took upon them armour before the coming of the Duke of Alva, although they had many and sundry opportunities and occasions offered them, both to possess many much and well fenced Cities and also to invade and spoil the king's treasure and Exchequer. But they would commit nothing, whereof they might not with a safe conscience make rehearsal before God, and all good men. But if any insolent persons either have gone about or done any other thing, or for some other purpose, as their doings were neither commanded nor allowed by those which were the chiefs of the congregation, let not so great a multitude of innocent persons be punished for the insolence of a few. For it does not appertain to us, what a few private men have committed to revenge their injuries taken before either of the Inquisitors, or

Of the overthrowing of images. of the sacrificing priests or of any other person. Much less does the overthrowing of Images and Idols appertain unto us, for we will easily prove that it was done without the commandment or consent of our Ministers, Elders or congregations, unless a few of ours (perceiving the Magistrate to agree thereunto) thought it likewise lawful for them to do the same. Although truly, whosoever they were that committed it, they have been more than sufficiently punished for their offence. For in place of one dead and blockish Image, there have been about 30 living Images of God (for whom the son of God shed his blood) murdered, destroyed, and burnt, and in stead of one rotten block more than ten living bodies, and yet the Images restored and renewed

Of new religion. by their common charges. As concerning the new Religion whereof they accuse us to be authors, every man knows how far our religion which we profess is from that kind of newness. For besides that this religion was delivered unto us by Christ, the antiquity of all things, the eternal Son of God, by his prophets, Apostles and Martyrs from many ages, it is manifest that above whole fifty years it has flourished in Belgium, and has been set forth in private meetings and Sermons. Neither was it at any time, either by lawful judgment or Edict rightly made condemned. For whatsoever judgments have been given against the professors of this Religion, the judges and Magistrates themselves were compelled by the severity of the Edicts to confess against their will and with great strife of conscience, to pronounce the same. Yea, they which were found guilty, were not suffered lawfully to defend themselves, but they had their mouths stopped with a ball and their tongues cut out of their heads contrary to the true order of Justice. It is manifest also that all the Edicts, which were made by Charles the Emperor and king Philip[57] are void and of none effect, because they were made contrary to the laws and statutes of the country without the counsel and consent of the estates of the provinces required in solemn assembly (as they were bound by oath thereunto) without whose assent nothing, according to the custom and manner of their ancestors could be established,[58] and were also thrust upon many of the Magistrates against their will, staying themselves upon most vain foundations, full of frivolous cavils, by false understanding, as we have before declared by the evident plain words of the Edicts. Therefore this religion can not by any manner of means be counted a new religion, nor they the professors of the same; since they were uncondemned as yet by any lawful judgment, accused of any crime, much less should they be esteemed as the authors of sedition and tumults of the people, and causers of this great and grievous calamity.

But what need we in so plain a matter to use so many words, seeing the case evidently shows itself, and every man perceives who ought to be accused as authors of these turmoils and calamities? We have heretofore declared what was the meaning and intent of the Spanish Inquisitors, and priests, what counsel they have taken, what help and ministers they have used, by what means they have aspired unto this tyrannical government and sovereign authority in Belgium, without any law or prescript. Though these things peradventure (because of their great modesty and equity, which they use in other provinces) may seem to some not probable (although truly they be daily sung in

Of things done after the Duke of Alva's coming.

[57] As early as 1521 the first Placard against the new Protestant heresy in the Low Countries was issued by Charles V. In 1522 the emperor appointed a general Inquisitor for the provinces. The first executions took place in 1523 when two Augustine monks from Antwerp were burnt at the stake in Brussels.

A placard was a governmental edict to which an original seal was affixed to confirm and sanction it. As such it is especially known in connection with the various 'edicts' issued against the Reformatory movements.

[58] Once again the *Libellus Supplex* referred at this point to articles 3, 18 and 25 of the Joyous Entry and to, as it added, 'infinite other ones'. See *Libellus Supplex*, fol. 41.

every child's mouth), yet if he weighs these present times, if he sees the effects of matters, these their doings and affairs, and notes this the incredible tyranny of the Duke of Alva, all which are most apparent to all men, he shall not doubt therein.

All they whom they called rebels, have forsaken their country, and although they might have had good occasions and opportunities to keep some stir, yet they chose rather voluntary exile, banishment and most extreme poverty, than that they would vex their country with most doleful war. But what? Have they anything, for all this, mitigated their cruelty? Have they not after all these things brought to pass in Spain by their devises, that the king (which in a solemn assembly at Madrid has sworn, that he would in his own person revenge the injury, which he thought himself to have taken of his subjects at Belgium, and for that cause made all things ready for his journey, and had fully determined to take his son and the Queen his wife with him)[59] should alter his purpose against his will, and (because they knew him by nature to be a Prince prone to all kind of mercy and gentleness) to continue still in Spain? Have they not substituted or sent an Ambassador in his stead (the king's son and many of the nobles were unwilling thereunto), the Duke of Alva, whom by his nature and manners they well knew to be very fit for their purpose, both by those things which he did in Germany, by the order of his whole life, but especially also by the deadly hatred, and rancorous grudge which he had of long time laid up in his stomach against the Princes of Belgium, for their valiant acts achieved in the wars of France against his will and meaning.[60] Have they not committed unto him the full power and authority, yea have they not caused the king's only son, lawful heir and Lord of the province of Belgium, to end his life shut up in a most horrible prison, because he was against the sending of Alva, and abhorred from the cruelty of the edicts set out against the religion, bearing singular favour and grace towards the lower Germans, bruiting abroad most vain and diverse rumours of the

---

[59] Because of the growing insanity of his son, Don Carlos, Philip postponed his departure to the Netherlands, and decided to send a commander to pave the way for him. After the Duke of Parma and the Duke of Savoy refused to accept the command of the Dutch mission, the Duke of Alva reluctantly accepted the commission. Philip never followed.

[60] At this point the *Defence* alludes to the rivalries during the war against France particularly between the Count of Egmont, who brought Philip the great victory of St Quentin, and Alva, who was the senior Spanish officer.

cause of his death.[61] What they have done unto the Queen, I had rather other men should imagine, then that we should report.[62]

This truly all men do behold, how this their faithful champion, the Duke of Alva, behaves himself. He comes into a quiet province, all those being thrown out or voluntarily gone into exile, whom he looked to have had as his adversaries. He is received most honourably of all men; neither was there anyone found, which, with his most ready obedience to the king's legate, did not testify his faithful heart towards the king. But he out of hand ordered them not as the king's loving subjects, but as enemies and traitors, equally raging and extending his cruelty both upon the professors of the Gospel, and papists, compelling, he constrained the chief Princes contrary to the authority of the laws, to the liberty of their privileges, and chiefly contrary to the decrees and appointments of the sacred and famous order of the golden fleece, of the brotherhood of Burgundy, to plead their cause in chains. And when they refused that kind of judgment as unmet and to be suspected, proffering themselves ready to stand before equal judges, he chopped off their heads.[63] The rest, which by their godly and wholesome counsels had defended the peace of their country, and by their wisdom stayed the tumults of the people, and effusion of blood, he pronounced as enemies and traitors to their king and country, and so compelled them (will they, nill they), by taking upon them armour, to try themselves unguilty of so great treason. The which their taking of armour (done by them for necessity's sake, as godly men may judge), he has since that time not only made as a just occasion of slandering us with his cavils, but aso as a godly title of Justice in executing his tyranny. And thereupon forthwith he put in practice that which he had before determined. Therefore he first put all the magistrates (which were thought once to favour justice) out of their authority and place, with great ignominy and reproach. He substituted in their rooms, contrary to their laws and orders, naughty

The Duke of Alva's doings since his coming to Belgium.

---

[61] Don Carlos died, in custody, on 24 July 1568.
[62] The accusation that Isabella de Valois, Philip's wife, had been murdered, was spelled out in William of Orange's famous *Apology* (1581). See H. Wansink (ed.), *The Apology of Prince William of Orange against the Proclamation of the King of Spain* (Leyden, 1969), pp. 44–5.
[63] This is an allusion to the decapitation of the Counts of Egmont and Hoorne on 5 June 1568. A year before, on 9 June 1567, both had been arrested. Their trial and subsequent execution, which jettisoned a number of privileges and their dignity as Knights of the Golden Fleece, became proverbial for Alva's tyranny.

packs abounding in all sin and wickedness. And he appointed as he thought good, a new senate house of Spaniards, before whom matters of life and death should be pleaded, the which for that cause should be called the bloody senate.[64] And by that means he deprived all the lawful and ordinary magistrates of their jurisdiction and hearing of matters granted to them by the laws. He filled the gallows and the Gibbets full of the poor people convicted of no other crime but of giving credit to the king's letters patents, to the governess' edict, and their granted licences, and to the magistrates consenting thereunto, and thereupon of hearing of sermons. He destroyed many with the sword, he burnt many alive with a small fire, he beheaded many before their causes were pleaded. Many he spoilt of their goods and possessions,[65] poisoned to death with the filthy stink of continual prison. But the ungodly persons, whose whole life had been stained with infamy, being before (as it is manifest) bought out with money, he gave them licence to plead with their witnesses. He cut out many of their tongues (whom he put to death afterwards), lest they should testify of so great injustice. He burnt many of their tongues with a hot pair of tongs, and to some he tied their lips together through with an iron, sharp on both sides. Others having their mouths most beastly set awry with terror and anguish, the matter and blood dropping down together, he cruelly drew to most pitiful slaughter. He pretermitted nothing of Phalaris' tyranny,[66] neither did he only with torments thus vex the professors of the gospel, but those also which most favoured the popish religion, and they which had endeavoured with all their power, that nothing should be moved against the king. As for those which could not behold the calamity of their country, but had for the avoidance of the present danger conveyed themselves away, he appointed them a day of appearance, and therewithal, scarce staying for the day appointed, he rushed in upon their goods, adjudging them confiscate to the king's Exchequer; [he was] not only spoiling poor widows, innocent orphans and very papists of their dowry and patrimony, but also deceiving the creditors of all their just debts and

---

[64] The Council of Troubles, soon nicknamed 'Blood Council', existed between 1567 and 1576. In connection with the 1566–7 troubles, about 12,000 people were put to trial; over 1,000 were executed.

[65] It is estimated that about 9,000 people were, either partly or completely, deprived of their goods and possessions.

[66] Phalaris (*c.* 560), the ruler of Acragas, had become proverbial for the cruelty of his tyranny.

lawful titles. He converted the inheritance of innocents from their kinsmen and allies (to whom for the beheading or civil death of the right and next heirs, they by law and right appertained) most wickedly to his own use and commodity. He took from cities and towns all their liberties, laws, statutes and privileges, he overthrew all order of humanity, he clearly took away all duties of Christian charity, chiefly commanded by the laws of God. For by edict he forbade that no kind of man, whether he were their father, son, kinsman, or whatsoever, should show any kind of charity to those that professed the Gospel or were banished for default of appearance at the day appointed. And thus he alienated and withdrew the minds of children from their parents, of parents from their children, and of wives from their husbands.

In the town of Maastricht he put a father to death, because he had for one night lodged in his house his own son, which had been for a space absent before. And likewise he murdered another well known citizen, because he gave the sixth part of a bz. of corn unto a poor widow, burdened with the keeping of four children, whose husband was before put to death for religion's sake. He bereaved also another of his life, because he sent his friend a little money over into England. He compelled honest and chaste matrons born of worshipful stocks, by flight and voluntary exile to save themselves, and by begging to provide meat for themselves and their children, only because they received their husbands into their houses. He threw down many men's houses, because they had received letters from their friends of their health and welfare. But what? Did he spare the dead? By his Edict he straightly charged, that whosoever died without shrift and auricular confession, his goods should be confiscated and his body hung on a Gibbet; then the which what can be thought or invented more cruel, more contrary to all humanity and Justice? Seeing it happened daily that many suddenly that have no time to bethink them of their former sins.

He placed over cities not soldiers, but enemies and thieves, which might violently abuse the riches, wives, children and lifes of the citizens, according to their evil lust. And he granted them licence to do what should please them freely without punishment. For was there any wickedness so heinous, the which the fury of Spanish soldiers has not committed in Belgium, and daily commits unpunished. In Ypres, a famous town in Flanders, when a minister of God's word was suffering death, the soldiers without any other occasion turned their weapons upon the miserable and unarmed people standing about them, and besides an infinite number whom they wounded unto death, there were 22 citizens shot through with bullets of lead, whom they left dead in the streets.

At Tournai a dissension happened between the Spanish soldiers and those other soldiers which were there for the defence of the castle, and two of the Spaniards being slain, the rest cried out 'Spain, Spain'. At the which voice, the other Spanish soldiers being called ran most furiously like mad men through the City, and killed all whom they met, in number about 15 of godly and honest Citizens. In the same night some of the Spanish soldiers, being persuaded that a certain widow called by the name of her husband widow Potier had a great sum of money in her house, broke into her house openly by violence at noon day and, most cruelly murdering her, her daughter and niece, they carried out of her house all things they could find. At Lilles, one of the chief cities of all Flanders, which has been always most addicted to the popish religion, when a Spaniard, going about by violence to ravish an honest citizen's wife, was let of his purpose by her husband and two of his neighbours, he cried out 'Spain' (a common byword amongst them for the avoidance of present danger in their wicked enterprises). The other soldiers, warned with that outcry came running and by force and violence, apprehended the Citizen and his two neighbours, and delivered them unto the Magistrate to be punished like rebels and seditious persons, with this threat, that unless they executed their commandments speedily they would set the whole City on fire. Wherewith the Judges being terrified, caused two of them to be hanged and the third to be whipped. But what availed it to reckon up particularly all the wickedness which the Spanish soldiers have committed, as there can not be imagined any offence so heinous, the which they do not day by day commit freely, without any punishment. And yet the Duke of Alva compelled them to maintain these soldiers at their own proper costs and charges. Belike that they might spoil and rob their coffers, ravish their wives, kill their children and families at their pleasure, and leave nothing free from their cruelty, avarice and horrible wickedness; then the which what can be imagined more unjust? Although truly, there is no injustice so great, from the which the Alva Duke does abhor. For lest he should leave anything holy and unpolluted, with his beastly boldness he dares profane the most holy rights of matrimony. He has dissolved (under the vain pretence of heresy) the lawful marriages of many, and made their children begotten in just marriage, to be taken for bastards and as illegitimate, to be excluded from the succession of their patrimony. He joined other men's wives (which were married before in the open assembly of the Church) to other men by a new marriage, or rather by most infamous adultery, because they had omitted a mass, or that the Priest was not courteously entertained at his coming to them. And therewith by his public Edicts he made manifest adultery and open bigamy to be accounted lawful. He has compelled widows against their wills and openly denying and withstanding the same, by force and violence to be married unto his soldiers and cut-throats, insomuch that many of them chose rather to forsake their countries, with the loss of all their riches, than once to consent unto such heinous villainy. But what? Has he left the most holy Religion of Baptism inviolated? He has commanded with great impiety, contrary to the Pope's decretals, that all they which were baptized after the manner of the Apostles in the primitive Church, and according to the just prescript of the word of God should be baptized again. For what avails it to speak of the most reverent order and religious keeping of the sepulchers and graves of those which be buried, the which from the beginning of the world has been amongst the most barbarous and fierce people most religiously kept, as he has not feared with most brutish cruelty to break up the graves of those godly and honest Citizens, which had been buried in the ground above 14 days before, and to take out their bodies, scarcely cleaving to the bones, hanging some on gibbets and burning the rest with fire. Neither suffered he the cities of the noble Empire to escape free from this, his odious kind of cruelty, for who does not know that even at Harderwijk in Guelders (which is the Emperor's lawful inheritance) there was the body of an honest Citizen which had been buried long before, drawn out of his grave, and cruelly plucked in pieces under a gibbet with great and bitter triumphing before the door, and even in the very sight of the miserable widow. But what is there holy amongst the living, or religious amongst the dead, the which he has feared openly to violate and pollute, the which after his own lust and appetite, has made profane things holy, and holy things profane, has made and abrogated laws, has spoilt the wealthiest of all their substance, has reproachfully slandered the chief of the nobility, has put to death those which were most innocent, has destroyed feeble, old men, young men, and tender virgins with most horrible torments, has oppressed Cities and the whole province with incredible exactions and unaccustomed tributes, which has wrung into his hands with his threats an infinite mass of gold and silver, and now exacts over all merchandises and usurps the Tenth penny, and by that means has diminished the trade of Merchants and taken away all licences of traffic with other nations. Was there ever tyranny since the first age of man so cruel and so covetous as this is? The wicked extortions, new and unaccustomed tributes wherewith Caligula oppressed his subjects are recorded in histories; yet notwithstanding he appointed a mean and measure of his covetousness, for he assigned to every kind of man by name their separate tributes; but this fellow [Alva], lest anything should escape him, be it never so little, besides the hundreds, which he has already taken away, and the new hundreds which he has of late commanded to be levied of all their lands, farms and other immovables, he doth exact the tenth in all kind of faculties.[67] And besides all this he required twenty hundred thousand crowns of gold, to be paid him yearly of the whole province. What need we any more, is there any man so cruelly wild or outrageous of mind, that he does not tremble and quake at the sudden remembrance of this unaccustomed cruelty, avarice, unfaithfulness and impiety? O, can there any man be found so void of sense and reason, whose understanding is so blinded, that he believes that these good and well disposed persons seek nothing else, but to keep the province of Belgium under the king's authority, to defend religion, and maintain laws? As all their actions and doings do openly pretend and show that they have no other king, no law, no religion but their own avarice, and most beastly covetousness. They make a glorious pretence as though all the Belgians were Lutherans, rebels, and traitors to the king's majesty, because forsooth they would not submit their necks to the yoke of the Inquisition, that is to say they would not willingly and of their own accord yield up themselves to the beastly lust and unjust tyranny of most pernicious persons. But truly if

---

[67] In March 1569 Alva proposed the introduction of three new taxes: a tax of one per cent, the so called Hundredth Penny, on capital assets, to be levied on a one-off basis; a permanent tax of five per cent, the so-called Twentieth Penny, on the sale of immovables and a permanent tax of ten per cent, the Tenth Penny, on the sale of movables. The States quite quickly accepted the Hundredth Penny, but the Twentieth and Tenth Penny aroused vehement opposition.

they had their king for their enemy, they would never have so faithfully observed their loyalty towards him. Neither would they so carefully have retained all their cities, towns, and castles in his fidelity and tuition. Neither would they so faithfully have given credit to the king's edicts, the king's name, the king's broad seal, and to the Governess, and in so doing should never have run into so many and so great calamities by their so light credulity. Neither should the Duke of Alva once have set foot into these countries. For they had infinite occasions and opportunities offered them of disannulling the king's authority, of alienating his cities, of striking league with other nations adjoining unto them, and of keeping back the Alvan duke from the borders of their province. And yet for all this dare not the adversaries affirm (unless they be most impudent) that this was once mentioned amongst them or spoken of. But let it be so that they were rebels, is it lawful therefore for the king to violate his faithful promise, to pervert the laws both of God and man, and to pollute all things, both holy and profane, with this unaccustomed tyranny?[68]

We read that in the time of our ancestors, many of the cities of Flanders rebelled against Maximilian, the most mighty king of the Romans, and the citizens did not only openly refuse his government and detained with them for the space of eight years his son Philip against his will, but also most contumeliously threw Maximilian himself into prison. But afterwards, being overcome by the help of Frederic the Emperor, and the other Princes of Germany, they yielded themselves again to his authority.[69] Then, this good prince Maximilian, in this so odious rebellion, and having been so injuriously handled, was so far from doing anything like unto the Alvan Duke, that he not only with great gentleness received his subjects again into

---

[68] The image of Philip II as a deviously misled but *au fond* virtuous prince, a highly traditional one, is suddenly dropped; now, with a rather scorning passage, the *Defence* makes the radical and unprecedented move of putting at least part of the blame directly on Philip.

[69] After the devastating 1477 defeat at Nancy, the States General recognized Mary of Burgundy, daughter of Charles the Bold, as the latter's legitimate heiress. Her authority, however, was greatly reduced by a series of privileges, amongst them the famous 'national' Grand Privilege (see pp. xiv–xv). Mary married Maximilian of Habsburg, who, after Mary's death, became regent for his three-year-old son Philip in 1482. Maximilian's relationship with the Dutch provinces was troublesome. Flanders in particular resisted Maximilian's expansionist policy towards France. During the second wave of revolts against his rule Maximilian was arrested in 1488 at Bruges. Having recognized the 'union' and confederation as concluded by the States General, he was released again, only to resume the conflict, which lasted until 1492.

63

his grace's favour, but also with great clemency worthy of so great a prince restored unto them again all their privileges and ancient immunities. By the which his incredible lenity, he made the whole province most obedient in all points to him, and his posterity forever. But these men never remitted any tribute, any subsidy, or burden, laid upon the king's most faithful subjects, whose loyalty towards the king could never with any crime be attainted, being always obedient to the king's commandment, who had offered up by humble supplication all their riches and substance unto the king's good will and pleasure, desiring to have nothing free from the king's commandment, but only a clear conscience in religion, the which they ought to keep unpolluted unto God alone. And they humbly desired to redeem the liberty of religion with an extraordinary and far more grievous tribute, than the Christians redeem their religion of the Turk, or the Jews obtain theirs of the pope.

Yet notwithstanding these men (I say) spoiling those faithful subjects of all their riches, forbid them the use of fire and water, air and land, as if they were the most deadly enemies of all mankind; and yet have they (God knoweth) committed no offence, but only given too light credit to the king's edicts, which in manner were established as firm laws, and never to be revoked. And so they simply believing the king's letters and name, kept diligently their sermons, in the which there was nothing preached but the pure word of God, and they daily admonished to show their obedience to the prince and his magistrate. Yet these tyrants do with most horrible cruelty oppress the whole province without respect either of the innocent or offenders, and with most insatiable avarice spoiling them, torment them with most barbarous tyranny.

Can any man now doubt, what it is that these men have heretofore laboured to bring to pass, or whereunto they have bent their minds, set their eyes, and applied their most ravening hands? Or is there any man so blind that can not see what has been the cause and origin of these aforesaid tumults in Belgium, or so blockish that he can not perceive that these honest men, I mean the good masters and bishops of the Spanish Inquisition, have from the beginning, only gone about to alienate the king's mind from his subjects, and by every small or none occasion to accuse them of rebellion; that as they have most furiously executed their tyranny in the kingdom of Naples, Sicily and the country of Milan, in new India, and in the chief part of Spain, so they might by some manner of means furiously rage in the low Germany, and by little and little when occasion shall be offered, in high Germany; and that under the colour of defending the Pope's religion, they might oppress the whole liberty of the citizens in Belgium, take away their magistrates' authority, and violate the whole power of their laws, bring the king's majesty subject to their authority, and that they themselves might, without law or order, at their pleasure command what they will, take what they lust, kill whatsoever should offend them, empty the rich men's coffers, and make themselves lords and governors of all things.[70]

But if any man shall think that these things, because they be present and not yet thoroughly finished, can not easily be judged upon, let him conjecture and take judgment of things already past. In the which we appeal unto your majesties, most mighty Emperor and you, renowned princes of Germany, call to remembrance, what they have heretofore done in Germany, what with what fetches and counsels they have wrought; you shall perceive truly their old arts, you shall know these old Spaniards, you shall know these old Inquisitors. For even these be they which with their grievous cavils and slanders and with the terror of the Pope's name, have oppressed the most famous princes of Germany before Charles the fifth, which kindled a most doleful firebrand of civil dissention in the very bowels of high Germany, and under the cloak of rebellion set the Protestant Princes together by the ears, being altogether ignorant of their treachery. The which have defiled all things in Germany with their wicked and flagitious acts, the which have gone about to overthrow the liberties of Germany and laws of the Empire, and even those be they at this day which vex and trouble the inhabitants of low Germany with the very same cavils, before the aforesaid Charles, his son king of Spain. They have deceived them with the same arts and subtleties and oppressed with the same enterprises. These be the authors and inventors of so great unfaithfulness. These also be guilty of their cruelty and avarice. These were the ministers and workers of all their mischievous boldness. For to whom is Granvelle, the Cardinal of the Germans

Of things done in Germany and in other places heretofore.

---

[70] At this point the *Defence* spells out what had been implicit before. It makes the important move of arguing that the conflict in the Low Countries was in essence not about religion, but about 'the liberty of the citizens' and the 'authority of the magistrates'. Thus the conflict with Alva is presented as an essentially political one, a fight for lawful liberty, against beastly tyranny.

unknown, and who knows not the Duke of Alva? Both the which have empoisoned the most noble princes of Germany, overcoming them partly by violence, and partly by their fraud and deceit, and have slandered them with most reproachful contumelies. These be the firebrands of the whole world, with the which the greatest part of Europe will most dolefully be set afire, unless your authority, wise doing and power, with speed foresees so great a mischief. These men therefore are only to be accounted as the authors of all the tempestuous broils seditions, tumults and miserable calamities which have happened in Belgium. But if there be any man that does not as yet understand, let him remember the saying of Cassianus ('to whom these things shall profit'[71]) and let him diligently consider not only to whom this public calamity of Belgium is now profitable, but also if there be any hope, that these things will be profitable to him here-after; since we could not but perceive that this danger was imminent either by loss of our religion or by wounding of our conscience, or by the grievous anger of our king, or by the doleful destruction of our country, which way soever it would have happened. For they have long ago hunted after their triumphs, their ruledom and Empire by any [of] these occasions. So that they have never ceased by their subtle devises to cause the subjects to hate their king, and the king likewise to hate his subjects, and with greedy mouths and stretched out ears they have taken the last suspicion of tumults and rebellion and have filled the king's ears and mind with their false tales, odiously amplifying their received news. The which, though it be so manifestly to all men that it need no longer proof, yet it is most manifestly confirmed by the king's Ambassador which was sent into France. For he in his letters sent to the governors writes on this wise: there will arise unto the king great fruit and commodity by the incommodious tumults of Belgium, because by this occasion, the king will bring them to full obedience and subjection, and reduce the state into that form and order of government unto the which his ancestors could never attain.[72] The which to bring to pass, the king has vehemently desired

A copy of this Epistle, word for word, is to be seen in the end of the Prince of Orange's Apology; confirmed with all their hands.

[71] The Latin original is 'cui bono fue rit'. Cassianus could refer to either Longinus Cassius, one of the leaders of the conspiracy against Caesar, or John Cassianus (360–430), a cleric whose *Collectiones* set the foundations for monastic life.

[72] Once more the conflict in the Low Countries is presented as a political one, and again Philip himself is said to play a major role. The purpose of the king is – and here the wording is rather striking – to change the 'state' (the *Libellus Supplex* used the word 'status', which obviously refers to 'the form and order of government'). For an overview

of long time, and therein has always hitherto spent his whole study and endeavour, and that there was no man (favouring the king's majesty) [who] would counsel him to let pass so noble occasion of the performance of this his worthy enterprise, etc. By the which words it is manifestly declared that the Spanish Inquisitors (which in the name of the king cloak and cover all their desires) have sought and gone about heretofore to get any occasion, whereby they might invade Belgium, spoil it of all his riches and goods, and rule all things as should best be thought to their lust and pleasure. So that no man can longer doubt from whence these have had their beginning, since it is manifest who they are that have long ago desired to reap the fruits of these our troubles. And it is also manifest that the Cardinal himself in a great assembly of many men, when it was objected unto him that it was to be feared lest if the people should be any more oppressed they would make some sedition, was not ashamed to answer that the king had no cause to fear. But rather to wish for the seditious tumults of his subjects: for by them the king's power and majesty was much increased, and the privileges of the Cities and liberties of the people very much restrained and diminished. Otherwise what is it that they should seek for by so many examples of such unaccustomed avarice and rare cruelty? Would they make the people subject to the king's authority? Every wise man sees, that then they take not the just and right way to obtain their purpose. For the subjects' hearts are won and reconciled to their prince by gentleness, humanity and Justice, not by terror, fear, or tyranny. And every man knows that the prince of Egmont and an infinite number of others which have been always and ever were most earnest favourers of the king's name and authority, and they which never spared the sweat of their brows or blood of their bodies for to keep the whole province safe in the king's subjection, and whom the king for this cause has always very much regarded, were notwithstanding destroyed of them for an old hatred conceived through an old envy of their noble acts so worthily achieved in their wars. But peradventure they seek by this means utterly to root out the religion of the gospel, which they (though the most part of them be of no religion) feign themselves so utterly to detest and abhor. Truly they mean nothing less, for then what cause had they with such

of the early modern history of the concept of 'state', see Quentin Skinner, 'The state' in Terence Ball, James Farr, Russell L. Hanson (eds.), *Political Innovation and Conceptual Change* (Cambridge, 1989), pp. 90–132.

infamy and reproach cruelly to put to death the aforesaid Prince of Egmont, the Earl Hoorne, and many others, which were both ignorant of this Religion and have been always adversaries of the same. Why do they still execute such tyranny, upon those which be altogether of the Pope's religion? But (most noble Princes) they desire nothing less: Their only fetch is to establish their kingdom in Belgium, that they may rule therein all things according to their lewd lust and pleasure, and contrary to all equity and right, as they have done, heretofore in Sicily and in the kingdom of Naples, that they being loaded with the rich spoils of so wealthy a province, may return home, and send others in their stead, they which should draw them dry of all their juice and blood. There is only one way to attain to this purpose, and that is their holy Inquisition, the which by good right is termed after the name of Inquisition, for by this they daily inquire and make search in the chests, bags and coffers of the rich men, in the beauty and bosoms of the virgins and matrons, in the throats, bowels and blood, and lastly in the souls and consciences of all men. By this they make themselves Lords and Monarchs of all things. They make all the princes and the king himself subject and obedient unto them.

They have used this means first in Spain, in the which by this art of Inquisition they have disannulled all privileges and liberties, the which were before very great in Spain. They have made subject unto themselves, all the authority of laws and the majesty of the regal sceptre. They have left only a bare name and title to the King with part of the tasks and subsidies, they challenge unto themselves sovereign rule and authority, and in capital causes they appoint unto the guilty either life or death at their own arbitrament. Whom they determine to destroy, no man is able to save, no not the king himself though he most earnestly desire it. Whom they take upon them to defend, neither the severity of the laws, nor Judgment sincerely given nor the king's commandment is able once to hurt his little finger. Therefore it is no marvel, if all estates, yea and the kings themselves, be very much afraid of them.

Afterwards they followed the same way in Naples, Sicily, Milan, and in the great country of India, and they openly (but in vain) put the same practice for to make subject to themselves all Germany. For they were withstood and prevented by your wisdom (most mighty princes) and by the wisdom, power, and virtue of your ancestors. But yet they cease not at this time by their crafty wills and deceits, to perform that which they have so long desired.

For that I may pretermit those of Groningen, the wise Frisians and those of Overijssel, Guelders, Cambrai and many others of the empire, the which always have obeyed to the jurisdiction of the Roman Emperor, have used his laws and statutes, and have appealed to the court of the Emperor, and submitted themselves into the government of the Duke of Brabant, only upon this condition, that they might retain their laws, customs and statutes safely without any appearing of the same. All which the Duke of Alva has deprived of all their liberties and privileges, and (as though they had been overcome by battle) appointed them new laws, created them new magistrates contrary to their ancient manner and constitution, has exacted unaccustomed tributes, has built castles in their cities, has vanished the chief of their citizens, seized upon their goods; that I may (I say) pretermit all these things and infinite more of like sort, in the which although he has no right or title, yet he pretends to have some kind of interest.

For what end (I pray you) does he seek openly to enlarge the bonds of his government without any just or shadowed title thereunto, even into the very midst of the empire? What causes him to seek, or rather by force to take upon him the government of the country of Kleve, and threateningly to command them to vanish out of their country, all the Belgians? What causes him by prescript to command Cologne, and the other free cities of the Empire, what they should do unto the low Germans? It is impossible that it should not be revealed unto you (most worthy princes) what cruelty he has committed, what fields he has destroyed, what droves of beasts he has carried away, what matrons and virgins he has deflowered, how many inhabitants he has murdered in the East country of Friesland, and the country of Emden. What should we think moreover, seeing he doubts not by his Edict to call home all the students of low Germany, which were gone abroad to foreign universities whatsoever (only Rome excepted) and all the young men which were departed to other places for the learning of some art or manual occupation, threatening perpetual banishment and loss of all their goods if they do not return, insomuch that he has spoilt the poor young men, travelling abroad for the knowledge of tongues, and getting the wisdom, of the fruit of all their studies and labours, making them unfit hereafter to take office upon them in the commonwealth, and has utterly beggared and undone many which travelled abroad to get their living by their art and occupation. In the which he showed himself utterly to denounce all humanity. For if all humanity be maintained by the mutual society and company of men, must he not need be the enemy thereof, which by violence seeks to take away that one gift, whereby man only shows himself to differ from the brute beasts.

For the knowledge of tongues, and use of reason, although it be peculiarly given unto man, yet the fruit thereof is not fully reaped, but in the company and society of men, and especially in our affairs which we have with other nations. Therefore seeing he goes about to bereave us thereof, what seeks he else but to destroy the tongue, and the whole use of reason. The which truly (so great is his inhumanity) he would do, if he could bring it by any means to pass. For what other thing does he seek by this his Inquisition? Why does he forbid the people the use of holy Scripture? Why does he refuse only the knowledge of God's holy will and Testament to the divines, that is forsooth, to his Inquisitors and bishops? Why does he forbid the people to pray in a known tongue? But that he desires rather to rule brutish beasts, than reasonable men. For he fears, lest if they should understand anything, they would at the length detest so great and unaccustomed barbarousness, and therefore he will have no cities or countries gone unto, but those unto whom he prescribes both laws and ordinances. It has been very well by the wise judgment and doings of our ancestors brought to pass, that young men studious in good literature, and liberal arts, should travel, unto other universities to see their cities and manners, and to learn their tongues. And for this cause, by the liberality and costs of kings and Princes, free universities were founded, and great liberties and privileges granted to them, that thither the young men of other countries might more often resort, and that by this means the faith, friendship and society of men among themselves might the better be retained. The which truly is no new custom, but has been used heretofore in all ages. For we read that Plato, and the other philosophers did with long and diverse travelling learn their wisdoms, whereof we all stand now in admiration, and from strange peoples and far nations carried the knowledge thereof into Greece. The Romans before times used to send their children into Greece and Asia for learning's sake, and that I may not only stay in those old examples, not much before the immunity of the Turk had overrun all Greece, the Germans, Frenchmen, Italians, and the Spaniards themselves were wont earnestly to go to Athens for study sake. The which liberty or custom whosoever takes away, he takes truly away all humanity and professes himself the deadly enemy of all other nations. For it is wont to be forbidden that any Citizen should inhabit or dwell amongst those, against whom our Harolds have denounced war. The which for this cause is done, because we think it not lawful for our Citizens and young men to resort to those people, whom we count as enemies.

Since therefore (right noble Princes) that he does forbid his Citizens and free young men to be brought up amongst you, and all other nations, only Rome excepted, what can otherwise be gathered, but that he misdoubts your faith, and suspects your meaning, and desires to deal with you, as with his open enemies. Let therefore all meetings or merchants and change of merchandise be taken away, let all your Universities be destroyed, abrogate all their privileges, suffer no hospitality to be kept. Let every man sit idle at home, in his own house, take heed lest anything be brought in from far countries, lest likewise you bring in somewhat which may at length hinder the barbarous trade of the Duke of Alva.

But we hope (most worthy Princes) that you plainly see what men are chiefly to be accused of this our injury. The Spaniard will not suffer our young men to come unto your Universities, your solemn markets and fairs, or to any of your provinces, lest peradventure they should return infected of some spot of heresy. By the which his judgment he openly condemns you and all your people of heresy, and impiety. Although in this his doing, he has besides this another fetch and purpose. For this is a new invention for to spoil the poor people of their substance. For when he sees them to have escaped the greedy jaws of his Inquisition, and it is not easy for him to accuse them, being absent, although many of them, in his judgment, worthily be accused of such heinous crimes, and had deserved to have their goods confiscated, because they were very rich and wealthy, he thought best to devise some way whereby he might likewise draw them into his net. And therefore he stretches out the veil of his Religion, the which he abuses to the full satisfying of all his appetites, as Gigas did his ring.[73] By this he drives some out of their country, and makes some return home against their wills. By this he takes from some all their liberties, riches, and life, to others he gives full licence to prey upon other

---

[73] Gyges was a shepherd who dethroned Candaules and became king of Lydia (716–678 BC), thanks to a ring which allowed him to become invisible. The story was told by Cicero in *De Officiis*, Book 3, Chapter 9, Section 38.

men's goods, and with all wickedness to shed the innocent blood. To be brief, under this pretence of Religion, he does whatsoever pleases him, though it be contrary to the laws of God and man. By this also, with most extreme and unaccustomed tyranny, he goes about to establish and to give all sovereign power in low Germany unto the Bishops of the Spanish Inquisition, that from thence, if it be possible, they might stretch the same, by their deceits and privy practices, throughout all Europe.

These things pertain as well to the Germans as to the Belgians. Do not you think (most noble Princes) that these things do not pertain unto you. For they do most especially bend their force against you, and your Germany. For there remains as yet, yea there is nourished (I say) in the Spaniards' hearts and bowels the great grief, which they of late conceived, when they saw the government of Germany (whereof they thought themselves in full possession) to be plucked out from between their jaws. They do as yet try their old counsels, whereby they make subject all the world to their holy Inquisition, and retain unto themselves the full superiority of all things; they have not as yet buried their old arts and crafty policies; they have not as yet abolished their leagues, societies and conspiracies; whereby they bound themselves utterly to subvert all those, whom they thought would withstand the increase of their tyranny. Who does not know the conditions of peace between the kings of France and Spain? Who does not know the confederacy made with those of Bayonne? Who knows not what firebrands have from thence been brought into France, low Germany, Italy, England, Scotland and into the furthest country of all the land Thulen.[74] Truly that long and deadly civil war in France was first moved and made by these authors contrary to the Edicts made by the estates of the whole Realm, and contrary to the will of the King and Queen, and by these also, the peace being broken, the leagues violated, and the fidelity of their oaths and agreements being trodden under feet. It was begun again the second and the third time, and by these men it has been continued almost ten years, to the great calamity of that noble province, and the great slaughter of worthy men and noble princes. Neither do they now at this time cease with their pestiferous counsels and most wicked practices by all their power to break and make void the peace appointed and concluded with the full good will of the king and all good

---

[74] Thulen stood for the most northern island or town in the world.

men. It is more manifest then that it needs rehearsal what persecutions they have done in Italy, what conspiracies they made in England, what seditious tumults and murders they have caused in Scotland, and what rebellions they have raised in Ireland. For what have they doubted even in England, setting up their Pope's bulls conviciously to call the most noble and virtuous Queen of England, the servant of all wickedness, the maintainer of most wicked persons, a heretic and favourer of all heretics, and do pronounce her cursed by the Pope's curse, to deprive her of the right of her kingdom, and jurisdiction to absolve her subjects and people from the bond of their loyalty and oath towards her, and generally to forbid that any man should obey her authority. By the which their judgment they have openly and plainly declared what other kings and princes, professing the Gospel should look for at their hands. But what, has this seditious flame contained itself within the bounds and limits of Europe? Has it not burst out and overreached the pillars of Hercules, has it not filled the shores of Africa with the dead men's bodies? Has it not stirred up the Moors to armour, and the Turks to battle? Has it not shaken the scaffold of the whole world with a most terrible tempest and does it not also now (most noble Princes) prepare itself to burst out amongst you, to arm yourselves against your own bowels if you do not take heed. Notwithstanding we do not doubt but that the Lord for his mercy sake will indue your honours with such wisdom and courage that you shall stand and withstand their mischievous practices.

But we (most mighty Caesar, and you renowned princes of Germany) beseech your honours not to neglect us the most miserable of all men, banished [from] our country, spoilt of our riches, slandered with ignomy, oppressed with poverty, through their great and unspeakable tyranny. Remember that Belgium is a part of Germany, whereof a great part is contained within the river of Rhine, and a great part also by most ancient right is obeying to the Emperor's laws and statutes. Remember that Brabant has been always in most ancient inheritances of the Empire, and the Dukes thereof have in all ages heretofore bound themselves to the Emperors, to be in their retinue and protection. And that Antwerp is accounted the chief Margraviate of the Empire, and that Guelders, Friesland and the country Groningen, Overijssel and Cambrai, are all under the jurisdiction of the Empire; and that Holland, Zeeland, Hainaut and other Towns of Belgium have appertained to the dukes of Berry, as their ancestors'

An earnest petition to the Emperor, and to the princes of Germany.

73

goods and inheritance. Do not you despise the friendship that is between us, by name, tongue, and continual society, and that we let pass all ambiguities. Remember most (mighty Caesar) that Charles the fifth your father's brother was lately chosen out of the midst of Flanders to the government of the Empire,[75] as though he had been by nation a German, and that Maximilian also your great grandfather, joined in alliance by marriage the country of Belgium, to the most noble and ancient house of Austria.[76] And that Charles the Emperor not long before caused that whole province to be accounted as one of the estates and limits of the Empire in the Parliament held at Augsburg, all the estates and princes of Germany assenting thereunto, and that they might be in the safeguard and defence of the Empire against all violence and injuries.[77] And that they by name have been sent as Ambassadors to all the assemblies of the Empire from the province of Belgium, and that they have paid tribute required of them for the repelling of the great Turk, and that it is until this day controversy whether the Duke of Brabant or the Bishop of Magdeburg should sit in higher rooms at the assemblies. So that without all doubt the province of low Germany should not be accounted as Athens from the Empire. Do not you therefore contempt (most mighty Emperor, and you noble Princes of Germany) the humble suit of us your friends requesting your trust and aid against the outrageous cruelty of those most proud and abominable men. We do not deny to be obedient to our king, to obey his commandments, pay our tributes, taxes, and subsidies, whatsoever to show our faith and loyalty towards him in all points. But in most humble wise we do desire that we may have our conscience and Religion left us freely, lest in that last judgment we be found guilty of violating the faith of Jesus Christ with an ungodly conscience, and that we may by the good licence of the king defend and keep the health of our souls.

And we, by the Immortal God, and by his only son Jesus Christ, whose name we profess in our public religion, pray and beseech your

[75] Charles was a native of Ghent. In 1570 Maximilian II was Emperor. He was a son of Ferdinand, Charles' late brother.

[76] The marriage between Mary of Burgundy and Maximilian of Habsburg in 1477 meant a fusion of the Burgundian and Habsburg dynasties.

[77] The 1548 Transaction of Augsburg turned the Low Countries into a so-called Burgundian Circle of the Empire, which above all implied the basic political and judicial independence of the Netherlands.

Majesties' highnesses, that we may defend ourselves, our wives, children and riches, but above all our conscience from the pride of the Inquisitors, from the avarice of the new bishops, and from the outrageous lust of the most mischievous ministers of the Inquisition, and rascal soldiers. And if the friendly name of the Germans can not move you, yet let that most straight bond wherewith we are knit together in Jesus Christ whose members we boast ourselves to be, move you. Let the duty you owe to all mankind, move you. Let the doubtful and uncertain condition of man's estate move you. Let crooked old men, now wrapped in sorrow, move you. Let miserable widows, unfortunate orphans, mourning virgins, let so great and so huge a company of miserable men, move you. Who altogether driven out of their houses, thrown from their possessions, deprived of the commodities of their country, spoilt of all estimation, violently plucked from the bosoms of their just careful parents, loving wives and tender children, wandering and scattered abroad in strange countries, not knowing what shall become of them, do seek waste resting places, small cheer and liberty of their conscience. But if no occasion shall be offered you, to restore us unto our country again, yet give no ear to our adversaries' accusations, nor place to their insatiable cruelty.

We know for a certainty, that they will never cease to urge you to deprive us of all the humanity and gentleness, wherewith you entertained and cherished us in your countries: So that there be neither air left to the living, nor earth to the dead, nor refuge to poor exiles. But we pray you, most noble Princes, to regard more the commandment of God (who command you to receive strangers and poor banished men, not only within your gates or walls but even in your houses, and to cherish them with all humanity) than the commandments of a few Spanish priests, which with the Duke of Alva, contend and labour to have us thrown out of your Empire. Suffer not the fear and terror of the Spanish name to be of more force with you, than the name and friendship of the German. For what should we speak of the agreement of our religion? The which truly should move you not to suffer us which be joined with you in the body of Christ, in one profession of faith, in one baptism, to be by the lust of a few (which have no religion but their greedy avarice) banished like strangers and enemies, lest that Christ, the King of all kings, in that last day of judgment take that done unto himself, which is cruelly exercised against us, being by his free grace and mercy united to his body and made his members. For though they do pretend the difference of our religion, there is no cause (most noble princes) why you should be moved. For we which do with you acknowledge one God the Father of our Lord Jesus Christ, true God and very man, one holy Ghost. And we which do rest ourselves in the only satisfaction of Jesus Christ, and for his sake we are banished [from] our country, spoilt of our goods, and appointed as sheep unto the slaughter; which acknowledge one church, one word of God, for the foundation of our health, and lastly, with you do look for one resurrection from the dead, and life everlasting, given by the free grace and mercy of God; do not you think that we profess any other religion than that which you do. But if we shall, by the exposition of some words, seem to differ, remember that the Apostles themselves, and their disciples did never so fully agree, but there was in some things a little dissension. Remember that even the ancient fathers of the primitive church have not only left in their writings errors, but also in many places open contrarities. The which truly by the deep providence and wisdom of God, is not without great profit appointed: that we, knowing the infirmity of our own wit may learn to forsake the judgment of man, and cleave only to the authority of the word of God, and not to prefer the authority of man, and our own judgment, before the authority of the word of God, but to bear one another's burdens, and with Christian charity to cover and wisely to bear one another's errors and infirmities. And yet notwithstanding what discord of Religion can there be amongst us, which do not only embrace the only word of God, but also out of that word take the form of our faith, and all things which we use in our religion. For we truly do with most joyful hearts receive and embrace the confession which our Ancestors delivered up to Charles the Emperor at Augsburg. And if we may give our judgment in anything, we subscribe in all points to the doctrine of those Divines, by whose labour that form of their faith was drawn out. We account them not only as our brothers, but even for the most divine and excellent prophets of God. And they likewise do embrace us with great and incredible charity, and with all brotherly love and piety. It is therefore you Princes a more cavil feigned of our adversaries, which say, that we profess a religion, diverse from the Germans. For they study nothing else, but that when they have set us together by the ears, they might tear the members of Christ in pieces, and so oppress us separated and dissevered, whom they were not able to overthrow, fast joined in amity.[78]

But you men and Princes, which have known long ago their crafts and subtleties, be you not therewith moved, neither suffer you the false cavils of our adversaries to have more power to tear and dismember the members of the body of Christ, than the word and commandment of the same Jesus Christ, than the sincere judgment of your Princes and Divines has power and force to unite and knit up the same. Neither let the diverse interpretations of one word prevail more with you, than the most sure and undoubted consent of the whole Scripture and faith. By the which faith and by the most holy body of the son Jesus Christ into the which he has joined us to himself with an knot indissoluble. We once again in most humble wise beseech and entreat you, that your charitable mercy, which has been always prest and ready to help all poor and oppressed innocents, benignly to receive us also with some tuition and safeguard, which for the name Jesus Christ do not only suffer all cruel torments, but also are overwhelmed with most false and unjust reproaches. And that you would only as long as it shall please God to chasten us thus with exile being spoilt of all our goods and commodities of our country, with your gentleness somewhat ease us, whom God's correction does keep low and in poverty. So shall you do an acceptable work unto God himself, the just judge of all things, and stir us up diligently to call upon his mercy and gracious favour for you and your people. Amen.

[78] The purpose of this entire paragraph is to play down the differences between German Lutherans and Dutch Reformed Protestants. As such it reflected the ecumenical policy favoured by William of Orange. Differences were, however, hard to deny. In 1566, Lutherans and Reformed Protestants had clashed in Antwerp over the issue of resistance, and in 1571 the Reformed Protestant synod of Emden self-consciously adopted a church model and a number of basic theological positions much more in line with Calvinism.

ADDRESS AND OPENING
TO MAKE A GOOD, BLESSED AND GENERAL
PEACE IN THE NETHERLANDS, AND TO
BRING THEM UNDER THE OBEDIENCE OF
THE KING, IN HER OLD PROSPERITY,
BLOOM AND WELFARE.
BY WAY OF SUPPLICATION.

TO THE HIGH AND MIGHTY, NOBLE,
HONOURABLE, WISE AND VERY PRUDENT
LORDS, MY LORDS WHO REPRESENT THE
STATES GENERAL OF THE LOW
COUNTRIES.

DONE IN THE NAME OF THE OPPRESSED
AND SADDENED COMMUNITY OF THESE
COUNTRIES.

ANNO 1576.

CAPTN: MICHIELS.

HIGH AND MIGHTY, NOBLE, WISE AND PRUDENT LORDS, MY
LORDS REPRESENTING THE STATES GENERAL OF THE LOW
COUNTRIES

If a beautiful and convenient opportunity to help the fatherland in its
greatest distress and to return it, from its impending spoilation and
destruction, to its flourishing prosperity has never before presented
itself, then it is offered to you now by the exceptional mercy and
favour of the Lord. It thus appears as though God, the Lord, moved
to pity by the wretched misery of the people, is now admonishing you,
and offering you his help to bring this affair to a good and blessed
end.

For it is certain and obvious that unless this Dutch war is rapidly
terminated by a good peace and a common treaty, we can expect first
gruesome bloodshed and harmful disruption, and then the total
spoilation and demise of our dear fatherland, together with the sad
yoke of foreign nations, which, due to our discord, will imprison us
and our offspring eternally. We shall become booty and loot for all our
neighbours, without meanwhile making any progress in that which we
intend to do.

For just as the disruption and discord, which has arisen amongst
the inhabitants of the country by means and violence of the strangers,
has caused all the present trouble and misery, so it is necessary to
decide that there is no other means in the world to rectify our affairs,
than to turn our disunion, dispute and discord into a good treaty,
accord and union; which will happen if you, regarding the misery of

the country and considering the proper duty of your office, will accept with candid heart the opportunity which now offers itself so wonderfully; and, casting off all idle fear and alarm, take charge of the matter. And if you make an end to this miserable war once and for all, by entering into a good, firm and binding accord and treaty with our neighbours and brothers from Holland and Zeeland, do not wait until the Spaniards, returned to their previous standing and government, take these wonderful means away from you and make the entire country a prey for themselves and other foreign nations.

In doing so you will not only deliver us from this bloody war and turmoil. More than that, by setting everything in good and proper order, you will resurrect our old privileges and the laudable customs and rights of the country (which, being sworn both by you and the King of Spain as our most merciful Lord, were nonetheless woefully broken and violated, under the pretended cloak of advocating the Catholic religion and exterminating heresy) and re-establish them on their old footing, just as they had been left us by our ancestors. Likewise you will establish anew the usual trade and commerce, and thus also the former prosperity and wealth of the country.

Therefore, as God Almighty has, against all human hope, opened this door for you so miraculously, and, by taking the Spanish commander from life,[1] has put the regiment of the country in your hands; so we, your communities, which you have sworn to champion, pray to you not to sleep through it, nor to let slip this wonderful opportunity, but rather to acquit yourself completely of your bounden and proper duty. This we confide unto you with all our hearts, hoping readily that none among you is either so unwise or so bewildered in his senses, or so contemptful of his fatherland's welfare, that he will not see and plainly acknowledge that you will thereby render an outstanding and most pleasant service to the Almighty and also to the King, the natural Lord of our country, but especially to the whole country and all your communities.

For this is demanded of you by the oath you have sworn unto God, the King, and your fatherland; requested of you, with burning hearts, by all your communities, and markedly indicated to you by the laud-

---

[1] Don Luis de Requesens, who had succeeded the Duke of Alva as Governor of the Netherlands in 1573, died unexpectedly on 5 March 1576. Officially the Council of State was now in charge of government.

able examples and footsteps of your and our ancestors. Some
malevolent and selfish enemies of the fatherland are trying to deter
you therefrom, and labour with veiled reasons to make you believe
that we in this country should wait for the advice and ordinance from
Spain, before we can decide on a good or fruitful course in so important a matter. This means only that they are seeking to make themselves grand and rich at the cost, indeed of the ruination, of the entire
country. And as they hope, the good favour of the Spaniards permitting, to obtain yet greater state, they would readily bring their own
fatherland and all of us into their eternal subjection and servitude.

We hope, however, that this will not move you to desert your
oppressed communities and to surrender them to eternal misery, and
so to please these self-interested flatterers. For all that they put
forward to keep you from such holy and useful work, has neither
ground nor importance to affect your wisdom and prudence or those
who wish to be true lovers of their fatherland and its faithful natives.

Now first, some say that it is not up to the States to ordain here:
that law and conscience should lead them to wait for the command
and instruction of the King, our natural Lord of the country; and that
they should conform themselves thereto in every respect.

Second, there are those who contend that although the law allows
the States to act, it would nonetheless be inadvisable for them to do
so, as the King might take and interpret it as an great deprecation of
himself, and, thus being angered greatly, might use his great violence
and invincible power to throw all of us and the entire country into
everlasting danger and misery.

There are others still who presume that, by virtue of their office,
the States are entitled to set everything in good order and that in
today's real peril, the King's opinion (for he, residing far away and
being completely controlled by foreign nations, can hardly be
informed about the state of the country) should be disregarded.
Nonetheless, as it seems that a common peace with those who have
deviated from the Roman Catholic religion, would produce a general
change in the country (which, due to the licentiousness of the Beggars, who seek loot and booty rather than the bliss of their souls,
might not only greatly harm the prelates and other clerics, but also
cast all Roman Catholic Christian folk into grave hardship and sadness), they therefore think it far more advisable to await patiently the

outcome of the present war, in the hope that God will help the strongest, rather than that, in order to avoid one peril, we let ourselves in for another, which might turn out far graver and worse.

We now want to consider, impartially and on the scale of truth, to what extent all reasonable people should regard these three objections as valid and important, and to present this as briefly as possible to you, beseeching you to set aside all bias and status of men, and to settle this matter according to the truth.

As far as the first part is concerned – that law and the States' office do not permit them to provide in this matter, or to make a common peace, without the King's command and order – the judgment of this question lies solely and especially in the reflection on the official rights and bounden duty of the States. For if we can correctly identify what is the States' entitlement by virtue of oath and law, and thus also what appertains to the Lord of the country by virtue of his office and highness, we will be able to solve this controversy without great difficulty, with good and complete arguments.

Now it is certain that, in order to discover the truth of this matter, we must turn to first origins, and note from whom the King, as a true natural Lord of the Low Countries, received his highness, and on what terms and conditions he was accepted and inaugurated by the country or by the States of the country; also what manner of status, faith and authority the States of the country had with his illustrious forebears the Dukes of Lorraine, of Burgundy and of Brabant, and with the Counts of Flanders and Artois, of Holland and Zeeland, etc. For it is undoubtedly true that the very power and authority, which both the Lord of the country and the States of the country have left to their respective descendants by virtue of God, law and oath, may and should be cherished, used, maintained and advocated with all possible means.

And in so far as one of them seeks to trespass his confines, he thereby falls into the culpability of either deliberate tyranny or rebellion meriting punishment. For as all power is from God, and as there is no power or government which God has not established, so God has also enclosed all power within certain confines and has decided and willed that everyone remains within the limits of the vocation to which he has been called, without in any way crossing it, out of licentiousness or recklessness. For he will not bear this, but instead punishes it with the supreme punishment of the downfall and ruination of towns and countries, and with the removal and change of kingdoms and principalities from one house to another.

Now first there are the word and law of the Lord; then come the laws of the country, the old laudable customs which have descended from father to child, arising from the mutual contracts and treaties made and concluded between Lords and subjects. And finally there is the oath with which both sides, the Lord of the country and his subjects, each on their part, have invoked God's holy name, and have made Him the witness, judge and punisher of their consciences, should they fail to follow and faithfully maintain point by point the sworn rights and customs, and the aforesaid mutual contracts and treaties for the common comfort and peace. Therefore God, who is envious and ardent regarding the honour of his name, neither can nor will tolerate that anyone disgracefully abuses the honour of his name and his majesty, and turns it into a cloak for wicked lust.

Now God's word, as well as all rights, privileges, old habits, usages and customs, and all mutual contracts, treaties, and alliances of the Low Countries, validated and confirmed by the Lord of the country and by the States, with God's word and with the holy oath, makes it clear and public that these Netherlands, fallen by the law of succession from the House of Burgundy unto the King of Spain, the natural Lord of the country, have never been governed as an absolute monarchy or kingdom, where the Lord of the country would have been allowed to manage the affairs of the country at his will and pleasure, without minding its laws or rights. On the contrary, the country has always been managed and administered, with right and justice, through a republican or rational civic policy, in such a way that the lord of the country has been like a servant and professor of the country's rights, laws and regulations, indeed, like a father of the fatherland, whose task it is to serve all, be they poor or rich, noble or common, with equal laws, justice and judgment. The Lord should tend the communities like a shepherd, governing not at his pleasure or will, but following the precepts of their rights, freedoms, privileges and old customs, by which he swore most sacredly upon his arrival, and by which he was inaugurated and accepted, committing himself with a grave oath not to deviate from them in any point, and especially never to do anything at will, but everything by right and order.

Therefore, though in these countries the right of governmental succession from father to child has nearly always been maintained and observed, it has never been considered to be fully binding, nor have the true legal heirs ever been acknowledged as Lord of the country, before they had been accepted by the States of the country in the name of the whole community, and had sworn to maintain the afore-said laws of the country in full, on the legal condition that if they failed to maintain our ancestors' privileges, and the freedoms and rights of the country, we would not acknowledge them as Lord of the country, nor render them any service or obedience, as long as and until the moment when they satisfied the countries and completely repaired the affairs in which they had erred.[2] And since it was impossible to convene the entire body of such a great community, in order to take the oath from the aforementioned Lord, or to assist in administering the affairs of the country, so some have been elected from the whole generality to represent the entire body, to do in its name what otherwise the generality should have done itself, to acquit themselves properly and faithfully in this matter with full powers, authority and command, and to defend and advocate the privileges, rights and freedoms of the community and the country in every possible way, without any connivance or regard of persons. Originally these were the two States, namely that of Knighthood or Nobility, to which some of the most principal nobles have been admitted; and that of towns, to which some burgomasters, jurors, ward-masters, pensionaries, and other similar persons have been elected from the communities of towns and other free jurisdictions. Later the clergy has joined too. Out of their company the clerics have chosen some distinguished prelates and abbots, who were supposed to represent the entire clergy and to defend faithfully its rights, privileges and freedoms with the other States.[3]

It is these three that one normally calls the States of the country. They assist the Lord of the country in accordance with his oath in all grave, important affairs, and help counsel that which advances the common good, benefit and welfare of the country, and its service and

---

[2] This passage is clearly inspired by the clause of disobedience contained in the Joyous Entry of Brabant, which is quoted almost literally.

[3] This outline of the Dutch system of representation does not seem to endorse fully the idea of the feudal order, with the States assemblies representing the first, second and third estates. It may be noted that here the first estate, the clergy, is only mentioned in the last instance. It should also be mentioned that the pattern of representation by States assemblies was by no means uniform in the Low Countries.

highness. They inform the Lord of the country of all forms of maltreatment that might in any way encroach upon the freedoms and rights of the country, in order to remedy them and to prevent all further inconvenience. They also hear the requests and desires of the Lord of the country and put them to the communities, as they are obliged to when any matter arises that might burden the communities, such as war, peace or truce, taxes or petition, raising or lowering the value of the coinage, the cession of territory or other like matters. They assemble the guilds and crafts, with their deans and heads in order to hear everybody's opinion and advice, and they announce and report these faithfully to the Lord of the country.[4] Furthermore, in all important affairs affecting the whole community they are empowered and obliged to deliberate, decide and carry out, in the name of the entire community which they represent, that which is thought best for the common good and benefit of the country and its inhabitants. Thus the entire body of the communities, consisting of clerics, nobles and of towns and franchises, have in good faith, prudence and wisdom completely committed to these elected States their welfare, well-being and liberty, to defend and advocate these against everybody in every possible way.

To this end there were elected in Brabant, by the Charter of Kortenberg,[5] 'four knights, the best, most distinguished and most experienced with the country's common good that one could find, and three good fellows of Louvain, three of Brussels, one of Antwerp, one of Bois-le-Duc, one of Tienen and one of Leeuwen.[6] Later it was agreed that Antwerp might send another citizen, and the town of Nijvel one too. Every three weeks they may assemble at Kortenberg. They are empowered to hear and know whether there are any short-comings, whichever they might be and however they might have occurred, which concern the privileges, rights and resolutions of the country, or which affect the country in some other way. And they

These are the very words of the Charter of Kortenberg.

---

[4] The process of consultation as described in this paragraph was rather typical for the towns in provinces such as Brabant and Flanders. In most northern towns, guilds and crafts were not directly represented in town government.

[5] The Charter of Kortenberg was granted in 1312 by John II, Duke of Brabant. It established the so-called Council of Kortenberg, consisting of representatives of nobility and towns, which had the task of protecting and advocating the privileges and customs of the Duchy. Because of its constitutional character, it has been compared to the English Magna Carta and can be seen as the forerunner of the famous 1356 Joyous Entry of Brabant.

[6] Such was the composition of the Council of Kortenberg.

87

always have full powers to provide for these matters and to improve them, and according to their best judgment, to do and ordain all good things for the benefit of the Lord and his country. And that which they so do and ordain is, by the aforesaid Charter, confirmed and sworn to them and their offspring with promise and high oath by Duke John, his son Duke John and Duke Wenclesas.[7] It was to remain fast and steady and was never to be curtailed, neither by these Lords nor by their descendants, even to the extent and on the condition that if he or his descendants, or someone else – whoever he may be – were to violate or cease to maintain something thus ordained, the aforesaid Duke agrees and wants, both for himself and for his descendants, that within his country no one shall pass judgment or render any service until the time that the very things which were violated are put aright and are maintained completely in every respect.[8] If this is not the case then all and each are ordered, admonished by their oath, homage and fidelity, mutually to uphold all aforesaid points, and to help to maintain them with concord, which should be achieved with power and force. This is sworn by oath and confirmed with their seals by the nobles until 1356, and by all the towns and franchises, as well as by the Duke.

Similarly, by the letter of the treaty between the country of Brabant and Flanders, and between the Duke on the one side and the Count on the other, concluded in the year 1339,[9] some good persons are elected from the nobility and the towns and two from the council of the Lord of the country. In the name of the towns and the communities, representing the States of the country, they are ordained and empowered to settle and reconcile any conflict or misunderstanding that arises, be it between the free Lords, or between the countries, or

---

[7] Duke John III governed Brabant between 1312 and 1355. The spectacular political crisis following his death ended with the acceptance of John's eldest daughter Johanna, married to Wenclesas of Luxembourg, as Duchess on the conditions as outlined in the famous Joyous Entry. For the full story see P. Avonds, *Brabant tijdens de regering van Hertog Jan III (1312–56). De grote politieke krisissen* (Brussels, 1984).

[8] At this point the *Address* reiterates the clause of disobedience as contained both by the 1356 Joyous Entry and the 1312 Charter of Kortenberg, using the formulation which gives every individual inhabitant the right of disobedience.

[9] The 1339 treaty was signed not only by the Duke and Count, but also by the cities of Brabant and Flanders as equal parties. It established a fundamental unity between the County and the Duchy, and strongly reflected the views of the dominant towns. In 1561 the treaty was rediscovered and analysed by Jacob de Meyere in his *Commentarii sive annales rerum Flandricarum libri septendecim*. In 1576 the treaty, which featured frequently in the political literature of the Revolt, was reprinted.

between the Lords and countries, in whatever way, or matter, however complex it may be. And the Lords of the country and the countries will regard the judgment they pass as good, firm and steady and will not thwart it in any way, on the penalty that if they oppose, the countries all together are bound to resist them with force and power.'

In this respect all other privileges, rights and charters of the countries concur, proving openly and irrefutably that the States – that is the men elected from both the knighthood and the towns (to which the clergy was later added by common advice) – have the power to observe and to settle the common affairs of the country, if some problem arises. And so this has been pursued and has been carried through at all times straightforwardly and without anybody's opposition, as appears clearly from all treaties, and agreements which the countries and towns have ever since concluded with each other, indeed, often if not always without having consulted the Lord of the country. This is clearly shown by the treaty and unity which those of Louvain and those of Brussels concluded between each other, without involving the Lord, after St James's and St Christopher's day in 1313,[10] only because of the good favour, great friendship and loyalty they have always borne and will always bear in the future towards their dear Lord the Duke and (as the words expressly state) 'noticing that this was to his honour and benefit, that he certainly needed his country to remain in concord and good order, and that the more the good fellows of the country are united, the stronger and more powerful the Duke will be, and they all with him. Therefore they promise one another to maintain mutual fidelity and friendship and to prevent, one and the other, all injustice that might occur between them, following the advice of the good persons of both towns. They furthermore mutually promise to protect one another's rights and to assist one another faithfully against anyone, whoever he may be, with the exception of their Lord, the Duke. And if (they say) our Lord, the Duke, should do injustice to any of the towns, we promise each other also to proceed against our Lord, the Duke, and his council, until the moment that the injustice is set aside. And should our Lord, the Duke, do or accept anything that is harmful and prejudicial for his country, we promise that the one who hears this

---

[10] In 1313 the city of Louvain concluded a number of individual treaties with Antwerp, Brussels, Bois-le-Duc, Tienen, Zoutleeuw and Maastricht. The purpose of these treaties was to reaffirm the unity of the towns.

first, will inform the other. Then they will present this together to the Lord and will proceed against him until the moment that he refrains from it'.

The same also appears from the compromise and accord concluded at Kortenberg on the day after St James's day in the year 1261, between the same towns of Louvain and Brussels, together with all other towns and franchises, such as Tienen, Antwerp, Lier, Herentals, etc., which was consented and confirmed with similar letters by thirteen in total.[11] Ditto by the charter of the four, in which the natives and the community of Brussels made an accord and union on 17 June 1368.[12] The charter also resolves, ordains and confirms, for them and their descendants in eternity, many different issues concerning the administration of justice and the maintenance of unity by the aldermen, guilds, and representatives of the crafts and other members of the town. Ditto by the alliance between the towns of Brabant and the towns of Maastricht, of Limburg, Dahlem, Roden, Kempen, Wissenberge and Speremont, concluded between the burgomasters, aldermen, sworn [jurors] and councils of these towns at Louvain on 8 March 1354,[13] who promised each other and their descendants 'to stay forever in concord, inseparable and undivided and to remain completely inseparable and in concord under one Lord if, after the death of their Lord they should have to choose a new Lord of the country; likewise to help each other to maintain their liberties, charters, privileges, habits, customs and usages, and, should somebody oppose these, to help to constrain him; and should one of them fall into trouble as a result of their unity, to help combat this trouble in concord, with body and goods'.

Ditto by the new union of all towns and franchises of Brabant, concluded at Brussels on 18 February 1371 (style of Cambrai), to stay with each other according to the charter of Kortenberg, the Walloon

---

[11] On 28 February 1261 Duke Henry III of Brabant died. As none of his children had yet come of age, the Duchy was faced with a grave succession crisis. On 24 July 1261 the main towns of Brabant, showing their civic consciousness, concluded their first main alliance with the solemn pledge to maintain union and concord.

[12] In 1368 a new council was established in Brussels, which marked the entrance of the guilds into town government, as its members were the delegates of both the old aristocracy and of the 'métiers'.

[13] As the sons of Duke John III of Brabant had all died before him, there were several daughters- and sons-in-law contending for the Duke's succession. The 1354 alliance, in the midst of the grave succession crisis, was to assure that Brabant would not be split up between contenders of Duke John III's inheritance, but remain one and inseparable.

charter[14] and all other charters and rights of the country, 'to uphold these forever, firm and unbreakable in all their points, without allowing anyone to oppose them. Indeed, if all or any of them, who has held by the aforesaid rights and unions, should be burdened or accosted as a result, or if somehow something should happen concerning the aforesaid matter, right and unions, then all together and each in particular shall proceed against it, shall help to bear and resist it, and all together shall stand in for any one of them at any time that this is necessary, as the alliances and unions made between us in ancient times also declare and contain.'[15]

Ditto by the accord of the three estates, concluded on 14 November 1415[16] by the abbots, nobles, towns and franchises, that they remain allies and help one another to maintain their privileges, rights, charters and usages. And also by the Act of conclusion and conveyance of the towns and the country of Brabant, concerning the privileges of the country, made on 16 February 1514 (following the style of Brabant), in which the States of the country negotiated, concluded and agreed amongst each other that, whatever commands or letters should be sent or attacks made expressly against the text and content of either the Joyous Entry or other privileges of the country, they would neither obey nor tolerate them. Furthermore many other acts, treaties, conclusions, letters and charters in Brabant about these issues have been made and concluded by the States, the towns and their members, without consulting the Lord of the country, indeed often against his will, in accordance with the rights and privileges of the country, as sworn by both sides.

This can also clearly be seen in the peace made and concluded by the States General of the Low Countries in 1488, which they have conceded to King Maximilian, the great grandfather of our King and father of King Philip, the natural Lord of the country.[17] As will appear

[14] The Walloon Charter was, together with the so-called Flemish Charter, granted in 1314. In return for the full recognition of Duke John III, Brabant received strong constitutional guarantees for proper government, and the (temporary) control over the ducal finances and administration.

[15] In 1371 and 1372 the Brabant towns took a concerted initiative with the purpose of getting the Charter of Kortenberg and the Walloon Charter reconfirmed.

[16] In 1415 Brabant was once again confronted with a succession crisis, caused by the death of Duke Anthony. His son, John IV, still under age, was recognized as the legitimate successor and precautions were taken to maintain unity.

[17] The policy of Maximilian of Habsburg, recognized in 1482 with great reluctance as regent for his son, the future Philip the Fair, was highly unpopular, especially in

openly from the authentic acts of this peace, the States of the country regarded it as a certain, clear and undoubted point that by right and by office the States are entitled to make peace, and to manage the affairs of the country to the country's greatest benefit.

In short, it is found public and true by all authentic and credible accounts, letters and charters that it is the function, office and bounden duty of the States to use their authority, name and power in the public questions and affairs affecting the country and community, in order to bring the country peace and union and to ordain, decide and do what is best for the common good of the country.

Therefore, verily, there is either too much wickedness and sly, clever connivance or too much coarse and crude ignorance in those who now want to deny that the States of the country are entitled to bring the affairs in this common destruction and confusion to a good, blessed and desired peace, without the King or his decree and ordination. Indeed, on the contrary, it is true that the States of the country neither can nor may in any way neglect to take full cognizance of the common affairs of the country and bring to an end the general ruin and misery, introduced by strange nations, without being disloyal and perjurious towards themselves, their Lord and the whole country, as they themselves pledged and, in the name of the communities and the entire generality have made the people pledge the privileges and rights of the country, presenting themselves as guarantors, observers and guardians of the common welfare of our fatherland. Indeed, this is so plain and certain that even the sworn enemies of their own fatherland – who have recently written and sent out a fictitious letter in the name of the King to you, my Lords, who represent the States of the country of Brabant, to make you forget and disregard your office and oath, thus seeking to take from you your right, power and authority, which you have received from God and from the rights of this country, and to hand them over to those of the council,[18] – cannot pass over or ignore this point completely. They say explicitly that the King prays to you and expressly ordains you to obey the men of the council as if they were his own person, and yet to ensure yourselves

Flanders. During the second great uprising against his rule Maximilian was taken prisoner by the city of Bruges. He was only released after he had accepted a 'union' of the States General which took from him his regency in Flanders and put restrictions on his rule elsewhere.

[18] The Council of State, which in 1576 was dominated by pro-Spanish councillors.

that the provinces are brought to peace and union. They thus signified sufficiently that by virtue of right and office you are entitled to do so. Their true slyness and duplicity are shown by the fact that they dare not deprive you openly and entirely of what is yours by virtue of the law and the oath of the King and yourself. They allow you this as given and granted by the King's ordinance and order, whereas, on the contrary, the King is obliged to render account to you and to put to rights that which has been done up till now against the common peace and welfare of the country and against all its privileges.

For in your hands the King, as a Lord of these countries, has promised, sworn and declared himself willing to take care of the country's welfare, peace and tranquillity in all possible ways, and neither to declare nor to wage war, nor, once it has been declared, to make peace, nor to make alliances, nor to introduce any innovations which reduce or change the laws of the country, without the common and well-considered consent and approbation of the countries and the States; also that he will not impose any tax, tribute or excise-duty upon the people without their free consent, which they will render him not as his right but by their grace, as the charters, made at various times concerning this issue, state explicitly. Indeed, he may not demand contributions from the community, except on the occasion of a knighthood, marriage or imprisonment, and then he will collect the contribution after due deliberation so that no good people will be hurt or burdened. And if he dares to act against this, the States will be bound to refuse and resist it. In your hands – and you are custodians and guarantors of this oath for the entire community – he also promises and swears to treat each individual not at will, but by right and justice, and everyone in accordance with the right of his town. And like the lowest of his subjects he himself will be judged in all disputes, without being allowed to breach or reduce another's right, privilege and liberty, nor to grant any right or privileges which could harm the countries, without the prior consent and approbation of the States.

In short, the States – that is you, my Lords – are ordained in the name of the community to ensure that the rights and freedoms of the country in all their aspects, and the common peace, are properly and faithfully upheld and that the Lord of the country nowhere exceeds his prescribed limits. It is your task to correct those who have been appointed to some office in contravention of the privileges and rights of the countries, or who have contravened these, in accordance with the fifth article of the Joyous Entry, as it was publicly effected at Louvain over the Council of Kortenberg at about 1420, and testified by Duke John himself in his Placard of 4 May 1421.[19] For verily, the States, that is the nobles and the towns, have on various occasions and with the highest obligation solemnly promised and sworn to maintain, for themselves and for their descendants unto eternity, all rights and privileges of the country and the common peace and union, in every possible way; and, if someone opposes or breaks these, to constrain him with force and power and to help put the matter to rights, as the lords of the country have prayed and commanded them to do. And to this end they have attached their seals as well as their oaths to the letters, for themselves and for their descendants unto eternity, as one can see in the aforementioned Charter of Kortenberg, whose words are as follows.

'And for the greater assurance and eternal establishment of these things, we beseech, command and call upon all garrisons of our country, all knights, both bannerets and all others, whoever they may be, who have some lordship or dominion within our country, and the good people of our towns, great and small, reminding them of the fidelity and homage they owe us, to promise – as we have promised before and with a similar oath to that which we took – that they will maintain all the aforesaid articles point by point, eternally, firmly and steadily, for themselves and for their descendants. Moreover, concerning the aforementioned fidelity and homage, we beseech, command and call upon all the aforesaid, those who are here now and those who will be in future, that if we, our heir or our descendants in any way violate or break the described articles and points, either in part or in total, they will neither render service nor assistance, nor be obedient to us, to our heir or to our descendants, until the hour that we have mended our ways and put to rights all the violations that had taken place, restoring the state or form described and declared by the articles and points above. If, now or in the future, some of our barons, knights, bannerets, or anyone who has lordship under us, or some persons of our towns, should oppose or break some of these aforesaid points, we, our heir and our descendants, will regard them as illegal

---

[19] In the *New Regiment* Duke John IV of Brabant conceded that, if he or his successors violated the privileges and rights of the country, the States were not only entitled to refuse any service, but also had the right to appoint a regent to govern until the Duke had mended his ways.

and unfaithful, both now and in the future, and they will no longer serve as witnesses, governors or judges. Furthermore, concerning the aforesaid homage, fidelity and oath, we beseech, command, call upon and admonish all our barons, knights, servants and persons from our towns, and each individual, to protect each other, to act in concord, and to help with force and power if anyone opposes or wants to oppose this in any way.'

Hereto the Lord commits himself, his heirs and descendants, and he renounces and relinquishes for himself and for his descendants everything, both in fact and in right, in general and in particular, which might somehow help or enable him or his descendants, to act against this commitment. He seals this with his seal, and all barons, nobles and towns swear the same and attach their seals to it, for themselves and for their descendants. From time to time this commitment has been accepted and maintained, and it has frequently been invigorated and confirmed, namely in the charter made at Brussels on the Monday after Ascension day in 1333 by Duke John, the son of Duke John,[20] and by two other charters given by Duke Wenclesas and his wife Duchess Johanna, one on St Lambert's day 1372 and the other at Brussels, on 13 April 1373. The latter expressly ordered and declared that 'all bannerets, knights and good persons of the towns and franchises and each individual of the country of Brabant should, on basis of the fidelity, oath and bond comprehended by and contained by the aforesaid charters, uphold towards each other, make to be observed and help to maintain with force and power the Charter of Kortenberg and the aforesaid Walloon Charter in all forms and ways declared and comprehended by these charters'.[21]

So it is obvious, public and beyond all doubt that the States of the country, that is the nobles, towns and clergymen, are entitled by right and by oath to maintain the privileges of the country and the common peace, and to uphold them against everybody, whatever the issue may

---

[20] Between 1332 and 1334 Brabant faced a profound crisis as almost all of the neighbouring principalities had united against it. For the sake of unity Duke John III made substantial constitutional concessions. For example, on 17 August, reconfirming the Charter of Kortenberg, he accepted an increase with two seats of the towns' representation in the Council of Kortenberg, which guarded the Charter and which can be seen as the forerunner of Brabant's provincial States.

[21] In 1372 the Brabant towns succeeded in obtaining the reaffirmation of the Charter of Kortenberg and the Walloon Charter. In addition it was agreed that all Brabant civil servants should swear an oath to maintain the charters.

be, as is also explicitly required by the letter of the alliance between Brabant and Flanders, and as has always been pursued in deed by our forefathers in the past. It also clearly appears from all the afore-mentioned charters, treaties, and unions, concluded between the towns and franchises, or between the countries amongst each other.

However, they made it especially clear when they publicly correc-ted at Louvain the governors and officers established by Duke John, who had acted against the rights and privileges of the country. Yes, even depriving Duke John of his government, they installed a regent, who was to govern the country with advice from the States until the Duke had given the States satisfaction on all points and had put to rights all misdeeds committed. Having done so, he granted them an Act, made up at Louvain on 4 May 1421,[22] by which he acknowledged that the States had the lawful power to do so: 'desiring and agreeing moreover, for himself and for his descendants, that if he or his descendants should wrong the three States of the country, or anyone of them, infringing with violence, force, power or wilfulness on their rights, charters, privileges, customs, usages and habits, they shall render no loyal service to him, nor be obedient or submissive, but shall be free from all oaths they have sworn to him, be it as town councillor or vassal. And that the three States of the country of Brabant may elect by majority a Regent of their choice for the com-mon good, welfare and profit of the whole country of Brabant; and that this Regent shall have full power to act in all matters like a Prince and Lord of the country. [Duke John] desires and orders all his subjects of the country of Brabant, high and humble, and each in particular, to be obedient and submissive to this Regent in all issues, in accordance with the ordinance and approval of the three States of the country of Brabant, until the moment that he or his descendants shall have completely restored and put to rights the impairment and defect concerning the three States of the country in question.'

I now omit Flanders, which has stood up so often against its Count, indeed, even against the King of France,[23] in order to maintain its

---

[22] Once again reference is made to the 1421 *New Regiment* as granted by Duke John IV of Brabant. See footnote 19.

[23] The King of France had feudal rights over most of Flanders which he only formally renounced in 1529, as part of the peace treaty of Cambrai. The French attempts to incorporate Flanders led to a series of conflicts. The most famous one started in 1297 when the Flemish count Gwijde of Dampierre cancelled his vassalage. It ended in the famous Battle of the Spurs of 11 July 1302, in which an army of Flemish artisans and farmers defeated the French noble army at Courtrai.

rights and privileges and to constrain the will and violence of the Lord of the country under the country's laws. I certainly do not want to tell here of how some rebels have unjustly acted against their Lord, but only of how the whole country has acted in accordance with the rights of the country, as has been later confirmed and affirmed with the succession of the next Lord of the country; when they expelled the Countess Richildis, because she had broken the privileges and accepted and inaugurated Robert the Frisian in her place as their Lord and Count;[24] or when they called Diederich the Alsatian, and took him as their Lord, expelling Count William of Normandy who wanted to govern by force, with violence and at his own pleasure.[25] If in these instances the Flemish have committed injustices, then one must conclude the present King of Spain cannot be the rightful, lawful Lord and Count of Flanders, having inherited the County from those who had held it unlawfully.

What would our old forefathers say now, if they were permitted to return to life, and saw what we, their children and descendants, have in our times suffered and accepted for so many years from the Duke of Alva, the Commander[26] and other Spaniards. How amazed would they be that we suffer and bear from strange nations so many infractions and violations of all those laudable privileges and rights that they left us with so much effort and carefulness, without even daring to speak up against it? How astonished would they be that we endure and watch with folded hands so much violence, murder, raping of women and young daughters, wantonness of servants, ordinations, levies, tributes, extractions, exactions of the tenth, twentieth and hundredth penny, so much miserable destruction and the arson of villages, franchises, towns and entire regions, without opposing? Indeed, that we still feed and help to maintain a war which was started, and until now waged, against all rights of the country and against all laudable customs of our forefathers. For not just that which has followed from this war is unbearable, but the whole war. Clearly its

[24] Richildis was the widow of Count Baudouin, who died in 1070. She was dissipated from Flanders by the latter's brother, Robrecht, who obtained the county in 1071.

[25] This is a reference to the famous crisis of 1127, which started with the murder of count Charles the Good by members of the powerful Flemish family Erembouds. In the subsequent conflict over the succession the Flemish towns prevailed. Their candidate, Diederich the Alsatian, was elected Count; he governed the country until 1168.

[26] The Commander was Don Luis de Requesens, who had succeeded Alva as Philip II's governor of the Netherlands in 1573.

entire foundation and basis tends to the total public violation and reduction of all privileges and laws of the country, and to the contempt of the oath which the king swore to you, as representatives of the whole country. The war has been started, and until now has been waged, without any prior advice or consent of the country, in opposition to the king's oath and obviously in conflict with the rights of the country. For as everyone knows, the Duke of Alva, having arrived here, has executed all his assaults and actions solely at his own will and with violence, without ever paying attention to the States of the country. Indeed, he has set up new councils, courts and tribunals and has openly declared that he regards all the States and inhabitants of the country as rebellious and restive. Thus the attorney-general was not ashamed to declare in front of the Duke, in the name of the King, that those who wanted the King to ordain in these conflicts, following the advice of the States, that which would be beneficial and salutary for the country, are using an improper and monstrous argument, which is in conflict with all laws and civil policies. It is therefore obvious that the entire beginning of this war is a singular infraction of the sworn laws and privileges of the country. Indeed, what is more – and you, my Lords, should take serious note here – the war not only started and has, until now, been waged without the advice or consent of the States, and is therefore unjust and in conflict with our privileges, but also, the causes of this common misery which has been followed by such great bloodshed and appalling destruction, were introduced from the beginning and in the course of many years at the sole will and pleasure of the Lord of the country, without any prior assembly or counsel of the States of the country. Therefore they are completely void, invalid and unjust.

For the very first Placard that ever was in our times concerning the religious question, from which the entire present conflict has risen, was drawn up and established by the Emperor Charles of highly laudable memory, in the year 1521 at Worms in Germany.[27] From there it was sent into these countries to Queen Mary,[28] who at that time was Regent here, to the court and to the members of the Council

---

[27] In the Edict of Worms Charles officially denounced the ideas of Luther as heresy, and ordered the persecution of the reformer and his followers throughout the empire.

[28] Queen Mary was Mary of Hungary, Charles' sister, who served as Governess of the Netherlands between 1531 and 1555. Her predecessor was Margaret of Austria, Charles V's aunt. In 1521 she was Governess.

of Malines,[29] to the Chancellor and members of the Council of Brabant, to the Governors of Limburg, Luxembourg, Flanders, Artois, Holland, Zeeland and Namur, to the presidents and councils of these countries, in short, to all governments, officers and States, members and inhabitants of the country, as a firm, strong, irrevocable command, decree and ordinance, as the printed text of the Placard puts it. So neither the advice, the counsel nor the consent of this country was expected there, as our privileges require. However, his Majesty declares that 'in God's honour, and in the proper reverence of his Vicar, our Holy father the Pope, and of the holy chair of Rome, it has been resolved, stipulated and deliberated to order, explicitly at his own authority (having merely received the advice of the princes and prelates of the empire, the Knights of his Order,[30] and members of his council, natives of many nations subjected to him, and now assembled), that the investigation and judicial trial of persons, who somehow contravened, opposed or refused to be subjected to his edict, command and proclamation, should be proceeded against each and all, regardless of state, dignity, distinction or the privileges they enjoyed'.

All of this was done to satisfy the papal sentence and bull issued against Martin Luther, as the words of the Placard explicitly state, declaring that all offenders be classed under the crime of lese-majesty,[31] with the appropriate indignation and penalties. So it is plain and clear to everyone that as the Placard was made up at the mere command, will and pleasure of the Lord, at the instigation, advice and determination of foreign Lords and potentates, and without hearing the States of the country, it has from the beginning always been *Ipso iure nullum*, indeed wholly powerless and void. Therefore the States ought not and cannot tolerate it, neither in the past nor at present, without notoriously breaking and violating their oath and bounden duty. Moreover is it not stated clearly in the second Placard, made in Malines, which established and confirmed the Inquisition, that this had been decided and ordained at the advice of certain men of

---

[29] The so-called Great Council, which resided at Malines, was the supreme court of the Netherlands.

[30] This probably refers to the order of the Golden Fleece.

[31] Heresy was interpreted by the Brussels government as treason against the sovereign (and God: lèse-majesté divine), which meant that, in the view of the government, normal procedures and privileges did not apply.

learning in the scriptures and that of the heads, presidents and fellows of the privy council, without even mentioning the States?[32]

On these Placards all the following were based and constructed, without the States ever being heard or assembled. Indeed, there are some which, on the sentence of heresy and penalty of lese-majesty, prohibit anyone from putting forward a request or supplication or from coming up with an advocacy or apology for something which falls under the aforesaid Placards. This is plainly against the articles of the Joyous Entry so solemnly sworn by the Lord of the country.

I shall hold my tongue about the fact that these Placards, on which all following ones were based and which are the cause of our present trouble, were made without the pleas of the parties involved ever having been rightfully and properly heard. What is more, they were made on the basis of information which is well known to be untrue and unfounded, to such an extent that nowadays nobody can deny that almost all accusations raised against Luther and his followers by the Placard of Worms are in notable contrast with their doctrine and with their true actions, as one can daily see. Indeed, even their most biased enemies no longer dare charge them with such accusations, but acknowledge that at the time this was the result of the vehemence of their own industry and thoughtlessness. Nonetheless these very accusations are the true, eternal and permanent foundation of the great inhuman harshness that has been used until now and is still used every day against those of this new religion.

Later the States of the country realized what great disadvantage and danger for the whole country the introduction of these Placards meant. However, although they have often humbly requested and remonstrated that it would result in the ruin and destruction of the country if the King would not repeal and cancel them, he nonetheless hardened his opinion. He did not listen to these remonstrances, and even used his will against them. He made the Placards more severe and ordered their sharp observance on penalty of falling into his disgrace and of being punished as a rebel. In addition he always refused to listen to the idea of convening the States General to discuss this issue.

Some nobles, following their bounden duty and sworn oath, assembled in Brussels and argued in a humble supplication that this would

[32] In 1522 Charles V issued a placard which established the Inquisition in the Netherlands. The first Inquisitor was a layman, Francois van der Hulst.

lead to total ruin.[33] They begged the King to annul the Placards and to shape other ones with the counsel of the States General of the whole country. In spite of the fact that his Majesty had sworn and had committed himself highly in the Joyous Entry, never to take ill a supplication or remonstrance of his subjects, he nonetheless declared the presentation of this supplication to be an act of rebellion against him, a crime of lese-majesty.

Likewise the league or Compromise the nobles had set up for this purpose, following, as recounted above, many examples of our ancestors (which, although they were far more sturdy and severe, were nonetheless welcomed and interpreted positively by the princes and lords of the country), has been condemned and damned as a notorious gruesome crime of rebellion. This appears clearly from everything that followed. It is shown especially by the written charges against the Lord of Egmont and Hoorne, handed over by the attorney-general, and by the fact that the house where the supplication was devised, was razed to the ground, as a clear sign that a gruesome conspiracy against the Royal Majesty had been set up there, and to make clear that the aforesaid address was regarded as an act of conspiracy and rebellion. Thus it is evident that the aforesaid Placards have broken the privileges, rights and laudable customs of the country in many ways, have hurt the welfare of the country, and have caused this miserable and pernicious war.

In addition there are many other and diverse novelties, such as the establishment of new bishops, the further strengthening of the ecclesiastical jurisdiction, the distinct reaffirmation of the Inquisition and the power and authority of the Inquisitors, the acceptance of the Council of Trent, etc., which he has introduced and violently established solely at will and at pleasure, and with the counsel of Spaniards or other foreign nations, not only over the heads but also in pure contravention of the will, advice, consent or acceptance of the States of the country and against many of their addresses. Later this has been followed by innumerable other acts of violence and arbitrariness, by which the privileges and sworn rights of the country have been overrun completely. In contravention of all laws of the country new blood councils, new jurisdictions and new tribunals have been set up. The offices of the country have been handed over to foreigners.

---

[33] This is a reference to the famous *Petition* of April 1566. See also the *Defence*, pp. 34–5.

The inhabitants and citizens have been treated in contravention of right and equity, and their goods have been confiscated although they were not confiscable. The country has been burdened with new, unheard-of tributes. Without in any way following the normal procedure, as contained in the laws of the country, much innocent blood has been shed. Towns and villages were destroyed with heavy and foreign garrisons, unreasonable taxes and various means of violence. And finally they have brought us this miserable and bloody civil war, and the complete disruption and destruction of the countries.

It is therefore high time for you, my Lords, to wake up from your long sleep and to stand up to remedy this great maltreatment, to follow in the laudable footsteps and precept of your forefathers, truly and seriously to regard your oath and bounden duty and, after laying down this childish pusillanimity and fear, to use your authority to do away with this harmful war, which has been started against every right and without the consent of the States, and which is being waged by the foreign enemies of our fatherland at great costs and to our utter ruin. You must turn it into a good, firm and unbreakable accord, alliance and union with your neighbours, dismissing all these bloody Placards which have been introduced at will, with violence, without any right or reason and without the prescribed approval of the States. With the common counsel of States General of the country you should deliberate and decide what will be found to serve best God's honour, the King's service and the common good and tranquillity. For in addition to the fact that God, law and your oath bind and oblige you to do so, you also have the beautiful and convenient opportunity that, with the King being absent and the Spanish Stadholder he had appointed having died, the entire government has fallen into your hands to attend to this in accordance with what you in good conscience think is beneficial.

At the same time you are also given the opportunity, not only to take care of this matter, but also to resurrect and re-establish, following in the footsteps of our forefathers, all the rights, privileges and old customs of the country generally in their former legality and constancy, from which they had been wilfully abrogated for a long time by foreign nations.

If you refrain from acting now, you are destined never to rise again, but rather to fall into an eternal and disgraceful servitude and slavery of foreign and envious nations. If, on the contrary, you seize this convenient opportunity, you will not only bring yourself, your communities and all your descendants unto eternity great advantage, profit and benefit, and will gain great and wonderful honour and praise from all nations, but you will also do the King himself a vast and useful service. For you will keep these countries together and prevent any foreign nation from filching them from him, which otherwise seems bound to happen, should you not step forward. Our opponents, the Beggars, have for once put their conflicts and troubles to the judgment and opinion of the States General and one may trust they will continue to do so, if we from our side also take the matter to heart. However, if we let this opportunity slip and, by our slowness, give them reason to alienate the countries and bring them under the power of another Lord, as it seems they will do if we do not manage the issue differently, then we shall cause the King damage and loss a thousand times greater and we shall drag us all, the whole country, into an exceptionally miserable and eternal desolation.[34]

Therefore if you want to do the King, our natural Lord, true honour and to show him love and obedience, instead of ruining him with feigned and hypocritical toadyism, then you should at present take much more account of what is truly his interest rather than what he himself thinks it to be. As you can see, in what is related, this is exactly what your and our forefathers have done, who declared in plain words that they could render the Lord of the country no proper service unless they had first of all made good and firm union amongst each other.

Even more than they did, you have to take care of this, for they had a Lord inside the country, who was himself able to judge what could usefully and profitably serve his interest. Our Lord of the country, on the contrary, being so long and so far away from us, cannot have a true and complete judgment of the condition of the country, for he only knows it by hearsay. It is also impossible – unless he frequently regards to be beneficial and honourful what may be greatly derogatory and ultimately unprofitable – because in addition, he gets advice and information only from Spaniards who are unacquainted with the country and its character. Therefore as you are very well aware hereof, being the ones who are observing it closely and by experience, you may not be excused later for great disloyalty and perjury for not

---

[34] At this point the author openly refers to deliberations in Holland to abjure Philip II, a possibility which the States of Holland had started to discuss seriously in October 1575.

failing to avoid the ruin of the country and the reduction of the King's Majesty, in order to please the King for a while in his misunderstanding.

However, if you, laying aside all gossiping and disputes, immediately realize now what will bring the countries into a good unity and a true obedience of their natural Lord, and subsequently bring it back into its old bloom and prosperity, then, although in the beginning the King will not be pleased, later, the outer shell having been cracked, he will start to enjoy the shell's fruit and will indeed find that you have rendered him good and faithful service and have kept the country together. Thus he will not refrain from thanking and rewarding you highly. And if he cannot or does not want to produce this acknowledgment, then you will have acquitted yourselves of your conscience for God and humanity, and at least you will gain from his Majesty's descendants and the whole country for eternity, not only great gratitude but also an honoured name.

For that some selfish toadies urge not to resist the King's will and plan in any way, regardless of whether he is well and rightly or wrongly and badly informed, is not only a great mistake but also a harmful, poisonous and false opinion by which the country and people, yes the King himself, whom they seek to please in this way, will be utterly ruined. For it is well known that Kings should stand under the laws and under the justice of the immutable will of God, who establishes all Kings and Princes to walk in his justice and will, not in their own. Likewise [it is well known that] all laws and rights are made for the good of the community, whose welfare and bliss is the supreme law, above all human laws and ordinations. Thus the Kings are established by God not to force the community to obey their own will but to serve the laws and justice of the Lord, for the community is not created and ordained for the Kings' sake, but the Kings for the sake of the community.

Therefore we read that God became very angry, when His people of Israel, unsatisfied with a legal government, wanted to have Kings, just like the pagans had, who would be worshipped by the community like idols and whose will and resolution would be regarded as the supreme and irrefutable law, without concern for what is right or wrong or what is or is not in agreement with God's law. This becomes clear from the fact that when God had promised to give His people of Israel a King, to govern them in accordance with his law, he comman-

ded them to choose one from the midst of their brothers, and instructed him not to make himself too powerful, neither with horses and
cavalry nor with gold and silver, and that he should not deviate from
God's law and word, neither to the right nor to the left side. However,
as they later hardly observed this command, and, paying more attention to the pomp of their neighbours, were dissatisfied with the
princes, governors and judges whom God delivered them, but wanted
instead a powerful and forceful King just as the neighbouring people
and nations had, then God's wrath was greatly kindled against them,
and he said that they had thus cast Him off, as they did not want to
accept that He would govern them at His own will. And He confronted them with the violence and tyranny with which they would be
oppressed by their King, in order to deter them from their plan,
saying that since they wanted a King, they should know how he would
treat and deal with them. It will be (He said) the King's right, or
rather his practice and his way of doing, which he will think his right,
to take your sons and to appoint them to his chariots and to make
them his horsemen. He will make them his servants who will have to
cultivate his fields and reap his harvest. He will take your daughters
and make them his bakers and cooks. He will give your fields and
vineyards to his servants and slaves. And on that day you will moan
and call for the Lord, and He will not answer you.[35]

So He proved that if a community is not satisfied with a moderate
and lawful government of its Lord, be he a Prince, Duke, Count or
something else, but wishes to have a King who is forceful and who has
the power to do what pleases him, without minding God's word or the
laws of the country, then it will bring on itself honourless slavery and
eternal ruin and destruction. So indeed it turned out a little later for
the people of Israel, who were forced by their King to practise a
religion at his own pleasure and profit. Following the ways of their
neighbours they built many images, altars and chapels against the
express prohibition of the Lord, and they were forbidden to go to
Jerusalem as God had ordered. Instead, each person was to make up
his own religion in his chapel or church in accordance with his own
devotion and opinion. This subsequently caused the complete
destruction and desolation of the whole people. Likewise Isaiah the
Prophet punished the people of Israel gravely because they were not

---

[35] This entire passage is based on 1 Samuel 9:11–19.

satisfied with the small and gently flowing waters of Shilo'ah,[36] but wanted to have the great and powerful streams of Euphrates with which to glorify and amuse themselves. This means that they, not contented with their mediocre King and with the power they had in their own country, wanted to allay themselves with the powerful Kings of Babylon and Assyria. For this reason, Isaiah says, the Lord will bring up against you the mighty waters, namely the King of Assyria and all his glory, and they will overflow all their banks. Their waters will rise to your neck, which means they will be completely oppressed by the great power and force of the Kings which they had sought themselves, as indeed has happened. We clearly see similar things in all other nations of the world, notably in the case of the Romans, who being seduced by the good days they had under the lawful council, from which every year some consuls, that is supreme governors or burgomasters, were elected, handed over all force and power to their dictator Julius Caesar and later to Octavian Augustus and his successors, to govern everything at their own will and pleasure, without regard to the States of the country, that is the nobles, knighthood and communities. In this way they fell into the gruesome slavery of their emperors, such as the one named Caligula,[37] who wanted the whole people to have only one neck so that he might chop it off with one stroke, and others, who looked much more like wild, senseless animals and unnatural human creatures than like reasonable men, as appears clearly from Claudius, Nero, Vitellus, Domitian, Diocletian, Heliogabalus and many others, who knew no law or rule but their own wantonness.[38] Thus Tiberius was not wrong when he exclaimed in astonishment, emerging from the council: 'O homines ad servitutem paratos', that is, 'O mankind, which does not seek but to bring itself into servitude and slavery'.[39] So the tyrant himself was vexed to find such a disgraceful and repelling slavish state of mind in the people,

---

[36] As the author indicates in the margin, this passage is derived from Isaiah 8:5–8.

[37] Caligula was Roman Emperor between 37 and 41 AD and well known for his madness and tyranny.

[38] Claudius was Roman Emperor from 41 until 54 AD. Nero, his successor ruled until 68. Vitellus was acclaimed Emperor in 69 AD by his Legions at the Rhine, but was killed in Rome in the same year, even before his rival Vespasian had reached the capital. Domitian was Emperor between 81 and 96 AD. Diocletian belonged to the later generation of Roman Emperors. His rule was between 284 and 305 AD. Heliogabalus, well known for his foolishness, was acclaimed Emperor in 218 AD. He was killed four years later.

[39] Tiberius ruled as Roman Emperor from 14 to 37 AD.

which ultimately also led to their total demise and ruin. We can see the same in the example of the Turks, Tartars, Muscovites and other Barbarians, who are mistreated by their emperors like dogs in their cages, not according to any laws or rules but at their will, forcefully and tyrannically.

I do not mean to say that when God grants a country some powerful and mighty King, that he should therefore be rejected or that this should not be seen as an act of great mercy, but merely to show that all princes and governors ought to stand under the laws of the country, and are tied to the laws and to their oath. Therefore the hypocrites who want to make them believe that their will should be above all laws and rules, bring the country and also its King into pitiful misery and total ruin.

It is, however, unnecessary to look for foreign examples in order to prove this argument, as we can observe it sufficiently in our own case. For as long as our princes and lords of the country, holding the Low Countries with the titles of Duke and Count, have been subject to the rights and laws of the country and have acted in wars and other important affairs of the country according to their oath, with the counsel and advice of the States, and have not governed with wilfulness or violence but with right and justice, so they have shown their subjects love and fidelity. Likewise they have enjoyed in return their fidelity, love, obedience, help and assistance, so that, growing in prosperity, they were able to resist even the most powerful Kings and Potentates of Christendom and have gained honour and praise from all other Potentates, Lords and countries.

However, enjoying glory for our prosperity, we then tried to make coalitions and alliances far away from our frontier with countries with which we shared neither friendship nor anything in common, only to obtain the glory of having powerful and mighty Lords. We wanted to cherish them in everything, accepting forever what they ordained, regardless of whether it accorded with right and equity, and regardless of whether the States of the country had been heard. Verily, from that time on, the state of the country started to totter greatly. As a furtive suspicion and mistrust rose between the lord of the country and his subjects, violence and wilfulness started to replace mutual love and fidelity. All sorts of Placards were made up at his will and authority, without even regarding the States. Indeed, the authority and standing of the States were turned into a false disguise and meaningless statue. Our privileges and rights were removed, changed, indeed completely destroyed. The towns were strengthened in the Italian way, with loghouses and fortresses against their own inhabitants, indeed they were attacked and oppressed with the help of foreign nations. Under the cloak of religion, innocent blood was shed in order to take goods and to force good fellows to take an oath to cruel lords and the Pope of Rome, whom before they had hardly heard mentioned. Finally, matters went so far that men would rather betray each other and bring one another to misery than to displease the Spaniards on any point. Eventually, this brought us this pitiful civil war and murdering amongst ourselves, as the true fruit of slavish adulation. Verily, when our forefathers first associated these countries with Spain in the affairs of maritime trade and commerce, their only intention was to have friendship and concord between both countries, and to enjoy maritime trade and commerce to the benefit of both, without enmeshing Spain in our laws, or our country in Spanish ways. To this purpose they confronted their Lord of the country with many good, clear and secure conditions which were sworn and confirmed with high oaths on both sides, so that just as the Spaniards would not accept that Dutchmen should control the government in Spain, the Spaniards for their part would not dare seize the government of these countries. For verily, if they had the right not to accept that from us, then what we put forward to maintain our rights and the old government of inhabitants is the more respectful and important, just as it is fairer that the woman follows the man, rather than the man the woman. For our Princes and Lords have married Spanish women and have extended their government from these countries into Spain; no Spanish Lord or King has ever subjected our country unto himself.[40] Verily, however, the great power and the reputation of Spain befogged us so much that we fell into the trap before noticing it. For our pious forefathers dealt with their Lords in such sincerity and simplicity that they never suspected that, under the cloak of the Spanish alliance, it would be attempted to bring this country under Spanish or other foreign rule. Eventually their good, sincere mind and fidelity cost them dearly. For at great cost and with heavy peril they made the

---

[40] The personal union between Spain and the Burgundian Netherlands was created by the marriage of Philip the Fair (1482–1506), son of Mary of Burgundy and Maximilian of Habsburg, with Juana of Castile, the daughter of Ferdinand of Aragon and Isabella of Castile. Due to dynastical chance Philip became King of Castile in 1504.

Lord of the country so mighty that by now they have almost completely lost their standing and authority, and the entire government has fallen into the hands of foreigners and of those whose hearts are so estranged from their fatherland, that, in order to obtain great status and to devour the blood and sweat of the country with all its fat and marrow, they try to strengthen the foreign tyranny and violence by all possible means, and to carry our descendants into an eternal slavery.

Therefore it is time now that the door is being opened for us, to see that we re-establish our old rights and customs. This is up to you, my Lords, if you will only take account of the welfare of the country and your bounden duty, without letting yourself be frightened off by vain imaginations, following the proverb that one should do good and should not be terrified by any King. For he who does good and fulfils his bounden duty in good conscience, has no reason to be afraid, as his rightful case will eventually rise like the dawn. However, he who wants to cherish the Kings and Lords, and spread honey around their mouths, setting aside the duty of his office in order to please them, he will not escape God's vengeance and will eventually get what he deserves, together with the disgrace of those he wanted to supplicate.

It is surely right to render unto Caesar the things that are Caesar's, unto God the things that are God's, unto the King the things that are the King's and unto the community the things that belong by right to the community. However, by God and by right, it is impossible that, in order to please Kings and Lords and to render to them more than what is theirs by right, one does not hesitate to bring the whole people into misery and distress, and ultimately to deprive the lords of their countries and people. So much for the first point.

We now turn to the other point put forward by those who feel that, although the States are indeed entitled by right to establish good order and to devise a general peace, it is still wiser to let the King have it his way, than to bring his disgrace and wrath over us and thus to make things even worse than they already are. This argument seems to carry some weight, but our daily experience and the state of affairs show the contrary well enough.

Verily, if the King wants to be a true Lord and father of the country, and wants to understand the matter properly, as can be suspected and as he is also bound to do by his oath, he will easily notice that the States have done him a great service by acting in this way, and he will accept it most gratefully. However, if he forgets the

fatherly affection he owes the country and, being stirred up by the
Spanish council, desires to oppress the authority and the right of the
States, and to govern and rule the country at his own will, without
regarding his oath or the laws of the country, then there is no reason
to be very afraid of his disgrace. For as has been said, it is better to fall
into disgrace with a Prince, who does not want to behave like a Prince
but like a tyrannic ruler, than to ruin one's own fatherland against
right and reason, and to incur the curse of the oppressed community
and the wrath of God, who will not forget the innocent blood.

Moreover, if one wants to take this road, who amongst the States,
may he beg and flatter the Spaniards as much as he wants, has not
already committed so much wrong that he has by now incurred disgrace and forfeiture of body and good? Among other things, the late
Lord of Egmont has been greatly accused of desiring that the conflict
which had arisen at that time over the religion should be settled by his
Majesty with the counsel of the States General of the country. Thus
he is imputed of having sought to bring the highness and sovereignty
of the King under the counsel of the States, which is (as the Attorney
General has put it) inappropriate, monstrous and in conflict with
nature and all civil and human laws. Likewise, he is accused of having
said that the Placards were too austere and rigorous and that there
were some Protestants in his family whom he had not turned in.
There were in addition many other points, too many to be recounted
here, because of which he was put to death. Now if this has been
willingly and knowingly done by the King, and if he wants to continue
along the same lines, then every man of the States, be he noble or
common, rich or poor, cleric or layman, may well take into account
that he will be paid in kind, for amongst a hundred persons there is no
one to be found who has not committed the same wrong, indeed, who
is not bound by God, by oath and by honour to do wrong, if it is
regarded as wrong (and it is undoubtedly regarded thus) to advocate
the rights of the States and the country where this has been confirmed
by the King's oath. Is it necessary to tell of the accusations which they
have levelled against the pious Lord van Stralen?[41] Let each search
his own bosom to find whether he is loyal and true to his fatherland,
or whether he has often committed this crime. Moreover, who of all

---

[41] Anthony van Stralen, a burgomaster of Antwerp and a prominent politician in the Low
Countries, was condemned to death by the Council of Troubles. He was executed in
1568.

Dutchmen[42] is so befriended and beloved by the Spaniards that, in their judgment he has not done enough wrong to forfeit body and goods?

Let us leave out further particulars and look at the addresses and remonstrances made up by, among others, the towns of Brussels and Antwerp. Is there anybody so ill-judged as not to notice that if the King blames the States for now trying to establish order in the country, and for trying to make a good general peace with the means God has granted them, he will find much more reason to become infuriated over previous requests and addresses which the States handed over to the Commander of Castile, in which they almost publicly denounced the higher and lower government as perjurious, and spoke so frankly that the Lord of Egmont would never have dared to think one hundredth part of it. However, why guess so much? For the Duke of Alva has often declared in public that all of these countries have lapsed into the crime of rebellion and insurrection against the King, as was confirmed many times by the general pardons, some coming from Spain, some from the Pope of Rome. So why should we neglect to do what is beneficial for the preservation and welfare of the country and indeed the King's service for fear of incurring his displeasure, when we have incurred it already for too long?

Indeed, when the Duke of Alva departed from here, did not many towns in Brabant, Flanders, Holland, Artois and elsewhere close their gates for the Spaniards, although they came from the King? Is this itself not enough to incur the King's displeasure and to be declared rebellious and insurrectionist by the Spanish council? Shall we still allow ourselves to be led astray by the false and double-hearted rancour of evil-minded enemies of the fatherland, to put our heads into the noose while asleep? After the proclamation of the general attorneys and the subsequent verdicts and sentences of the Duke of Alva, given in the name of the King, which state that it is inappropriate, monstrous and in conflict with nature and all civil and human laws to desire that the general conflict concerning the issue of religion might be settled by the King with the counsel and advice of the States General, do we still not see how they will judge the third member of

---

[42] At this point the author is one of the first to use the rather modern term 'Nederlander', to denote all inhabitants of the Low Countries.

Brussels,[43] which has announced to the Commander of Spain and declared by final resolution that they were not bound to render the King any service, indeed, that the States had the power to appoint a Regent for the country, and that they would no longer endure the force, violence and injustice described by them. If the Count of Egmont has been taken as a rebel and has lost his life for having tried to get Cardinal Granvelle out of the council, then how do we think the Broad Council of Antwerp[44] will be judged for having openly answered the Commander that it was unwilling to pay unless the unfaithful castellan was deported, the audit office, the Governor Champagney[45] expelled, and all novelties were annulled for now and forever? In addition it desires that the descendants will find nothing to remind them of this impertinent and unfaithful Spanish government, which eternally defames and disgraces their ancestors, and it greatly denounces the government, both high and low, as perjurious. Do we think that this can ever be forgotten or forgiven? Then truly their character and nature must have changed dramatically. For as they have already taken revenge in such an inhuman way for the small things mentioned above, surely they will never let pass this matter, which touches their entire honour and reputation.

For a while they may very well simulate and put up a good face, but as soon as they see their chance they will not refrain from taking revenge. Do we not know that the wise say that the wrath of the King is the message of death? It is for this reason that the schoolmaster of the Spanish and Italian governments, Niccolo Machiavelli, teaches so diligently, proving it by the example of Cesare Borgia,[46] that Kings

[43] The third group of members of Brussels' town government consisted of representatives of the guilds. In contrast with most northern towns, the guilds were part of town government in most of the towns in Brabant and Flanders.

[44] The Broad Council of Antwerp was the assembly of the town's four members. Thus it consisted of (a) the town Magistrate, (b) the former Aldermen of the town, (c) representatives of the citizenry, and (d) representatives of the guilds.

[45] Frederic Perrenot (1536–1602), Lord of Champagney, Granvelle's younger brother, had become Governor of Antwerp in 1571. He was dismissed by Requesens in 1574. In 1576 he was one of the southern nobles pleading for reconciliation with Holland and Zeeland.

[46] The *Address* refers of course to Machiavelli's *The Prince*, of which chapter 18 discussed 'How rulers should keep their promises'. See Quentin Skinner, Russell Price (eds.), *Machiavelli: The Prince* (Cambridge, 1988), pp. 61–3. In general Dutch authors depicted Machiavelli in highly negative terms, as the master teaching Princes to lie, cheat and discard justice. In fact it was quite common to present the alleged Machiavellianism of the Spaniards as the ultimate cause of the Revolt.

and Princes should never let the harm they feel they have suffered go unavenged, whatever promise, oath or treaty they may have given. They should hide their passion behind a pleasant visage, and cover it with all sorts of beautiful promises, until the moment that, having gained the confidence of their tormentors, they find the occasion to exterminate them and their whole family and following so completely, that they have no reason to fear them any longer, but have so much strengthened their state and kingdom by these means that all others, taking this as an example, will refrain from doing harm or being hostile. This is the foundation of the tyrannical power and greatness which the Spaniards seek to rear with all possible means.

Therefore one should either not incur their wrath or, if one has done so in good conscience because the right and welfare of the country required it, one should settle the affairs and put everything in good order with manly bravery and constancy, and constrain the power and force of the King under the good laws and policy of the country, so that they will have no means thereafter to fulfil their wrath and revenge wilfully or injustly.

Remember the fables our old forefathers used to tell. When the deer, who had come to salute the lion, the king of the animals, felt that he had been seized by the lion to be torn apart, he so violently shook his antlers that he escaped from the lion's claws and teeth. It kindled the wrath of the lion so much that the fox, fearing that it might spill over onto his head, took it upon himself to soothe the king, promising that he would bring the deer once again under the lion's power. Indeed, his flattering and buttering up made the deer docile, and he returned to the king, hoping to receive mercy and pardon from the king, as the fox had promised. However, as soon as he had approached to salute the lion, the latter put his claws around him, and all other animals encircled him, so that he was devoured and torn apart straightforwardly. Then the fox struck and secretly stole the heart of the lacerated animal and ate it. However, thereupon the king sent out to look for the heart of the animal, being the nicest morsel, and when it could not be found, the fox was accused by the other animals of having taken away the heart. He strongly denied. Eventually, however, seeing that his excuses were of no avail, he said: 'I am falsely accused, for it is impossible for me to take away a heart which was not there. Had this animal ever had but the smallest piece of a heart in its body, it would, having escaped from the power of our merciful king and seeing his anger, never let itself be persuaded, as it has done now, to return to him. Thus it is obvious that it never had heart nor reason.'

The same can now be said of all those who remind us that they have been granted pardon once, and that having been hostile to the Spaniards, they nonetheless still stand in the King's mercy. They let themselves be persuaded by these selfish foxes, who would love to feed and fatten themselves on their flesh and blood, and do not understand in time that hereafter they might be oppressed with violence. Thus they make it clear to everybody that they have never had any heart, courage, reason nor sense.

However, I now assume, as is to be hoped, that the King is well-disposed towards the country, and has been seduced by evil counsel and wrong information rather than by some evil will. Nonetheless, nobody will make him believe anything else but that all towns and provinces which have refused entrance to the Spaniards and have been ill-disposed towards them, have fallen into the crime of insurrection and rebellion; unless one can find the means and opportunity to tell him otherwise, which forsooth will never happen as long as the States do not deal seriously with this matter and seize the opportunity frankly to defend their rights and good case, with the privileges and the laws of the country. However, assuming still that this were not the case, I should really like to know whether the disapproval of the King with regards to an act which in good conscience one is bound to perform and on which the welfare of the country depends, is as much to be feared as the damage, misery, distress and ruin which are apparently bound to follow from this war if the States do not accord with those of Holland and Zeeland. Regardless of whether French, English or German horsemen take the matter at hand, do we really think that the mercy of the King, which we now want to buy with our ruin, indeed with his own detriment and loss, will release us from their hands? Verily, it is commonly said that one should choose the lesser of two evils. Now I think, and every sensible and impartial man will agree, that to neglect the good opportunity which is now at hand to make a general peace, will be incomparably more harmful and ruinous, to both the King and the entire country, than the King's disapproval; for regarding the King's disapproval there is still some remedy or at least some good hope available. One may inform the King of the great need that has forced us to act. One may remonstrate with him that his service and the preservation of the country depended on it, and one may subsequently soften and rectify his heart with good order, policy, service and obedience. And if all of this should be to no avail, the example of Holland and Zeeland still shows us that if the countries remain united and of one mind, in all years to come the King's disapproval can never cause such great harm as this civil war will cause us in one year, if we do not take proper care of it. If, on the contrary, foreigners become involved, there will never be any remedy. For one sees that the end of civil wars is normally that both parties fall to the foreigner, as is shown by Aesop's fable of the frog and the mouse, which being both prepared and equipped for battle, were both grabbed and torn apart by the harrier. This also happens, one finds, in history, as is shown particularly by the pitiful dispersion of Christianity in Greece and Asia, where the cruel Turks managed to introduce their gruesome tyranny only due to civil discord, which made both parties look for the assistance of foreign nations against their enemies. This caused Italy to become a prey of the Goths, France of the Franks, England of the Saxons, Spain of the Vandals, Moors and Saracens. The word of the Son of God, which is the eternal truth, cannot fail in saying that a kingdom, country or town which is divided against itself, will eventually decay and be destroyed. What else can we expect if the English, French or Germans join our adversaries, but that everyone will have the worst end of the stick and that the poor country will be miserably destroyed and torn apart? The Germans will want their pay from both sides. Those of Brunswick on the one side and those of Holstein on the other will revenge their grief at being sent home without pay, indeed their grief at being almost mocked. The French will try to extinguish at the cost of their neighbours the fire and coal which almost burnt down their house. The Huguenots will try to strengthen their party. The English will not tolerate the French so close to them. The Spaniards on the other hand will not want to lose their share and will benefit from such discord and disruption. In short, on all sides we, poor Dutchmen, will have to pay the piper with our life. Except then that God will rightfully punish us for not having seized this marvellous opportunity for a common peace.

Therefore, in this respect the King's disapproval does verily not weigh as much as God's, and the ruin and destruction of the whole country. It is a mistake to belittle our opponents of Holland and

Zeeland, as if they could be easily defeated. They are not so emaciated: they are in fact much stronger than they were before they had Middelburg, Arnemuiden and Rammekens in Zeeland and Geertruidenberg here on Brabant territory as strongholds. They have been able to offer resistance and it has not been possible to take one substantial town from them with the exception of Haarlem, which has cost both King and country so dearly that we, our descendants, indeed the Spaniards themselves will lament it forever if they should have to conquer more towns in this way. Moreover the Beggars have now such good relations and friendship with the Huguenots in France, whom the treaty of the King's brother and the King of Navarre[47] has made so powerful that they will always have recourse to assistance and relief. This will mean the ruin and destruction of Brabant and Flanders, for it will be impossible to prevent them from letting the French come into the country, as often and as many times as they want or as will be necessary.

Besides the Prince of Orange is neither so bad, inexperienced nor so imprudent that he does not know perfectly well how the land lies and how he can resist his enemy. Even the slightest advantage he can gain over us will immediately harm us enormously, as far as both our means and our honour and reputation are concerned. If, however, we can gain a small advantage over them it will be to little avail, because they altogether are determined rather to die one after another than to abandon their religion and its worship. Therefore there is hardly any need for us to insist on Zierikzee, for it will take a lot of work yet to conquer it.[48] And things can go rather oddly, considering that we cannot know how close we are to our goal. The Spaniards made us believe that they wanted to take possession of Zierikzee before Easter, or there would be no money. Yet they are still where they were before. The Beggars boast openly that there are still provisions for another

---

[47] On 6 May 1576 the 'Peace of Monsieur' was concluded in France. It ended a disrupting rivalry between King Henry III and his brother the Duke of Anjou. The peace was accompanied by the extremely liberal edict of Beaulieu, which allowed the Protestants the exercise of their religion throughout the realm and permitted them the construction and possession of churches. The peace proved to be temporary, if only because it gave a major boost to the formation of the so-called Catholic League.

[48] The siege of Zierikzee (a town in Zeeland), which had started in the autumn of 1575, was regarded as crucial by both sides. The siege continued after Requesens' death and on 2 July 1576 the exhausted town had to surrender. However, the victorious Spanish troops, deeply dissatisfied with their poor pay, decided to mutiny in order to gain a full settlement. Within hours they left the town again and invaded Brabant.

three months. Be that as it may, we have still not got the town. And even if we had it already, the same would happen as in the case of Haarlem. We thought then that if we could conquer Haarlem, everything would be won and the war would be over. However, having conquered Haarlem, and in addition also Leerdam, Buren, Oudewater and Schoonhoven and almost the entire country of Schouwen,[49] we have not yet come half way. We see that our opponents become increasingly stronger. The number of their friends grows. Day to day their religion spreads. Their power does not wane. And their courage grows more and more. Indeed they have taken Krimpen[50] from us when we thought they were exhausted. Every day they launch new attacks on our main towns. If one of them succeeds, we will be lost, and the hope for peace eternally gone. They might already have some secret understanding with the English and the French, which is hidden from us, for we see that notwithstanding adverse promises made to us, they get as many soldiers and guns as they want. Moreover we should remember that we can only wage the war at a cost ten times higher than theirs, for we have to protect a much greater territory than they do. And as we are the attackers, we have to gain still more (especially if we take the sea into account) than we have at this hour. We should furthermore consider that among us, most of the communities sympathize in their hearts with the Prince, because of his gentleness and kindness. And there are many who hold the religion of the Beggars, and almost all equally hate the Spaniards. Therefore we are in permanent fear, suspicion and danger. Indeed, it is to be feared that their religion will make so much progress that we will not be able, not with any violence, to defend or advocate our own in these, our countries. In short, whatever may happen, the Beggars of Holland and Zeeland are too quick to be netted easily.

Therefore we should cast off the frantic and senseless boasting of the Spaniards, with which they have made themselves and the King believe that it is a simple and quick thing to subject the entire country of Holland and Zeeland. Indeed, the Duke of Alva may have boasted that he would fry them all in the butter of Holland, but forsooth, he has not yet been able to eat very much of the fried fish, and to his

---

[49] Leerdam, Oudewater and Schoonhoven were towns in the eastern regions of Holland. Buren is a small town which is now part of Guelders, while Schouwen is one of the isles of Zeeland.

[50] A town in Holland, close to Rotterdam.

companions the butter has not yet tasted very nicely. They have launched many heavy attacks but still have not made much progress, the only result being that they have emaciated and exhausted the whole country. They have extorted us and held us under ransom so often, that it should cry to heaven. Nonetheless it has pleased them greatly, as they seek nothing else but to impoverish and weaken the country, so that it will be so much the easier for them to keep it under their subjection. For their sole intention is to use this country as a place for garrisons, to maintain here, at the cost of the country, ten or twelve thousand Spanish soldiers, whom they can then dispatch and use as suits them best. Therefore we will of necessity be ruined forever unless we seize this opportunity to make a common union. Some persuade themselves that we will receive relief from Spain, in the form of money or otherwise to help us prosecute the war, but this is merely a little fib. For when the last fleet arrived from Spain, they declared it would be the last one we could expect, as they have neither financial means nor sailors left. Indeed, they announced that they aimed to protect the Spanish coast against pirates with these ships, knowing full well, as they themselves acknowledged, that otherwise they could have found no men for the job. Therefore the King ordered the Commander by way of his Secretary Dommingo Ravilla, whom he had in fact sent to Spain for this reason, that he should try to continue the war with the means of these countries, as nothing more was to be expected from Spain. And truly, even if they had all the means of the world, they will take care not to exhaust their country for our sake, also because (as argued above) they do not seek, and from the beginning have never sought anything else, but to impoverish this country and to strip it of all its plenty, welfare and commerce, so that they can do with it as they like.

Why then should we exhaust ourselves any longer with waging war against our own friends and neighbours? To damage our commerce and trade and to ruin our own fatherland, in favour of the Spaniards? And what injustice it would be if we should bear the costs of the war, while meanwhile the States of the country would not have the right nor the standing to make peace and to protect the country from an invasion of foreigners when such a marvellous opportunity presents itself? Verily, in this case even the King himself is asking too much from us if, that is, he wants to be a just King. If he does not even want to allow the States to discuss the matter to make peace with their neighbours without his command, just as they argue that the States are not permitted to give counsel, then let us decide not to bother ourselves with this war and to make no further costs, as it is none of our business. But those who have woven it together should make certain that they unwind it.

For us to expect that the King will enter into any treaty with those of Holland and Zeeland, as is often feigned and pretended, is futile. He has decided once and for all to lose all of his kingdoms and countries rather than to permit them the exercise of their religion. They, on the other hand, have once and for all decided rather to accept help from the Turk, and to put their last man at stake, than to conclude some treaty without being assured of both their religion and life. They do not want to slaughter the deer, we have mentioned above, to be persuaded by the fox. Therefore it is pointless for us to expect peace, unless we set ourselves to work and enter into such a treaty with them that they will have reason to feel secured by us without any suspicion. Presumably they will be much more willing to do this, now that they have handed over the case to the counsel of the States General of the country. For this reason we may hope to find them prepared and ready to show every sort of equity and modesty, just as we want to show modesty towards them. For it is wrong and mistaken to think of violently forcing another to accept a religion, be it for the sake of the King, the Pope or something else, which he in his conscience can not regard as true. Nature teaches, reason testifies and experience shows that religion and the service of God exist in the conscience and should be cultivated with God's word, faith and firm persuasion, not with human commands or Royal Placards, violence or arms. For more than fifty years much innocent blood has been shed for this sake, in Germany, France, England, Italy, Spain and our fatherland, which, now calling for vengeance to God, has brought the world everywhere in uproar and war, and has thus done little good. Indeed, the religion they wanted to destroy and suppress violently has grown and risen all the more, so that we clearly see that it is not God's will to proceed any further with such methods.

It is therefore high time for us to give the matter due consideration and to choose another way, before we are ruined completely and become the mockery of the world. We should frankly and freely allow them their religion, as they want to account for it before God, and should make an accord with them that they will not hinder us in our religion, but that each, be he cleric or layman, will keep and hold his religion peacefully and quietly, and serve God in accordance with the reason given him, and as he wants to account for it on the day of judgment, as long as and until the moment when a free general council, having heard both parties, may decide and determine something else.

Some are of the opinion that this will not happen because of the Beggars, as they will never want to tolerate the clergy and those of the Roman Catholic faith. This is the third objection, which we introduced above, and it too has no foundation. It is likely that if they attack this country with adroitness or violence, they will not spare churches or cloisters, nor will they have much regard for the clergy. However, if we enter into an accord and treaty with them, it is easy to take precautions so that both religions will remain free and secure, as one can see in many countries and kingdoms.

Moreover neither the Prince nor those of his council are so unfair that they do not want to tolerate others in their religion, as they ask theirs to be tolerated. Nor are they so unfaithful that, having once committed themselves to this, they would break their oath and promise, and derogate their honour and reputation with other nations. To argue that they acted differently in Holland and Zeeland carries no weight, for there the necessity of war forced them to do so for their own protection. Otherwise they would have had to deal every hour, yes every moment, with the danger and peril of a thousand betrayals. Notwithstanding this, one sees that even here they did not expel the clergymen; they left themselves out of idle fear. Those who remained, were granted a fair pension from the church property, and it is still so today.

However, as the States of the country themselves saw the general support of the people, and the small number of Roman believers, they publicly issued the directive and command to tolerate only one religion. On the other hand it is well known that the Prince [of Orange] deals with no question concerning the common country without its common advice and assent. In this case he will have to and want to do the same, especially as he has promised to do so before. Therefore there is no problem at all here, as is clearly shown by the example of France, where the Huguenots have been a hundred times more cruel and embittered against the Catholics, and displayed infinitely more enmity towards all clerics than was ever the case here. Nonetheless, as soon as they entered into a treaty with the Lord of Damville,[51] and both parties promised each other that each could freely live in his religion, one did not hear any more of a hair on a cleric's head being harmed. We have the same example in Germany. There the bishops and prelates are almost as powerful as some Princes and Lords. Now since the religious peace has been concluded,[52] they are very well tolerated by the Protestants, whereas before none could bear or tolerate the other. One has seen the same thing in the Kingdom of Poland, in Bohemia and in many other countries,[53] where by common treaty and agreement both religions are tolerated. Why then can we not follow the very example that has produced such a blessed peace and concord in all countries? Yet, if we are afraid, let us accept their good caution and assurances to reassure ourselves so that some idle argument, which we imagine without reason, does not prevent us from doing such a holy, blessed and useful work. Only then will the King realize that he has not been well advised to let his beautiful patrimony deprave rather than permit the worship of the religion to those who do not seek (so they say) but to serve God and the King in good conscience. The same happened to the Emperor Charles, who was also of the opinion that he should put all of his kingdoms to risk rather than tolerate the religion in Germany. However, he then saw the Princes and the States of the country take up arms for the second time. Having taken him by surprise and having forced him to leave Germany,[54] they took the matter in hand and concluded a treaty among each other. He was later contented with it and until the last moment, when he handed the empire over to his brother, he let them live in good peace and tranquillity. From the beginning his brother, King Ferdinand, has followed this example. Likewise the present Emperor Maximilian, who recently tolerated the religion in the Kingdom of Bohemia and later also in Hungary.[55]

---

[51] In 1574 Henri de Montmorency, Lord of Damville, concluded an alliance with the Huguenots, as his authority as governor of Languedoc was disavowed by the crown.

[52] This probably refers to the famous 1555 Peace of Augsburg, whose motto, 'cuius regio, eius Religio' gave German Princes the freedom to introduce the religion of their choice, either Catholicism or Lutheranism, within their territory.

[53] In 1573 the Pax Dissidendum granted freedom of religion to all denominations in Poland.

[54] After a resounding victory over the Lutheran Princes in the Schmalkaldic War, Charles V was confronted in 1551 with a new uprising, which forced him to flee to Innsbrück.

[55] In 1575 Maximilian sanctioned, as King of Bohemia, the 'Confessia Bohemica', a rather loose Protestant association. Hungary was also notable for its religious toleration,

Thus this is the sole means to re-establish our poor oppressed fatherland in peace, tranquillity and its old welfare and prosperity: that we enter into a treaty with each other and make such an agreement that, both religions being free, each may serve God and the King as he in his conscience thinks he is bound to do.

This is what the whole community, now so miserably exhausted and oppressed, wholeheartedly and for God's sake ask from you, high and well-born, noble, honourable and prudent Lords, my Lords the States of the Low Countries, as they call nothing but 'peace, peace', which you may give them and all of us. If you do not, then they cannot refrain from declaring with great heartfelt grief that the blame for the ruin of the country and for the eternal slavery and disgraceful servitude, to which they are bound to be brought under the Spaniards or other foreign nations, will now and in the future be with you forever. Not only we, but all our descendants will have to lament that the liberty, rights, privileges and laudable customs, which our ancestors have left us after great difficulties and so many wonderful, courageous deeds, have been disregarded and neglected by you. May God forbid you to do this, and may He give you His Holy Spirit so that in all of your counsel and deeds, you may serve His honour and the welfare of the country. AMEN.

especially in independent Transylvania where legislation provided Catholics, Lutherans, Calvinists and Unitarians alike with religious freedom.

BRIEF DISCOURSE ON THE PEACE NEGOTIATIONS NOW TAKING PLACE AT COLOGNE BETWEEN THE KING OF SPAIN AND THE STATES OF THE NETHERLANDS.

*

CONTAINING ALSO THE ARTICLES OF PEACE AND SHORT ANNOTATIONS TO EACH OF THEM.

AT LEIDEN

BY GREGOIRE PHILERENE.

1579

NOTICE TO THE READER[1]

Among the other duties which those who love their fatherland and try to assist and succour their neighbours, have to fulfill, it is certainly not the least to instruct and inform them about the affairs that might affect them. For this reason I have willingly written down what I can tell you about the affairs of the Netherlands, about the negotiations on the pacification of the troubles and on related matters. It is not meant to be a formal discourse, but merely a proposal which might serve as an aid to memory for those who want to lead pertinent debate and comment on these matters. For I regard this subject as so important as to be worthy of being addressed by learned and wise men, who have the leisure to devote to it the required industry and time. Whereby this memorial, if not as an address, serves at least as an argument and reminder to others who are provided with the suitable qualities to undertake a great responsibility.[2]

Now since the truth has no need of grand arguments and tinted reasons, I hope that the reader will have regard only to the importance of the matter in examining the reasons in the scales of a just judgment, adding his own to what has been pondered, for one or the other side, with total loyalty, sincerity and frankness. Then he himself will, by his own reasoning and unhindered by passions and affections of prejudice, have constituted and approved that which right and reason command. He will assure me that God, who has done him the grace

[1] This heading stands at the top of the first page of the *Petit Traicté* but is missing in the *Brief Discourse*.
[2] This probably refers to those in charge of the negotiations, i.e. the leading politicians of the Netherlands.

to have a good will and a sincere understanding of what is beneficial for his own good and for the common good and general conservation of the country, will also give him the strength to continue on this route and the power to maintain himself in sacred and good resolution.

What I propose to argue here contains three main points. First, that the King[3] has no intention whatsoever of giving his subjects a good and secure peace. Second, that the States General have dutifully done everything possible to arrive at such a Pacification, and that it is not the States but rather the King who has thwarted peace. Third, the claims of the King, the results he seeks from the peace negotiations convened at Cologne and their effect.

However superfluous and poor this distinction may be, my intention is none other than to inform those who are not well instructed about the affairs of the country and the circumstances of this peace. And without letting my attention dwell on anything else, I will proceed with this distinction and start with the first point.

---

[3] The King was, of course, Philip II, who is directly and vehemently attacked by the *Brief Discourse*.

The nature of kings is, as other men's, desirous of vengeance. And as this appetite grows by the power one has to satisfy it, it is well known that the Kings, who combine authority and force, are more devoted to the desire of vengeance than any other man. That the King of Spain thinks he has legitimate reasons for vengeance, I consider to be so well known to everybody, that there is no need to discuss it at any length. For there was no other motive but the fact of his having been reduced to the necessity of pursuing his intention by warfare and the opinion formed by him that his subjects have taken up arms against him without cause. For this sufficed to evoke a lasting and perpetual hatred. Far more than particular acts committed during the war, such as the demolition of castles, the Placards of rebellion published against the Governors sent by him, even of his own blood, the quashing of commands and orders issued with his approval and the establishment of the practice of the Reformed religion, it has moved him to an irreconcilable hatred against the subjects of his countries. Thus he does not want to give peace. Rather, under the pretext of simulated peace negotiations, and through the practice of his ministers, he wants to bring us under their absolute power, in order to punish us afterwards. This appears quite clearly from the articles proposed by the Duke of Terranova,[4] which will be discussed more fully in the proper place. It is not for us to presume that the King of Spain is of a different nature to other men, and even that of most other Kings, as he has made his vengeful desires sufficiently known

---

[4] Charles of Aragon, Duke of Terranova, was the principal Spanish diplomat during the Cologne peace negotiations.

by the cruelties committed in Spain, in Italy, in the Indies, and even in these countries, where he had an infinite number of his subjects massacred and burnt alive, without sparing the greatest Princes, as the death of the Counts of Egmont and Hoorne testify. By an extraordinary and unseen novelty to render them even more ignominious, the heads of these Lords were put on iron stakes, serving as a sad spectacle. We know, following the great affection the King shows himself to have for his Roman religion, that by its rules he is under an obligation to make war with his subjects who do not want to follow this religion. For it is been resolved that he cannot grant liberty in his countries for the practice of any other than the Roman religion, and that having given himself to such unjust and tyrannical things as the laws of this Roman religion, he will not want to act against his conscience in order to accommodate his subjects, to whom until this hour he has shown so little affection. In addition to this the general and continual alliances he has with the pope, especially against the Reformed religion, whose adherents are considered by them as worse than the Turks and other enemies of the Christian name, do not permit him to reconcile himself with his subjects of any other religion but the Roman; to such an extent that he is pushed by his supposed religion to satisfy his supposed conscience, to continue the war against us or to trap us by a feigned peace. Everybody can experience himself what the forces of this religion are; he can then judge whether the Kings would abandon a war, which they consider holy and necessary for the salvation of their souls and of which he can not hear, even less see and feel the calamities. For as one has seen and still sees every day, an endless number of men let themselves be miserably massacred in order to maintain their religion, even if it is bad and wrong. Since it seems to him that his claims are well founded, how does it seem for him to abase himself to the point of confessing that he was wrong, as he would be obliged to do according to the conditions of peace, as the justice of the States' cause and the security of the subjects require.

Moreover does not one see that the King makes no preparations at all to come to peace? For with regard to the mission of his ambassadors, the Baron of Selles[5] in the first place, who came to the country just before the defeat of Gembloux, God knows that he has been

---

[5] The Baron of Selles, brother of the Baron of Noircarmes, served as an envoy for Philip II. As such he played an important role in the negotiations of the late 1570s.

nothing but the instrument in corrupting some of those who had command of the army and who have unfortunately let it be defeated since. He has never proposed anything that could help to bring peace and tranquillity. For instead of bringing about the King's consent to the liberty in the practice of religion, which is, following the example of the neighbours of these countries, the sole remedy to redress the affairs, he has publicly declared that the King wants to maintain nothing of the Pacification of Ghent. And instead of bringing about a general peace, he has gone to negotiate in particular with those of Artois, Hainaut and other provinces, creating dissensions and divisions, in order to subject the provinces separately by these means so that, eventually, they do not have the convenience of a united and co-ordinated defence. Therefore, as he did not intend to be frank and sincere, he has dealt in none but a cunning way with the aforesaid provinces. Omitting, for the sake of brevity, a discussion of the ruses and tricks, forgery and bribery he employed to secure the treaty of Arras,[6] made and concluded on, as it seems, the 17 March last, but examining this treaty and the supposed ratification by the Prince of Parma, carried out before the city of Maastricht,[7] one finds that this is nothing but pure fraud and that in fact these provinces, under the colour of this treaty will have surrendered unconditionally to the Prince [of Parma], to use and dispose of them as he would find convenient according to the circumstances. For much as it seems that there is an absolute contract and that there is nothing left open to interpretation, unless in the execution and implementation of the articles of the pacification any difficulty should arise, one finds that the Prince of Parma has not been willing to admit it absolutely but has put forward various problems, by which he has revoked and once again put into dispute the whole treaty. And despite the fact that the deputies who were commissioned to sign and avow with him the so-called articles of Arras, declared, by their instruction that they were in

---

[6] With the treaty of Arras of October 1578, the provinces of Artois and Hainaut took major steps towards a reconciliation with Philip II by reaffirming their loyalty to peace, the king and the Catholic church. The treaty marked the discord amongst the Dutch provinces.

[7] The town of Maastricht, now in the south of the Netherlands, was besieged in 1578 by Alexander Farnese (1545–92), Prince of Parma, who succeeded Don Juan as Philip II's Governor in the Netherlands. In contrast with Don Juan, Farnese was both an able diplomat and a brilliant military strategist, who exploited the tensions within the States General with great political skill (see also 'Biographical Notes', p. xxxviii).

no way to be authorized to change, elaborate or restrict anything, they have nonetheless tolerated that the oath of the aforesaid Prince is restricted to what is still to be agreed in the future and is entirely conditional as much in the obscurities he alleges as in the points put forward in writing by the Prince of Parma. And they have made the oath reciprocal, as one can see in the writings, already distributed and published, of both parties. By the same token one may consider two highly remarkable things. First the deputies charged with the ratification have exceeded their power and commission. For instead of appointing commissioners, as was laid down in the so-called convention of Arras, to understand, sharpen and settle the problems that may arise during the implementation, the deputies have moved on, to the point not of effecting the implementation and form of the treaty, but indeed of making the whole treaty the subject of controversy and debate. Moreover they have allowed the prince to put forward new points, which should first be resolved. The fact that they have permitted that the Prince of Parma, despite his oath, be in no way committed with regard to the conditions, demonstrates clearly that the parties do not yet agree and that, from his side, the Prince has not yet consented to anything, so that, according to law, the contract can not be valid. Thus it becomes clear that, since the Prince of Parma has been unwilling to acknowledge what the deputies concluded at Arras, the Prince is not of good faith and that the commissioners, who negotiated at Arras, have exceeded their power in order, by all means of trickery and deceit, to deliver the provinces, the governors and all other Lords and inhabitants into the hands of the Spaniards, their enemies.

And with regard to the so-called general peace negotiations going on at Cologne, they neither act in better faith nor with fewer ruses and tricks as they have done in dealing with the individual provinces. In the first place, with regard to the Duke of Terranova, who was sent to this end by the King of Spain, after long negotiations as much in Italy with the Pope as in Germany with the Imperial Majesty, what else has he tried to achieve but that his Majesty [the German Emperor], instead of sending neutral mediators has deputed ecclesiastical Princes who obviously would not want to do anything either for the liberty of conscience and the practice of the Reformed religion or for the security of his subjects, be they of one religion or the other.

Furthermore one should consider his tardiness, for despite the continuous solicitation of the Duke of Aerschot,[8] he had been in Cologne
for more than three months before one could get any resolution out of
him. Now that it has at last been declared, it has become evident that
the Duke has no intention of drawing up and concluding such a
necessary and desirable peace; for he who proposes conditions
neither tolerable nor acceptable at all, does not wish to reach an
agreement. It will be apparent that the conditions proposed by him
are in no way either feasible or admissible, inasmuch as he demands
that the people shall be disarmed completely so that they will be
unable to guard the towns, making it possible for the enemies or their
adherents to surprise them and to put garrisons in the places where
one is accustomed to having them. Which would mean everywhere,
even in the towns of Antwerp, Brussels, Utrecht, Groningen, Ghent,
Bruges and elsewhere. For there is no town that was not frequently
garrisoned. He demands that all towns and fortresses be restored to
the power of such a Governor as the King pleases to send; that all
magistrates, indeed all subjects will be obliged to take the accustomed
oath, which was usually sworn by all, upon the Roman religion; that
the practice of the Reformed religion should desist, except in Holland
and Zeeland where it will be permitted for only a certain time, and
under conditions which are such that one may well claim to annihilate
it everywhere, just as was initially done at the first opportunity in the
year sixty-six. This would present itself and would be exploited as
soon as the towns and fortresses, as demanded, would have been put
in the hands of the Governor (to be sent by the King). One should
also re-establish those who have betrayed their fatherland in their
estate and good name, so that they have the means, authority and
standing to realize in time of peace what they could not accomplish
with arms. Moreover they want to treat with my lord the Prince [of
Orange] separately, in order to keep the principal treaty in abeyance
in the meantime and to deprive the States of the person of my lord the
Prince, knowing that, after God, he alone is the hope for the preservation of the state of the country and the link by which the Provinces are

[8] The Duke of Aerschot was the official leader of the States' delegation in Cologne (see
'Biographical Notes', p. xxxvii). Although Aerschot promoted the 1576 reconciliation
between the provinces, he did not agree with Holland's independent political course. As
a Roman Catholic he probably favoured a moderate monarchy, which respected the
privileges and the political importance of the States.

connected and united. By his authority, prudence, counsel and experience he sets about redressing the affairs and restoring union and concord in order to defend by common forces and good mutual wisdom the fatherland and the just cause which the States have taken up against the common enemies.

Thus, considering these pretensions and other unreasonable demands, one evidently sees that they do not want to settle the problems but rather augment them, as it is shown very clearly that they want to accommodate themselves to no reason whatsoever. Likewise the Duke of Terranova has limited commission on the issue of religion, as may appear from the act of his commission. For inasmuch as it contains a general clause, this is, however, limited by a special clause, reiterated in the same commission, by which he is ordered to conserve the Roman Catholic religion. As generally determined by law, general clauses inserted in commissions and similar procurations are limited by specifically declared conditions.

As for the mediators, the ecclesiastical princes,[9] their quality and profession make it perfectly clear what little fruit the States can expect from their intercession, and until this hour they have not dared to touch upon the issue of religion. On this point they will give themselves over to the manipulation and orders at the will of the Duke of Terranova, for they separate the political affairs from the points concerning religion, as if the issue of religion does not touch upon and has nothing in common with politics. Thus it is easy to judge and conclude that the King seeks nothing less than peace, for he has sent commissioners who have no authority whatsoever to deal with the principal issue; likewise the mediators are not at all empowered to dispose of their authority in order to attain a remedy appropriate to the wound. Consequently as will be deducted at greater length in the following chapter, it is to the King, and not to the States, that is to be imputed the fact that the poor inhabitants are being deprived of the benefits a good, lasting and secure peace might bring them.

Those who presume that the States General are the cause of the continuation of this war, be they the subjects and inhabitants of the provinces which remain united and allied, or the enemies, that is to say the Spaniards and their adherents, judge, either out of ignorance

---

[9] The Elector and Archbishops of Cologne and Trier and the Bishop of Würzburg were amongst the mediators.

or malice, the affairs otherwise than is advisable for the health and conservation of the whole state.[10] With regard to the inhabitants of these united provinces who tend to believe that the States are protracting this war, one should think that they do so on account of their being insufficiently informed of what is going on, and otherwise carried away by the great desire they have to see the country restored to peace and returned into a flourishing state. Since this stems only from a good and laudable intention, it is to be excused if, prior to arresting their judgment, they make the effort to inform themselves in order to understand the reasons for the duration of these troubles and internal wars. By doing so they will find that the States General are those who sit together and assemble on behalf of the nobility and the towns of the country, so that it is the inhabitants themselves who have delegated them and who also have the authority and power to delegate others, if those who are commissioned at present or in the future do not fulfil such a duty as their state and charge requires. Thus to slander them is to wrong oneself, above all because nothing in the world can move them [the States General] to maintain dissension and war. For regarding them it is well known that they have neither had nor have now any money in their hand of which to dispose for their own profit and advantage. From the very beginning of the assembly the scarcity and need of money has continually been such that it has always been allocated for some necessity of war even before its receipt. The States have found themselves in this situation throughout the last peace negotiations, as is well known to everybody. In fact they have kept aloof from all financial administration, as much because the revenues of the general means were due to the merchants as because all other means are specifically devoted to the maintenance of the forces of those on horseback and on foot, who are still in service. Thus neither the management of finances nor any other ambition could have made the States desirous of keeping these countries in these disasters of civil wars. For in bringing peace, the States will continue to exist forever, be it as provincial States or as States General, and the provinces and towns will always have the same power to delegate and employ whomsoever they please, having

---

[10] At this point the *Brief Discourse*, following the *Defence*, seems to use the word 'etat' (state) in a striking fashion, not merely connotating the condition of the country (as at the end of the following sentence) but equating it with the country as such. See *Defence*, note 72, p. 66.

no obligations to any person. The town pensionaires[11] or councillors will neither be short of work (as they have always been before) nor will there be fewer possibilities to advance themselves in times of peace than during hard and changing times such as those caused by a detestable civil and intestine war. One cannot imagine that there would be people so wretched and miserable that, if they could possibly avoid it, they would want to put the whole country in peril and danger for the little good the war might bring them. He who reflects on the state of public affairs, the financial problems, the damaging and ruin of the whole countryside, the poverty of the towns, and the complaints lodged every day at the States, both about soldiers, who, for lack of pay, commit a thousand follies and insolences, and about the payments of debts, will easily see what little pleasure there is in being involved in such perplexing and difficult affairs, without having the means to apply the appropriate remedies, and whether the States have any reason to deprive the whole country and themselves of the prosperity and happiness which a good and secure peace could bring.

The enemies themselves and their adherents, who out of malice give a negative interpretation of all actions of the States in order to give lustre to their own unjust and tyrannical designs, have no basis for saying that the States have ever set back the cause of peace. Therefore we leave such discourses and excuses to the barbarians, to those who take delight in human blood, and to the enemies of the country, for we think that there is no need for the States to justify themselves before such insubstantial charges. Let us discuss the facts, namely the efforts the States have made in order to obtain a good peace from the King of Spain, these being infallible evidence of their will. This consists of two principal points, namely in whether the conditions and articles of peace the States have asked for are reasonable and are such that the King should have accepted them, and in the means used to induce the King and his ministers to agree to these conditions, supplications and demands.

First, concerning the articles and conditions proposed by the States to attain a good peace, the instructions which were given to my lord the Duke of Aerschot and the other Lords, who are deputies at Cologne, show clearly that the States make only just and equitable claims. And in turn they offer the King total obedience, which in

---

[11] The town pensionary was the highest-ranking civil servant in the expanding town bureaucracies.

effect is nothing else but to submit themselves to the King, with the exception of the conservation of the liberty, rights and privileges of the country.

That it is just to take up arms for the defence of one's liberty, one's goods, wife and children, is approved by the judgment of all men, who judge sanely on the duty of Princes and States or magistrates, who represent the people. And it is already approved without contestation by the King himself, having acknowledged the resort to arms by the States by the so-called agreement based on this fact, as comprised by the Edict which was dubbed eternal,[12] and there where this could be put in debate around the issue which is in question in the provinces. Consequently all actions of the States since the beginning of these troubles should be discussed.

It would take too much time to discourse upon all points of the instruction given to the deputies of the States, in order to show that the conditions proposed are necessary to maintain the privileges, the liberty of conscience, the practice of the Reformed religion, and to assure and secure the observance of the promises which would be made in this respect. I will here only mention what the States have put forward with regard to the practice of the religion. Which is that the practice of the Reformed religion will continue in those places where it exists at present, until a legitimate assembly of the States disposes otherwise. This is the article most disputed and flatly rejected by the ministers of the King. Therefore it should be seen whether the States demand something wrongful in this matter and whether the King's reasons are well founded in its complete rejection. As far as the States are concerned, it is easy to show that their demand is just and well-grounded, for everybody can see that the greater part of the inhabitants of the country profess the Reformed religion.[13] As the States represent the whole people and all inhabitants of the country, it is reasonable that, for the common good of this country, they conform themselves to the dispositions and desires of the inhabitants in just and proper matters. Of old, as long as people can remember, the

---

[12] The *Eternal Edict* of 12 February 1577 was the outcome of negotiations between the States General and Don Juan, whom Philip II had appointed Governor.

[13] This was a slight exaggeration. In spite of their preponderance in politics and culture, Reformed Protestants remained a minority in the Low Countries and in the Dutch Republic. For detailed statistics see Alastair Duke, 'The ambivalent face of Calvinism in the Netherlands, 1561–1618' in Menna Prestwich, *International Calvinism 1541–1715* (Oxford, 1985), pp. 109–11.

States have represented all people in the Low Countries in order to defend their right and to maintain them in peace and tranquillity, and to guard them from all outrages, violence and oppression against everyone, even against their own Princes.

It is hard to imagine a Republic, Kingdom or other sovereign government without a subordinate magistrate and States which represent the country. However, following the privileges and constitutions that provide for such magistrates or States, this is much more obvious in one state than in another, to the extent that in some provinces the venerable name of States is almost extinguished, because of the limited authority the States have. Nothing of the sort has occurred in the Low Countries, where the States have always held so much authority and respect that the Dukes and princes have not been able to make any alterations in the matter of sovereignty such as levying salt tax or other duties, or minting new coinage, or making peace or waging war, without the express consent of the States. This and many other rights and prerogatives can be derived from their privileges, laws and constitutions of the country. Even what the States have granted to their Princes for some necessary war against an open and declared enemy, have been called requests,[14] instead of aid or taxes of the Prince, in order to demonstrate that the States were in no way obliged to anything, but that they had given their consent to the requests of the Prince. In order that the States might always be respected and maintained in their authority, they have never given perpetual or absolute consent, but have always limited it to a certain sum and time. Thus it is clear enough that the States are authorized to take up arms against the Princes who exceed the limits of their office with open tyranny. There can be no doubt that they are entitled to propose and demand things which, in their view, seem appropriate to the good of the inhabitants of the country and which by consequence, they should also obtain from their Prince. Thus the justice of their demand on behalf of the multitude of inhabitants who adhere to this Reformed religion is clear from the fact that they are obliged to stand equally for all subjects of the country, giving equal favour to all in their demands if these are not unreasonable, which in this case can only be concluded if one could prove with sufficient reasons that two religions should not be suffered in a single country and, since in such

---

[14] The Dutch word is 'bede', the French one, used by the *Brief Discourse* 'praires'.

a case one should maintain the true and reject the false religion, it would be necessary to convict the Reformed religion of falsity. In my opinion there is no need to debate about the toleration of two religions, as great countries of Christendom are practising it, and have practised it for several centuries. It is certainly true that it is more desirable to have but one religion, just as it is that all men were of the same opinion, will, condition and wealth, in short, that all were virtuous and happy. Yet, if this cannot be brought about, one should govern the country in the best way possible, setting up such laws on the issue of religion that as far as the state is able, all are satisfied. Therefore, seeing the multitude of those who profess a religion other than the Roman, should the States, following the example of their neighbours, rather allow the King to ruin the country, to chase and massacre the subjects, than to tolerate both religions? And having then seen that the unjust stubbornness and cruelty of the King serves to no effect, and that in spite of the fact that the King has had innumerable people burnt alive, and has chased and banned an infinite number of men and women of all ranks, has confiscated body and goods and has sent the poor children out to beg, the Reformed religion has been extremely popular, with the number of those dedicated to this religion having rather increased than diminished, should the States forever suffer, or rather oppose such barbarious tyranny for the defence and protection of the subjects of the country?

Now if it had been shown that there are no grounds for permitting two religions in this case, one would necessarily have come to the point of examining which is the true one. As those of the Reformed religion say that they are prepared to allow their articles of faith to be examined by a free council, and offer to show that these are in accordance with the Holy Scriptures,[15] should one not rather hear them than condemn them unheard? For the Council of Trent has only served the Ecclesiastics, who can not be judges in their own cause. Neither France, nor Germany, Poland, England or other countries and kingdoms have obeyed or are still obeying this council. And as far as the King is concerned: he must have it one way or the other. Either he grants his countries the practice of the Reformed religion, or he cannot, because it would seem to him the desecration of his conscience. If he can do it without any remorse from his

---

[15] This had been suggested in a 1578 supplication of the national synod of the Dutch Reformed Protestant churches.

conscience, then of what use to him will this long war be, the shedding of so much blood of his poor subjects, if it is not to use the difference of religion as a pretext for the extermination of all good people, for the complete ruin of the country with fire and blood, in order, in the words of his late Secretary Escovedo,[16] to have the possibility to reduce this country to extreme servitude. If he cannot permit the exercise of the Reformed religion, because it goes against his conscience, then what else should this country expect from him, except a firm and resolute determination to continue the war and to achieve his ambitions either by force or by tricks and intrigues, and give hope of peace in order thereby to cause discord and to deceive one side and the other. The result in any event is that he wants to force his subjects to abandon him and to look for other ways to protect and defend themselves. In this the King's alleged conscience, his desire and will do not merit any regard. For he is not established over the consciences and the States of the country, which have reserved unto themselves the power to decide on all matters concerning the sovereignty; have they allowed the King to dispose on his own of the consciences of the subjects? And could such permission be given, as neither the King nor the States either, but each individual must answer before God for his faith and conscience? After all, is not everybody ordered to study the Scriptures, to the extent that it is much more advisable to regard the whole country than the will of a single King and that, as far as the salvation of the soul is concerned, one should obey God, not men or Kings. As it appears that the King of Spain has permitted, through the Eternal Edict, the practice of the Reformed religion in Holland and Zeeland, and offers to extend it here, it should be said that the intention of the King is to abolish the practice too in these countries, either by force or intrigue. Otherwise he is doing wrong to his other subjects by refusing to grant them the same benefit. In any case, one cannot hope for any justice or good treatment from him. Indeed he demonstrated this in the year sixty-six, by the massacre, ruin and misery that ensued as the King, in spite of the promises that were made at the time, which he then had revoked

---

[16] Escovedo was a Spanish councillor, who served as a member of the Council of the State. The interception and subsequent publication of some of his letters to Spain, which revealed Spanish ambitions to subject the Netherlands to harsh Spanish rule, made him the prototype of a Spanish evildoer and a welcome victim for the propagandists of the Revolt.

by the Duke of Alva, had an endless number of people of all ranks murdered and driven out, and has put into effect rigorous and tyrannical placards. And recently the late Don Juan has in fact publicly declared that he charges my lord the Prince of Orange, and the States of Holland and Zeeland, to abolish the practice of the Reformed religion, to subjugate the country of Holland and Zeeland, in order that he might later give the laws he has wanted to all the provinces. To this the States did not wish to yield, with the result that he decided to attack the castle and town of Namur, and to renew the war in order to oblige them by force. Moreover it is of no use to say that, as King and Prince of these countries, by the accords these constitutions of the Empire,[17] he can ordain upon the issue of religion according to his will. For, first, the accords do not speak in such terms. Second, the King has never wanted to hold himself to these constitutions dealing with the issue of religion. Third, the Princes of the Empire do not resolve upon the issue of religion absolutely, without a measure of consent from their estates, towns and countries. And, fourth, even if they did so, one should consider that it is not very likely that the said Princes will set their countries alight and ablaze and put their subjects to the sword, rather than endure two religions in their countries, or that, rather than coming to terms with this, they would prefer to wage war against their subjects for so many years, at such a great cost, with the ruin and desolation of towns and whole countries, such as this miserable war of the Low Countries has brought about. And fifth, if one should find Princes so cruel and obstinate and so closely allied with the Pope of Rome, should one still follow their example? Are not the States of the country founded to use all their power and all the help of their neighbours, even to take another Prince as Lord of the country, rather than to suffer such a barbarous resolution?

There is another very important reason, the sixth, to prove that the argument concerning the constitutions of the empire has no bearing with regard to the King of Spain. Namely that the Princes of Germany have never persecuted so rigorously those, in their countries, who were of any religion other than the Roman, or another generally observed one. Likewise they have never let themselves be seduced to the point of contravening their promises, whereas over many years,

---

[17] Probably the author of the *Brief Discourse* was thinking of the 1555 religious Peace of Augsburg whose famous dictum 'cuius regio, eius religio', gave the German princes the right to determine the religion of their countries.

the King of Spain has had more than a hundred thousand people killed under tyrannical placards: most were burnt alive, having been previously deprived of the use of their tongues by an extremely cruel iron machine, in addition to the torments to which they were subjected before suffering the final torture. In spite of the promise to moderate the placards and the permission given to practice the religion, he has ever since renewed and extended the placards even more rigorously than before, hunting down all those who, with the permission of the Governess, have attended Reformed sermons. For this and similar reasons he had an infinite number of men tracked down and killed, even the principal Lords of the country,[18] and forced others, allowed to stay alive, to accept the letters of pardon, thus, as shown by the placards published on these issues by the Duke of Alva, condemning at a stroke all provinces, revoking all the privileges.

Therefore it is small wonder that the countries, being so brutally treated for the cause of the so-called Roman religion, would not want to submit themselves once again to the latter under the pretext of moderation and regulations to be made up by the Prince who has treated them so badly and has so seldom kept his previous promises.

To these considerations a seventh point should be added. The majority of the Princes of Germany declare themselves to be of the Reformed religion, which they regard as founded upon the Holy Scriptures and command of God, whereas the Roman religion is founded upon the authority of the Pope of Rome and the opinions of men.

Eighth, it should suffice for all that the Low Countries have different privileges and that the States are merely doing their duty and that in this country the King of Spain is not seen as King of Spain, but only as Duke of Brabant, Count of Flanders, Holland, and in each country respectively in accordance with their constitutions, decrees and privileges. It is not my intention to dissect this question in detail, nor the others, but only to pass it on with what has already been said. Relying on what numerous learned people have argued regarding the right of magistrates and States against a tyrannical king, the toleration of two religions, even the distinction between the good and wrong one, I will go on to discuss with the same brevity the reasons, for which in my opinion the States cannot and must not accept the

---

[18] The most famous example here, of course, was the execution of the Counts of Egmont and Hoorne in 1568.

conditions proposed on behalf of the King. I will add the sad articles in order to give my opinion on each one in particular. Let us go on to the first article, whose tenor is as follows.

> *1. First, the Pacification of Ghent, made and concluded in the town of Ghent on 8 November 1576, and the following Union of Brussels of 9 January 1577, as well as the Eternal Edict published in the same year in the town of Brussels on 17 February, together with the confirmation and ratification of the King will be upheld and executed in all their points and articles.*

It should be noted that the King does not promise to observe the Pacification of Ghent solely, absolutely, and plainly, but the Pacification of Ghent together with the following Union and the Eternal Edict. In doing so, he publicly declares that his intention in this is not to maintain the Pacification of Ghent; for the Pacification is either dispensed with completely or subjected to so many capricious interpretations, due to the restrictions contained in the Union and the Eternal Edict, that the force of the said Pacification comes to an end. Since the principal good the Low Countries expected from the Pacification of Ghent consists in the preservation of the Privileges, rights and customs of the country, by virtue of which the King could not decide anything without the consent of the States with regard to the Reformed religion, one neither could nor should have the authority of the States prejudiced with regard to decisions concerning the liberty of conscience and the practice of the Reformed religion. Nonetheless, both by the Union and the Eternal Edict, one sees, on the contrary, that at least fifteen provinces swear and promise to uphold the Roman Catholic religion. If only those of the Roman religion would like to admit that the practice of the Reformed religion can be accorded without the least violation of the Roman religion, and that one can preserve the Roman religion while granting freedom of worship to the Reformed religion. However, they do not yet want to admit to this – in fact they are demonstrating the very opposite by persecuting those of the [Reformed] religion everywhere they have regained control. Why then, one will say, are they usurping the title of the Pacification of Ghent? It is to mislead the simple folk, by letting it be known that at least the people will have liberty of conscience. In this way a meaningless liberty of conscience would have been established by the Pacification of Ghent, which is an abuse. For in Ghent one has obtained the liberty of the country, the re-establishment of the authority of the States, in order to withstand the inconveniences which have already come into being and brought so much ruin and calamity to the country, and which could still grow due to the diversity of religion and other reasons. Now therefore, as the States have found it advisable to accord the free practice of the Reformed religion, one should for the same good, the security and prosperity of the country, ensure that it is maintained and upheld without lingering on a holy name of the liberty of conscience, which the ignorant hope to enjoy under the fine title of the Pacification of Ghent, Union and Edict, which, however, will be found to be true means of an even more immaculate inquisition, than ever ruled in Spain. We will return to this later.

No one can take seriously the suggestion that by consenting to the Pacification of Ghent there would be more liberty than before. For, first, the effect of the Pacification is restricted by the Union and the Eternal Edict, subjecting the inhabitants of the country to observance of the Roman religion. Second, eliminating all practice of the Reformed religion, both in private and in public, will mean a return to the previous placards, as in fact desired by Don Juan, and shown by the spilt blood of a citizen of Malines, with the effect that the Pacification will be annulled. Those who will be found to have acted against the Roman Catholic religion will be punished. Only they will be exempted who will know how to enjoy the liberty of conscience in hiding; they have always been free, even at the time of the Duke of Alva, for although he was a great tyrant, he could not punish his hidden enemies. Those who boast of this fine title of liberty of conscience act like those who allow one to do good on condition that nobody knows of it, like those who promise thieves not to punish them if they steal so secretly that nobody comes to know of it. Thus it is not his Majesty's intention that the Pacification should be maintained. For it is also evident that the so-called articles of peace contradict the Pacification in many places.

2. *Like and in addition to what happened at the time of the first troubles, since the time of the treaties, the Pacification of Ghent, the Union and the Eternal Edict, several other things have occurred and have been said and done by one side or the other, both in general and in particular. Therefore a perpetual oblivion is ordained by the*

Pacification not only of what happened since the conclusion of these treaties, but also of what has happened before, to the effect that this will never be mentioned, criticized or investigated, as if it had not happened, under pain of exemplary punishment for all subjects who act in contravention, as disrupters of public order.

Regarding the second article, containing a general pardon, it remains only to say that this article depends on the degree of assurance the States can have as to the observance of the treaty, given that the subjects were treated so badly in 1566 and that the calamitous war has ever since been continued without reason. It may be added that this article is also subject to captiousness due to the exceptions mentioned in article 13, speaking about the approval of the decrees of his Highness[19] and the States.

3. The Catholic King will guard and maintain his vassals and subjects. If this seems necessary he will time and time again approve everybody's rights, usages, customs, immunities, franchises and privileges, and the privileges of each province, town, village, community and of other places, both in general and in particular, just as he promised and swore both when he took possession of the provinces of the Low Countries and in the tenth article of the Eternal Edict.

The same consideration is to be taken into account with regard to the third article, as with the preceding second article.

4. That all foreign soldiers, that is to say Spaniards, Germans, Walloons, Burgundians, Englishmen, Scotsmen and all other foreigners, as called by both sides in the present troubles, will leave the provinces of the Low Countries together and at the same time once the Pacification has been published on terms that can be accorded them by all sides.

See how by this fourth article, and by many others equally uncertain, it is quite clear that not only are the conditions unacceptable, but they still reserve the right to revoke them completely, while keeping the subjects hopeful of obtaining peace. For what else is it if the deadline for the departure of the foreigners is not mentioned and

---

[19] Matthias, Archduke of Austria, from the Austrian branch of the Habsburg dynasty, had been appointed Governor by the States General in 1578, after the break with Don Juan who had been declared an enemy of the country.

if many other points are left without final resolution, but in this way to make the whole treaty an illusion. The more so since by law treaties are not absolute and concluded until everything is resolved. The result is that the Spaniards could still demand a term for their departure of three, four or five years, and other unreasonable things.

> *5. For the greatest relief of the afflicted subjects, the King commands with regard to the native soldiers that all soldiers, both on land and at sea should be dismissed and discharged at the same time, so that from now on they may live privately at peace. Only the ordinary garrisons are maintained in competent numbers, so that all subjects, citizens and inhabitants of these countries may return without the least delay to their trade, manufacturing and jobs; and in this way they can honourably take care of their wives and children, without doing wrong to their neighbours, and also relinquish and abstain from the practice of arms, anomalous and improper in times of peace.*

This fifth article declares plainly enough that the King wishes to place garrisons everywhere where these have normally been, which would mean even in Antwerp, Utrecht, Ghent, Groningen and everywhere else. And he wants to disarm the inhabitants, in order to have the possibility to take the towns by storm.

> *6. That all demands, impositions, and other exactions, and unjust charges, which have been introduced in one way or another because of the troubles, will be suspended and annulled. That is to say that if one finds the continuation of some imposition necessary for the public good, as soon as the States table a remonstrance to this effect, the King will willingly conform to their counsel and desire.*

The sixth [article] is merely a lure to mislead those who are less informed that they would not be subject to taxes. Where it really leads is made quite clear in the last clause, declaring that there will nonetheless be taxes and excises.

The Duke of Alva clearly demonstrated his intention by demanding the Tenth Penny, which he wanted to introduce not only without the advice and consent of the States, and also against their will and express protest, not just for a defined period but in perpetuity, to the effect that the late first Bishop of Antwerp and others boasted of having found a fountain of subsidies, which would flow forever. It is also clear enough that the Prince of Parma will not spare the country any more than the late Duke of Alva did and wanted to do. For the nature and constitution of the Italian Princes is characteristically devoted to finding a thousand devices to exhaust the purses of the subjects. Thus he wanted to mention the feigned discharge of the subsidies, thereby depicting the cause of the States as loathsome, as if they were burdening the subjects with unnecessary taxes. In this subject one should consider that there is a great difference between contributions made voluntarily to safeguard one's liberty, property, wife and children against a manifest tyranny, and the subsidies given to maintain the tyrant and to subject oneself, one's property, wife, children and offspring to an exceeding barbarous servitude, and to make war against one's fellow-citizens and colleagues. Considering this, all men of virtue and good character will not find anything bad in paying, even if it were as much as half of their property. For if all are held to employ their own life for the preservation of the fatherland, then how much more are we obliged to employ the property God has given us to provide for all our needs, which cannot be greater than that at hand, the defence against such a barbarous and cruel enemy. It is also explicitly stated by the Pacification of Ghent, by old and new alliances that we should employ all our property, even our own life, for mutual assistance. Moreover it is within the power of the country to suspend and abolish, if they so wish, the taxes levied by the States, whose administration is also in their own hands. And everybody can assure himself that the money is used for no other purpose but the necessary defence of the country.

This can only mean that nowhere else does one see the effects of the good will of the States so well as in their means. Therefore bad patriots do everything to hamper the taxes under the pretext of privileges, as if such a great war against such a powerful monarch could be carried on without continual contributions of truly great sums, and as if the privileges prevent the inhabitants of the provinces from employing their riches to secure and defend themselves against such an unjust and barbarous violence and slavery, with which one seeks to oppress not only their body and goods, but also their consciences and souls.

The privileges were made in order to have the liberty of doing what right, reason and virtue commands, not to be so tied and constrained that it is not possible to dispose of one's riches for one's own defence.

This would be a real and abominable servitude. We see many towns, even those of the Holy Empire, which are free and exempt from taxes, but yet they do not fail to contribute towards the public good if necessity requires it. The war of the King of Denmark and those of Lübeck against the King of Sweden is still fresh in our memories. In this war the people of Lübeck, though a town completely free under the laws of the Holy Empire, spent a mint of money. The subjects and inhabitants of the town were taxed in various ways and measures, even by a hundredth penny,[20] which they have paid more than ten times in but a few years, not only of the inheritances they had in the town and its territory, but of all their possessions and properties both within their jurisdiction and without. It is indeed a very different and more considerable contribution than that which the States, nonetheless with the consent of the towns and provinces, have practised until now. Did not the people of Lübeck, whose quarrel with the King of Sweden concerned only certain rights and prerogatives affecting commerce, have only a hundredth part of the justification to make war as the Provinces have to maintain it against such a cruel tyrannical enemy, against whom they are forced to defend themselves in order to prevent themselves from being forced to act against their consciences, from being returned to harsh servitude, from seeing a million of souls massacred and exiled.

The flourishing town and republic of Nuremberg prides itself in its liberty. However, even in times of peace it still annually contributes the hundredth penny, to be paid in silver coins at the old value, which means that this Hundredth becomes the Twenty-fifth Penny. The towns of Strasbourg, Ulm, Augsburg, Frankfurt and innumerable others are neither exempted from taxes, although they are privileged and free. And if every politically well-ordered town and republic must be rich, as is affirmed by all wise political thinkers, and if this should be the case in times of peace, then is there not much more reason to have means of general subsidies to be employed for the common good in such a case of necessity as war. For one cannot wage war and maintain the discipline of the soldiers without prompt payment. Moreover these general means and the resulting taxes all return, if they are paid at the right time, to the purses of the community, in

---

[20] The term 'Hundredth Penny' must have reminded the readers of the *Brief Discourse* of Alva's highly unpopular fiscal proposals, depicted in the political literature of the Revolt as an essential part of the Duke's gruesome tyranny. See for example pp. 62, 97.

addition to the obedience and good discipline one may enjoy if the soldier is content with his pay, by the relief of poor villagers and townspeople who are forced to endure garrisons because of the vicinity of the enemy. That which one contributes to the States is thus for the country and for the inhabitants themselves, as the deputies who are at the States in command of the towns, in order to represent for them what these might like, are in control of the distribution. In consequence everything the bad patriots could concoct on this subject, in order to stir up the treason against their fatherland, is refuted.

> *7. Moreover the freedom of trade, and passage through all manner of places, towns, villages, over rivers, streams and bridges and by all seaports of the Provinces will be completely re-established in the state they were in before the present troubles. Wherefore the new taxes and impositions levied because of these new troubles without the consent of the King will be stopped and annulled.*

On the seventh article no other solution is sought. For the States are also of the opinion that all impositions should cease as soon as the necessity of war disappears and that commerce should be as free as it was before the troubles.

> *8. In order to oust and extirpate the causes and origins of all grievances and complaints, all ecclesiastical and secular persons both from the Low Countries and abroad are reconfirmed respectively in their ecclesiastical and secular movable property, being still in kind, together with all immovables, titles, debts and holdings, in order to enjoy and possess them undisturbed in the state and quality in which they will presently be found. Everything will be done without fraud and deceit and notwithstanding any mortgage or other alienation made to the contrary since the time of the Pacification of Ghent onwards, leaving what happened before the Pacification at its decree and disposal.*

> *9. Similarly all subjects from both sides are re-established in their honours, dignities, benefices, governments, charges, functions and offices as it was at the time of Eternal Edict, leaving what happened before the Edict at its decree and disposal. However, excluded are the persons who have been provided with some position contrary to the franchises, rights and privileges of the fatherland.*

Yet it should be clear that if the persons who were deprived of their position were reinstated, they are bound and obliged to take the oath as mentioned in the following article, just as those are who will be appointed to any new office or position from now on. In doing so everything both sides have done, decreed or decided to the contrary is revoked, quashed and annulled.

Passing over the eighth, we come to consider the ninth [article], whereby on the one hand all those who held office in such a bad way in the time of Don Juan are reinstated, while on the other hand those who have been appointed by the States General are put into dispute under the pretext of the privileges, which will be interpreted at will by the future Governor and also by means of the oath, to which all who are and will be henceforth are bound. Remarkable also is the general clause, by which everything done and decreed to the contrary is quashed and annulled, by virtue of which they might annul and cancel whatever they please in the future.

10. No persons are admitted to the government of provinces, towns, castles, fortresses, military commands, neither to the Council of State, the Privy Council, the Council of Finances or to other important offices, other than natives of the Provinces comprised by the general government. Before their admittance to office, these persons will be obliged, in addition to and above the old oath which it is customary to swear to the King, as to the natural Prince, solemnly to swear as well the present articles, both to the King and to the States and to promise to maintain them faithfully and without infraction, on pain of the statutory punishment for perjury.

As far as the oath mentioned by the tenth article is concerned, the words 'in addition to and above the old oath' make it abundantly clear what they are up to. For as the majority of the governors, officers and magistrates were accustomed to take the oath to the conservation of the Roman Catholic religion, that is the Spanish Inquisition, this article would like simply to plunge the whole country back into subjection and servitude again, in order to tyrannize not only the body but also the soul.

11. That all prisoners still held by the two sides at present because of the existing troubles will be released immediately without ransom, unless an accord or agreement to the contrary has been concluded previously by the parties.

12. The Count of Buren[21] will be released and will return to the fatherland three months after the Prince of Orange has accomplished and effectuated that which has been negotiated with him.

We shall also pass over article 11. However, the twelfth, speaking of the return of the Count of Buren, kidnapped and taken from the country during his minority against the rights and privileges, is entirely unreasonable. It shows clearly that the Spaniard retains all means to infringe all conditions that could be agreed, and that in addition to the other divisions he stirs up everywhere, he also tries to draw my lord the Prince of Orange away from the States, in order to achieve the ends of his enterprises, which are thwarted by the authority, prudence and counsel of his Excellency.

13. The ordinations, decrees, edicts and resolutions taken by my lord the Archduke Matthias, his collaterals[22] and the States General, published on behalf of his Majesty, will be considered valid and legitimate, and will come into full effect as far as benefices, dignities, offices and similar things are concerned, which used to be in the power and at the normal disposal of those who occupy the position of Governor of the Provinces, but not with regard to those reserved to the particular person of the king, or with regard to those made contrary to the rights, privileges and immunities of the fatherland, both in general and in particular, or those which redound to the disadvantage or detriment of another.

The thirteenth article declares clearly enough the intention of the King's ministers regarding the general pardon discussed in the first article. For by bringing into dispute what has been done by his Highness and the States, by refusing to approve this absolutely, and by excluding those things reserved to the King, which in their view comprises all resolutions concerning religion, the demolition of castles and all other similar things, they have ample pretext to be able to accuse and condemn those who have employed themselves for the good of the country in these and like areas. As they can otherwise declare things to be to the detriment and prejudice of others, there is ample room for every sort of calumnious interpretation.

---

[21] Philip Willem, Count of Buren, the eldest son of William of Orange, was arrested in 1567 at Louvain, while studying at the University, and sent to Spain. He did not return to the Low Countries until 1596, when he came back to Brussels. He remained in the southern Netherlands.

[22] This probably refers to the Collateral Councils, such as the Council of State.

14. Similarly the magistrates, officers of towns and other places, deprived of their offices in a way that was either illegitimate or unrightful, or contrary to the privileges of the towns, or by extraordinary and unaccustomed means, are re-established and reinstated in their dignities and offices. In choosing the Magistrates in the future, it will be proceeded as before in following the rights, customs and privileges of each province, town and place so as not to abide the wrong done to anyone.

The fourteenth article tends to re-establish the bad patriots, who followed the late Don Juan or have otherwise declared themselves against their fatherland and those who have been established in dignities and offices and magistracies by the late Duke of Alva. It does not speak, however, about the good ones who have been and always will be respected and honoured by good men.

15. The authority of and the obedience to the King will in the first place be re-established and maintained as they must be, following divine and human law, the privileges, usages and customs of the country, and in accordance with the Pacification of Ghent, the following Union, the Eternal Edict and this present treaty, to the effect that they will be observed as before; so that justice be administered properly, the subjects governed in all reason, justice, peace and obedience, and this in such ways and manners as were observed according to all recollection of both the late Emperor Charles V, and his predecessors and the time of the King up till the beginning of the troubles. If authority is not re-established entirely, with the obedience of the subjects, it is impossible to maintain the people in union, concord, rightful justice, peace and tranquillity.

The re-establishment of the authority of the King as proposed by the fifteenth article tends to put back into effect the old Placards, to relight the fires, and to set up the Edicts against those of the Religion, in order to drive from their fatherland those whom it will be impossible to entrap in order to kill them cruelly, just as was done at the time of the Emperor Charles. And if this is not their intention, then to what purpose is the mention of the time of the Emperor without any exemption or restriction? As the Pacification is being held together with the Union and the Edict, it can serve no other purpose than to mislead those who still stand in awe of such a considerable treaty,

which has given the Generality of the Dutch Provinces the beginning
of their liberty.

> *16. Moreover as far as the government of the Provinces is concerned,*
> *the King will choose a Prince or Princess of the blood, who through*
> *experience will have the requisite virtues and qualities to undertake*
> *such a difficult office, and with whom the subjects should have good*
> *reason to be content. He will govern in all justice and equity, but*
> *above all in accordance with the usages, rights, customs, and privile-*
> *ges of the Provinces, including the Pacification and the Edict of the*
> *present reconciliation, as he will be bound to promise and swear.*

It is a strange thing, and one that posterity will talk about, that these
countries have a Prince who, maintaining his residence in Spain, has
been neither willing nor deigned to comply with the requests of so
many Provinces for the choice of a Governor, who would be agreeable
to them, as it is discussed in the sixteenth article; not even with a
Prince who is as close to his own blood as possible, the Archduke
Matthias of Austria, although the Provinces have such good reason,
because of the cruelties and other indignities suffered in the past, to
mistrust the Governors that it is desired to give them. Such are truly
unjust desires of Kings, who think that the people are created for the
satisfaction of their unbridled will and appetite, not to be governed in
justice with their consent and approval instead of with force. Therefore the States have asked in this respect to leave the Archduke in
Government to govern the Countries in accordance with their privileges, and according to the articles sworn by him.[23]

> *17. Each and every town, city, fortress and other place, occupied at*
> *present by one side or the other under whatever title or pretext as*
> *may be the case, together with the patrimony belonging to the King,*
> *artillery, provisions, weapons, supplies and ships will be delivered*
> *completely, entirely and without further delay to the Governor; so*
> *that he, following the advice of the Council of State, can put the*
> *places which since time immemorial have had garrisons, into the*
> *custody of native Dutch. These Dutch, in addition to and above the*

---

[23] A detailed treaty stipulated the conditions on which Matthias was accepted by the States
General on 8 December 1577 as Governor. For the articles, which clearly established
the political dominance of the States, see Kossmann and Mellink, *Texts*, pp. 141–4.

oath that one is accustomed to take to the king as natural Prince,
will take the oath and swear allegiance both to the King and the
States, to observe and maintain the present articles or whatever else
the Governor will decide to be most advisable for the service of the
King, for the benefit and security of the Provinces or for other
reasons, as it should be done and as it was before the present
troubles.

This is the principal goal of the Spaniards' designs, to have all
ammunition, every fortress, and the control of everything in their
hands, in order to be able to command absolutely at their pleasure.
This is completely against the articles of the Pacification of Ghent,
and also against the privileges of the country, which do neither allow
the Princes to put garrisons everywhere at their own pleasure, nor to
decide on matters of war and peace as it suits them. There is even less
reason for this because of what has happened in the past, where great
opportunity has been given to continual diffidence. What else could
one expect if the Ministers of the King were absolute rulers, but new
Parisian licentiousness,[24] or another day of Carnival, during which the
Duke of Alva had everybody arrested in the Netherlands who was
suspect to him in some respect? Until now the States have never
wanted to debar either the King or the Governors from the country.
They have only wanted to assure that the Provinces were governed in
accordance with the privileges and rights, and to obviate the
inconveniences in which the country has fallen in the past; all because
the Ministers of the King have governed according to their fantasies,
without any regard to the States of the country or to the common
good of the people.

18. Nonetheless the King agrees (purely for the benefit of this
reconciliation) that what has been previously collected, drawn and
taken from his patrimony or the subsidies of the people will remain
collected and received as such, while nobody will be further hounded
or prosecuted; on condition, however, that in future no similar
detention, collection, apprehension or seizure will take place.

19. With the Pacification of Ghent, the general Union of the
States and the Eternal Edict of Brussels remaining valid in their

---

[24] Probably a reference to the Massacre of St Bartholomew's Day of August 1572, during
which Huguenot leaders were killed on the orders of the French government.

entirety, the States will renounce all other alliances, accords and reciprocal agreements concluded because of the troubles, both inside and outside the Provinces.

The Queen of England and the Duke of Anjou[25] are to be included in this present treaty.

As far as remaining points regarding the completion, confirmation, publication, dissemination, and firm and perpetual observance of this Pacification are concerned, these will be negotiated if everything else has been solved and concluded.

We pass over the rest of the articles, the eighteenth, nineteenth and twentieth, for the sake of brevity, appending only that the last condition, declaring that one will discuss in greater detail the publication, confirmation and implementation when everything has been resolved, demonstrates once again what has been said elsewhere – that a door is being kept open to retreat everything, as the Prince of Parma did at the so-called ratification before Maastricht, mentioned in the first chapter of this discourse.

The Articles concerning the Religion

As regards religion, which must be very rightly highly recommended to all true Christian Princes, the King can in no way do anything else but, following in the steps of the Catholic Kings, his superiors and predecessors, to desire strongly and to command that the apostolic and Roman Catholic religion be upheld and practised in his patrimonial provinces as they have always been received and under which the subjects of the provinces have previously been so flourishing; and under which, as is also well known, both the King and his predecessors, before taking possession of the provinces, have been received under solemn oath as natural Princes. With exclusion of all others, this religion will be taught and practised freely, peacefully and without any hindrance by the provinces of the Low Countries, as the States pledged reciprocally and solemnly in their general Union, in the Eternal Edict and in several letters written to the

---

[25] By the 1578 Treaty of Mons Francois, the Duke of Anjou and brother of the French king, Henry III, had promised military assistance to the States General. In return the States declared that Anjou was the first candidate to succeed Philip II as lord of the country, if the States should decide to abjure the Spanish king.

King, both before and after the beginning of the present troubles, and as they have also written to his Imperial Majesty. The result is that in a matter of such importance they cannot contravene in any way their own writings without great blame and without subverting the whole political state. And as far as Holland, Zeeland and the town of Bommel are concerned, this is referred to the decree of the treaty of the Pacification of Ghent, yet on the condition that the Roman Catholic religion will be re-established in the towns and places where it was practised at the time of this treaty.

As for the subjects of other provinces of the Low Countries comprised in the present treaty who have abandoned the Roman Catholic religion, the Catholic King, having regard to the present state of the Low Countries, grants them by his Royal Commissioner the possibility and permission to remain and live in these provinces without any punishment or harassment on account of the placards promulgated on the issue of religion. These will remain suspended until the King or his Governor-General, upon the counsel of the States, lawfully and properly assembled at a secure place where they can speak out freely, has decided otherwise regarding the Placards' moderation. On condition, however, that such subjects should meanwhile refrain from scandal and emotion and from any service or practice of any other religion but the Roman Catholic, but they will enjoy all their goods, both movable and immovable, their rights and assets. Regardless of the quality of these goods they may transport them elsewhere, sell or alienate them as they see fit. And in case they should like to retain their goods, they can, should they be absent, choose at their own discretion Catholic receivers for the supervision, administration and receipt of these goods. Moreover they can return to the provinces as often as they want (while living, however, in a Catholic way, behaving as Catholic persons should). Such visits and the power to administer one's goods will be permitted in good faith to everybody on condition that they have informed of such an intention the pastors, officers and magistrates of the places to which they will return to.

By nature of this Royal permission everyone may see clearly that the King wishes nothing less than the confiscation of the goods, the ruin and loss of his subjects. Neither does he intend to oppress them with the rigour of placards, given that he is very well prepared to moderate and mitigate them on counsel and advice of the States and, similarly, to do everything that is proper for a human and Christian Prince to further the honour of God, and the peace and tranquillity of the provinces.

Let us discuss the point of religion, as resumed above. Who does not see that the intention of the King of Spain and his ministers is to extirpate the Reformed religion completely, as he explicitly declares that he wants to have the Roman religion maintained to the exclusion of every other one? Whether he is well founded in this respect, is argued elsewhere and has been discussed by many others. The same argument could be used by the Turk, the Muscovite, the Tartar and other Princes, who have also been received by their subjects in the religion they practised, on which they also took an oath to their Prince. However, it does not therefore follow that their subjects have promised always to remain in the same religion, or that their faith and religion is good. And as far as the Union and the Edict are concerned, these were not accepted by all provinces alike, with the result that these alleged Unions and Edicts, which do not include all provinces, could not serve as a general peace but as the beginning of new, even more dangerous discord, as was in fact shown by the late Don Juan, who had planned to renew the war against my lord the Prince of Orange and the States of Holland and Zeeland under the pretext of the said Union and Edict.

Moreover, a proper reading of the Union and Edict shows them not to prohibit the practice of the Reformed religion. Also the Union was not acknowledged absolutely but under restriction, by the delegates of the States of Guelders, Friesland and the Ommelands.[26] In addition the delegates of the States of Holland and Zeeland have protested explicitly against the Union, and my lord the Prince and the States of Holland and Zeeland have sent a truly solemn protest and declaration to the assembly of the States General against the Edict, which they do not want to accept, except under conditions, whose adoption has in no way been accepted. As for the letters of the States, written to the King, the States, being still assembled and gathered, have sufficiently clarified the intention and the true interpretation of these letters in a discourse, upon which I am drawing, called *True Answer to the letters*

---

[26] The so-called 'Ommelands' was the area surrounding the northern town of Groningen. Throughout the sixteenth century Groningen and its 'Ommelands' were in continuous dispute with each other.

patents and abusive arguments of Don Juan of Austria, given at Heure on the 15th day of February 1578.[27]

The Union serves to no purpose if one wants to understand it in the Spanish sense to debar every other practice of religion, but to an outright Inquisition which is even more rigorous than the Spanish. By virtue of it the late Don Juan wanted to force all subjects to declare their faith and Religion, making them sign the Union as token of faithfulness to the Roman Catholic religion, so that those discovered to be of the Religion, could be subjected to a general massacre. By giving the same interpretation to the Union, one wants to accomplish the same with the above article, for it was made in order to maintain the Roman Catholic religion, to the exclusion of all others. The oath all will be forced to take should be further added here, in order to confirm the said intention of the King, making it clearly known to everybody that they do not seek in any way to remedy the inconveniences, but rather to increase them and to enable the King to decide on the moderation of the Placards on advice of the States (which he is not obliged to follow), which means that instead of burning all alive, they will be hanged or murdered in some other way. That one should meanwhile refrain from any scandal means that one should do everything the Spaniards command. In other words, if one passes an idol without paying it honour, this will be a scandal worthy of death. And the verdict that everybody of the Religion is exiled, has already been pronounced and declared. The rich may sell their goods or have them administered by Catholics, by whom they are taken care of as if they were people without will and who, according to their law, are not obliged to remain faithful to them. The others, that is to say a million poor people, will be forced to go begging everywhere with their wives and children. For as they have nothing else but their craft and trade, which they neither can nor know how to practice anywhere else, are they not destined to die of misery and poverty? Just like a great part of those driven out of 1566, who could make themselves a good living with their hands and crafts in their proper fatherland, but in other countries were afflicted by calamities worse than death itself. The indignity of such iniquitous things does not allow me to demonstrate more fully the tyrannical pretensions of such an unjust

---

[27] The *Responce veritable aux lettres patentes et persuasions subsives de Jan d'Austrice, données à Heure le XV. iour de Feburier M.D.LXXVIII*, was published in Antwerp by Plantin's office. The author of this treatise, also published in Dutch, is unknown.

demand, but I reassure myself that those who wish to be called Belgians or low Germans, lovers of their fatherland, will not, for fear of a war, allow persons who do not have the slightest knowledge of the foundation of the Reformed religion and of the just and equitable desire of those dedicated to the Religion, to do such horrible and abominable things. They do not want to deliver their brothers to the slaughter, or have them hounded out and exiled as was seen in the past.

Enough reasons are put forward by this small discourse to point out why the States General cannot approve the accord reached by the provinces of Artois, Hainaut and Lille, Douai and Orchies. For not only are individual agreements dangerous and harmful, in that they hamper good mutual understanding and cause dissension, but one also finds that this accord precludes all practice of the Reformed religion; that all bad patriots are re-established in their state and office; that the rebuilding of citadels is allowed only with the approval of the States of those particular provinces who will be under the command of the Governor; that this Governor will be an Italian; that the return of the Spaniards is allowed as well, should the King be involved in a foreign war, which he can start whenever he likes, for the opposite has not been negotiated, and neither have the privileges of the country been reserved in this matter: along with several other prejudicial conditions, as appears from reading it. Add to this that, as mentioned at the beginning of this treatise, the Prince of Parma has not yet approved the articles, and one may very well presume that the sting is in the tail.

Above it has been demonstrated briefly that conditions are proposed on part of the King, which the States cannot accept in any way. On their part, however, only conditions necessary for the preservation of the liberty of the country have been demanded. Nonetheless, their humble requests and supplications have borne no fruit at all.

It would be a good idea to touch briefly on the endeavours they have made to obtain from their Prince, the King of Spain, a good, secure and salutary peace. One should know, while on this subject, that the States, although they have discussed it, have not been able or did not dare to send any distinguished embassy to Spain, as my Lords the Marquis of Bergen and the Lord of Montigny, having been sent there, were, against every human law, detained, held prisoner and later put to death. To the best of their abilities they have written many letters to his Majesty, begging him to be willing to have compassion and pity for his subjects, presenting to him all the changes which should occur if he were to persist in his decisions. They have also humbly begged the emperor to be so gracious as to mediate the accord with his brother the King, both by means of several letters to this end written to his Imperial Majesty and also by a distinguished embassy, a task of which the Count of Nieuwenaar[28] has taken charge at the request of the States. The States have implored the same through special ambassadors, namely the Lords of Aubigny and Mansart,[29] to the King of France, the Queen Mother, my Lord the Duke of Anjou and also several times, both by letters and by the dignified embassy of the Marquis of Havré, her Majesty of England.[30] For this purpose her Majesty of England has also sent her ambassadors to Spain. To the same end the late King of Portugal and his uncle the Cardinal, who is the present King,[31] has also been beseeched by letters, which were handed over to his agents. In short, the States have left nothing undone, which they imagined could have helped to address themselves to the very person of the King himself, in order to induce him to be so gracious as to accord tolerable peace conditions to his subjects. And as the King has sent here the Baron of Selles, the States have also continuously offered him to begin a parley for peace. The Prince of Orange, the Duke of Aerschot, and several other lords have often negotiated with him and the States have since deputed the late Count of Bossu, the Lord of Oirschot from the house of Merode, the Lord Louvigny and many others to enter into a parley with the Baron of Selles in the town of Malines, which they have carried out. However, instead of proposing some ways to arrive at an agreement, he has, amongst other things, declared that his

[28] Adolf, Count of Nieuwenaer and Meurs, was later to become Stadholder of Utrecht, Overijssel and Guelders. He died in 1589.

[29] Aubigny and Mansart served as envoys of the States General to France from the autumn of 1576. They played an important role in developing contacts with the Duke of Anjou.

[30] Charles-Philippe of Croy (1549–1613), Marquis of Havré, was the brother of the Duke of Aerschot. After he had served Philip II in a similar capacity he worked as an envoy to England for the States in 1578, negotiating financial and military aid with the English government.

[31] After King Sebastian of Portugal was killed on 4 August 1578 during the battle of Alcazar-Kebir in Morocco, a long-term succession crisis began, due to Philip II's claims to the Portuguese throne. When Sebastian's successor, his great-uncle Cardinal Henry, died in February 1580, Philip invaded Portugal; he was formally recognized as king in April 1581.

Majesty was in no mind to uphold the Pacification of Ghent, which, as mentioned before, his Majesty still refuses to do. Later, when from the side of his Imperial Majesty hope had been raised that one could reach an agreement in the town of Louvain, the States immediately showed themselves to be ready and willing, deputing several prominent persons.

Moreover they have requested that the ambassadors of his Imperial Majesty, of the King of France and of the Queen of England should employ their authority, thus showing the good hope and great desire they had to reach peace. However, instead of negotiating, Don Juan (who had nonetheless made it look as if he from his side was also willing to work towards peace) after several delays, would declare that the King was to send the Duke of Terranova and that he had passed all negotiations to his Imperial Majesty, who would send neutral ambassadors for this purpose to Cologne. The outcome has been that since that moment the arrival of the ambassadors has been continually awaited; in the end the Princes and Lords who are at present negotiating the Pacification of Cologne were appointed by the emperor. And how the States could have mistrusted such ambassadors, how much reason they had to excuse themselves for not entering the peace negotiations! – for they were not such as his Imperial Majesty had promised to send, all being the principal ecclesiastical Lords, bound to their religion, as experience has also shown, so that they did not want to deal with the issue of religion, even though it was the principal problem to be settled, as they could very well have been aware before they left their houses. Thus it is, however, that in order to avoid all obstacles and not to block any way which could lead the inhabitants of these countries to a good peace, the States on their part have immediately requested my lord the Duke of Aerschot, as principal lord of the country, and in addition to his lordship the Duke, several other Lords and renowned persons, to attend the negotiations, after they had first assembled the States in greater number to deliberate seriously on the conditions of peace, which eventually were determined by common pinion at three separate readings.[32]

What has happened since the last negotiations is partly clarified

---

[32] Other members of the States' delegation were the Abbots of St Gertrude and Marolles, Gaspar Schetz, Lord of Grobbendonck and the Frisian humanist and lawyer Aggaeus of Albada, whose annotated *Acts* of the Cologne negotiations, published in 1581, became one of the highlights of the political literature of the Dutch Revolt.

hereby, and it is to be hoped that if the negotiations have finished light will be thrown on everything. Here I do not want to talk about the efforts of the States to obtain, in order to facilitate the peace also in this way, the assistance of their neighbours, such as the emperor, the Princes of the Empire, both individually and also at the Diet of the Empire as assembled at Worms,[33] the circle of Westphalia, the States of the Country of Liège and even the King of France, Monseigneur the Duke of Anjou and the Queen of England; to the extent that all these efforts alone of the States would require a big volume. I think that what has been said suffices to demonstrate that the States have not rejected any means in order to accomplish peace. For in addition to having proposed equitable conditions, they have also done their duty in submitting these to the King. They have used all possible manner of requests, supplications and intercessions to remove the subjects from the necessity of war. The States are not, and never have been, to blame for the fact that the peace, so desired by all, has not been effectuated, and that the negotiations set up for this purpose have not yet produced any result.

Having discussed and demonstrated in the briefest possible way that the King has little desire to grant a good and secure peace to his subjects, and that the States of the country have made every possible effort to obtain it, one should examine successively what might prompt the King to negotiate and to enter into conferences on a Pacification, as he is already quite decided not to grant it. First, as the King and his Council know very well that the nature of men is strongly inclined to peace and that they are slow in taking resolutions on the contributions necessary for war, they feign and will feign continually and deliberately to be willing to negotiate, in order to prevent that decisions necessary and appropriate for the necessity of the time are taken, whether in general or in particular. And in order to further confirm the hope of those who let themselves be deceived, they made it look, under the false mantle and pretext of peace, as if they are now willing to observe the Pacification of Ghent and to concede some false liberty of conscience. This has been refuted

---

[33] Marnix van St Aldegonde was sent to Worms to plead the States' case. His oration at the Diet was published in 1578 under the title *Oraison des ambassadeurs du serenissime prince Matthias archiduc d'austriche &c. Gouverneur des pais bas: & des Estats generaux desdits pais*, by Plantin's office in Antwerp.

sufficiently yet as summarily as possible by this discourse. The same applies to their willingness to withdraw the Spaniards and other adherents, as if evil proceeds only from a handful of soldiers of Spanish nationality, rather than from the bad and tyrannical laws, which they want to introduce once again, implement and maintain in the country.

The Duchess of Parma found no difficulty in retracting all her promises in 1567 without the presence of the Spaniards, who were sent by the king as and when it pleased him. And after Don Juan had made the Spaniards leave, he called them back and had them returned to the country at will. The Prince of Parma will do the same, if he has them withdrawn, which seems in no way likely. Such promises are of no other use but to make good cheer, as it is said, and to create under this fine pretext the possibility of starting talks with particular towns. He will even be quite content to negotiate with these towns on the condition that the agreement will not come into effect until the Spaniards have left. But why? Because in this way they are drawn into talks, whose effect will always be discord. Those who are confederated cannot, under any pretext whatsoever, negotiate with the enemy about a reconciliation, which concerns the generality. Likewise they cannot pledge themselves to remain neutral, for he who wants to be neutral abandons the confederates, whom he is bound to assist, and eventually he will be, incidentally, the prey of either the one side or the other.

Let us turn to the other advantages the King gains from these so-called peace negotiations. I contend that in addition to the fact that he thwarts all good decisions, due to the vain hope of peace that is concerned, as all lightly believe in things good, desirable and wished for, the King also has the possibility to deal freely with one or the other, to win them over with promises of money, positions and false inducements. Above all the principal benefit the King hopes to obtain from the peace negotiations is the increase of discord and division. As he knows very well that it is not easy for the Provinces to be of the same opinion as far as the articles of peace are concerned, he assures himself that, just as religion has been a cause of dissension between some of them, the diversity of opinion regarding the articles and conditions of peace will have the same effect of discord amongst others. Do we not see the beginnings in the towns of Malines and Aalst, who let themselves be seduced completely, and the danger in the town of Bois-le-Duc, that it should be misled by the same route. And as the Prince of Parma has made no final agreements yet with the Provinces of Artois and Hainaut, Lilles, Douai and Orchies, the supposed general negotiations and the hope this Prince gives them, is one single grand design to keep these provinces devoted to him. Given this one should surely weigh up the dangers of these particular talks, for even the smallest opening to specific treaties will lead step by step to complete discord. Once the enemy has accomplished that one is willing to lend him an ear, he will easily achieve the aim of his designs. The provinces of Artois, Hainaut, Lille, Douai and Orchies have also been tricked in this way. Until now they have not sought to force the other provinces to abandon the religious peace. On the contrary, they have often protested and declared that they surely wished the King would consent it, and they themselves have entreated it. To this effect they asked a resolution that would leave them free to maintain the religious peace. Thus they found convenient what the States had given them. Nonetheless, by these talks they have, until this point, let themselves be led astray to the extent that it is to be feared they are now willing, against all law and reason, to assist the Spaniard in making war against the other provinces so that these will be obliged by force to abandon the practice of the Reformed religion. As demonstrated above these provinces simply cannot do this. It should suffice then that they are left in the real liberty they desire, just as they have no right to prescribe the law to the other provinces, especially not when it is evidently unjust. There are plenty of examples from their neighbours, who, after having shed so much blood, were eventually content to permit the practice of the Reformed religion. Since they have not been brought to their senses by such vivid reasons as the results they have seen and still see daily, there is no doubt that they will bring upon themselves the miseries, calamities and misfortunes of this war, unless they quickly change their minds, quit the unfortunate society of the Spaniards, created to oppress their compatriots and brothers, and reunite and recombine with them in order to provide, in good mutual understanding, by common hand what is beneficial for the good and preservation of the whole country in general.

Thus in no way should one allow oneself to be misled to the point of starting some communication separated from that of the Generality of the country. Neither should one even make particular agreements with the enemy, even though he would be willing to grant one single, particular province everything it could ever ask for. For one should not abandon his brothers. One should also look not only to the present but also to the future, and should reflect that by means of these particular treaties the enemy aspires to nothing else than the separation of the Provinces. So that, having broken their good mutual understanding, he should have the means to command each of them at will, to cast them ultimately into intolerable servitude, forcing them also to submit the means for making war against their neighbours, their compatriots and friends, with whom they have no quarrel at all. These then are the pretensions of the King and the ends to which the so-called negotiations are directed, whereas, on the contrary, had he loved and desired the good and prosperity of the subjects, he should have proposed such conditions of peace, as were equally acceptable to all provinces and which could have comprised them all, without any wish to dismember the provinces, which have been closely allied and united for so many years and which, with common forces have resisted the most powerful monarchs of Christendom in various times and seasons. This should be given mature thought by those who are thus in flight and who have separated themselves so lightly.

Also because of its location, the convenience of its places and rivers and the necessity of commerce, the Low Countries have and should have an alliance closer and a mutual understanding better than any other country or republic. The calamities the war brings to one place, will by consequence damage the whole rest of the country, so that those who wage war against their neighbours will do so as against their own body and bowels, and will ruin their own subjects. Meanwhile they will be forced to receive garrisons of Spaniards, or of others, whom the Spaniards will introduce whenever they please. Who believes that the Spaniard will leave, or that, if he leaves, he will not leave bands worse than himself, with the assurance of being able to return when the time will come to subject the country completely, misleads himself greatly. He acts like one who wants to believe that he would find people who are so stupid that they would make war and suffer a thousand hazards and travails in order to hand over the possessions and usage of their conquest to their very enemies. The provinces of Artois, Hainaut, Lille, Douai and Orchies may be unaware that they have been enemies of the Spaniards, and that they are still considered as such by the Spaniards, whatever they feign. Let us leave all of them there in great diffidence, in the firm hope that God will soon open the eyes of the inhabitants of these Provinces, of which the greater part are of good affection, having not the least intention to make war with their neighbours; and that they will soon have means to discover the false practices, by which the adherents of the Spaniards have let themselves be misled; that the true patriots, and those who have shown such affection in the past to the fatherland against the Spaniard, having known that he attempts only to surprise and entrap them, will in time take other better counsel, and reunite with the rest of the Provinces, for in the long run the Spaniard will well know how to find the opportunities. Meanwhile the Provinces which still remain united should also, from their side, be on their guard. And as they are strong enough in countries, in men, in riches, in commodities of all sorts, both sea- and river-ports, and town fortresses, nothing else is needed but a good and firm resolution in the defence of such a good and equitable cause, as they have maintained right until now. If they do this, their enemies will soon see by experience, they have not yet fallen so low that they do not have the means to bring down evil, fall and ruin on the heads of those who should seek to bring it upon them. As God did not desert the countries of Holland and Zeeland laid low at other times, but nonetheless remained determined and constant in the defence of their liberty and their just cause, so likewise one should rest and confide in God, who is the God of forces and armies, without losing one's nerve because, for a time, the enemies seem to enjoy fortunate success and seem to prosper in their tyrannical designs. For soon one will see that things will change, and they will be put back in the best order, perfect harmony and obedience; that the enemy will not reap the fruits of his designs, as he desires, having always in his mind Psalm 37 of the prophet David, which teaches us not to marvel at the prosperity of the wicked.

> Fret not yourself, if during this life
> you see the wicked prosper often:
> and do not envy the wicked who are doing well:
> for in the end they will go to ruin,
> they will soon fade like the grass.[34]

---

[34] This final poem, featuring only in the *Brief Discourse* and not in the *Petit Traicté*, was evidently inspired by the theme and wording of Psalm 37.

POLITICAL EDUCATION

CONTAINING VARIOUS AND VERY IMPORTANT ARGUMENTS AND PROOFS,

founded on God's Word, and on written
Imperial Rights and on authorities of pagan authors,
which demonstrate forcefully that not without cause
and very good motives, His Excellency and the
States General of the united Netherlands
request to forsake by means of a new oath
the King of Spain and his adherents,
and to promise, against him,
Homage and Fidelity to the present Government,
the Country and one another,
because of which this Oath
should be taken and solemnized
by each one (wishing to be a good Patriot)

And in order that no one pretends ignorance of the Oath,
the Form of the Oath is enclosed here.

Cicero, De Officiis, Book III

'For our ancestors were of opinion that no bond was more
effective in guaranteeing good faith than an oath'.[1]

Hebrews, 6:16

Men indeed swear by one who is greater than themselves, and
and in all their disputes an oath is the final
confirmation.

At Malines,
BY JACOB HEYNDRIX.
1582.

---

[1] Cicero, *De Officiis*, Book 3, chapter 31, section 111 (Cambridge, Mass. (Loeb edition), 1975, p. 390).

NOBLE, HONOURABLE AND MOST PRUDENT LORDS

The sincere patriot wishes salute and welfare to the Lord Governor, Bailiff, Burgomaster, Aldermen, and Council of the City and Jurisdiction of Malines, being principal advocates of the fatherland and loyal patriots.

As nobody has ever been able to behave himself in his profession in such a way that he suited and served everybody, for what seems good to one normally seems bitter and reprehensible to another, there is no doubt that my work will not please everyone. It will be praised and despised according to the diversity of humours and passions of men. Moreover, as nothing is so sure as that there will always be found Momists and Zoilists,[2] I cannot but expect reprimand if something is uneven, and envy, when the matter is found plain. Nonetheless, I can neither approve of passing my time in silence and negligence nor of employing it so that I would serve or benefit no one but myself. Considering 'quod homines hominem causa sint geniti',[3] that is, that one man is created for the cause of the other, that we should not live for ourselves alone, but also for the fatherland and posterity, I have

---

[2] Momists were followers of Momus, a son of the Night according to the Greek poet Hesiod, the God of mockery and criticism, who became the personification for fault-finding and unfair critique. Zoilists are followers of Zoilus, a fourth-century critic of Homerian poetry who became proverbial for his narrow-mindedness.

[3] This is a quote from Cicero, *De Officiis*, 1. 7. 22 (Loeb edition, p. 22) and/or Plato, *Epistle IX (to Archytas)*, 358A – see Plato, *Timaeus, Critios, Cleitophon* ... (Cambridge, Mass. (Loeb edition), 1966), p. 603 – to whom Cicero himself refers.

thought it advisable and indeed necessary briefly to put into writing and to print this Political Education, and Instruction, concerning the new oath, which his Princely Excellence[4] and the States General of the united Provinces of these Netherlands have conceived, in the form set out below, and have ordered to be solemnized and sworn by every good loyal subject and patriot, so that the government, the country and we together would be caused to resist, with considered courage, the Spanish tyranny and the mischief and perjury of the Malcontents,[5] as a consequence of which our towns would be better secured; moreover that all good subjects who raise objections against taking the oath, shall be instructed about the moral rightfulness and the usefulness, righteousness, lawfulness and necessity of this oath, so that they may know its origin and purpose, and with what confidence and clear conscience they not only may but also should take the oath. I hope that my work will be taken at its best (although not all matters are as thoroughly discussed as the subjects require) by all lovers of the fatherland, and those who love their liberty, wives, children, body and good, and that its mistakes may be forgiven, if only because of the good assiduity and great affection which I bear and have always borne my government, his Princely Excellence, the fatherland, my fellow citizens and their welfare. So God Almighty knows, may He give your noble, honourable, wise and most prudent Lords his Godly mercy and a long and godly life.

From Malines, 13 January 1582.

---

[4] His Princely Excellence refers to William of Orange.

[5] Troops, mostly commanded by Walloon nobles, who mutinied in 1578, as they were horrified by the rise of radical Calvinism in Flanders (with Ghent as epicentre) and Brabant, and who disagreed with the policy of William of Orange. From October 1578 there was an open war between the Ghent Calvinists and the Malcontents, which strongly contributed to the disruption of the frail unity created by the Pacification of Ghent of 1576.

One says with a common proverb, 'There are as many opinions as there are men', and 'Each bird is known by its note'. Isocrates, however, with whom I sympathize, says that all those wanting to judge an unusual and questionable matter, on which a lot can be said and debated on both sides, should be free of all affections, which can easily confute reason.[6] For a mind driven by passion is shrouded with such a dark mist that it can neither see nor understand what course in the matters under deliberation is the most expedient and apt. However, a free mind, in which an unrestrained intellect governs, can see and observe, sharper than a tapeworm as they say, what is honest, profitable, righteous, lawful, proper, possible, feasible, and necessary in such matters. For experience shows that eyes overcome by heavy humours, catarrhs and other illnesses can scarcely see what is lying on the nose. Similarly the mind, inflamed by the fire of passion, cannot judge rightly, neither in private nor in common matters. Thus the Emperor Theodosius, when he erred in ordering the killing of a great multitude to take revenge for a knight who had been killed, opened his ears and gave place to anger (which is an evil counsellor), and therefore acted unfairly, without profit, rightlessly, unlawfully and wrongly, as he himself (having understood the reasons) repented in sorrow afterwards. Therefore, Gaius Caesar is greatly to be praised: he, when counsel was held concerning which penalties one should use to punish those guilty of Lucius Sergius Catiline's conspiracy,[7]

---

[6] In this section the author probably dwells especially upon the *Antidosis*, a discourse on Isocrates' own trial which the latter wrote when he was 82, in 354–3 BC.

[7] The story of the conspiracy of Catiline, an impoverished Roman patrician who tried to seize power in Rome in 63 BC, was the subject of Sallust's famous work *The War with*

argued in full meeting that each should judge without passion, saying 'it is necessary that all those (lord senators) who have to judge questionable matters, should be free from hatred, friendship, anger and mercy, for it is difficult for the mind to discern the truth, where such affections dominate, and no man has ever been able to serve both desire and utility'. And this is the cause for saying that no one may be both witness and judge in a conflict. Therefore it is also normal in all courts that judges, if they are related to one of the parties, rise and leave when their case is being heard, although, God save the mark, this [rule] is not always fully observed. I therefore pray to each to take this work for the best and to judge it without partiality.

It is known to all that his Princely Excellence, the States of the country and the country's council have thought it advisable, for the greater security of the country and to remove all mistrust, to present to all inhabitants of the country, of whatever state, condition or quality these might be (I mean male persons and those who can carry arms), a certain new oath, which has the following form.

The Form of the Oath

I hereby swear that from now on I will no more respect, obey or accept as my Prince or overlord the King of Spain, but that I will leave this King of Spain and consider myself dismissed of all duties and bonds, with which I may have been tied to him previously in any way on behalf of this country. I furthermore promise and swear to be loyal, obedient and generous to the United Netherlands, e.g. the Provinces of Brabant, Guelders, Flanders, Holland, Zeeland, etc., and also to the country's council and government established by the States of the aforesaid Provinces. And I will render them, after my power, all help and assistance against the aforesaid King of Spain, his adherents and all other enemies of the country, and furthermore do all what good and faithful inhabitants and countrymen of the aforesaid united countries owe their government and fatherland, so help me God Almighty. The above being discussed and decided in the meeting of the States General of the United Netherlands, in The Hague, 29 July 1581.

Under which was written 'By decree of the aforesaid States', signed Houfflijn.[8]

Catiline. The following sentences are a direct quote from this work. See Sallust, 'Bellum Catilinae' in *Sallust* (Cambridge, Mass. (Loeb edition), 1985), 51. 1–4 (p. 88).

[8] Jean Houfflijn was one of the clerks of the States General.

As I can readily understand, this puts various persons in great problems. Some take the oath with anxious heart and frustrated mind, others under protest, a few refuse it flatly, leaving their post and office, to their great detriment, disgrace and confusion.

I, on the contrary, find the form of the oath honest, profitable, righteous, lawful, proper, possible, feasible and that it be taken (as requested by the government of the country) necessary. I find, after good deliberation and speaking without passion, that one should accept this form of oath without exception and that all should be summoned to take it. For I am sure that with this oath the common affairs of these Netherlands are greatly glorified. To prove this, the purpose and aim of requesting this oath by the government of the country are to be considered, which are (as said) that those who have the government of the country in their hands will thus more strongly subordinate and tie the hearts of the subjects to themselves; that those who until now have worn masks, will be known, so that there will remain no cause for difference and distrust; that those who do not know (although the streets are still red because of the blood shed by them) the tyranny of the King of Spain, his bloodhounds, and all our enemies, be they Malcontents or Biencontents, will learn to know them and (as necessity requires) have the boldness to resist the enemy so that the country, government and towns will be better secured.

What is more honourable than to be loyal to and to advocate, after God, father and mother, one's fatherland? He who can bear to watch with good and patient eyes as his own fatherland is disturbed, tormented, trampled on, burnt, spoilt and torn apart by rebellious inhabitants, perjurers and traitors, by tyrants or by strange soldiers: he must be an abject, infamous and depraved man, for by rebellion and war all good teachings, wonderful arts, and virtues are removed and, on the contrary, force, violence, murder, theft, usurpation, arson, robbery, cursing, disgrace and perjury are established. In short, every evil, big as it may be, stems from this.

Oh! let those who remain in such foolishness remember and consider that they still glorify and fear the King of Spain, and therefore neither want nor dare to forsake him by oath, nor to take an oath of fidelity to those who risk body, good and blood for their welfare. Those who do so have to be convinced in their hearts, that they do not promote honour but an unfair cause, and that they love their true enemy, indeed their mortal enemy, more than their protectors. For to those whom I love and desire to assist loyally, I will confirm such by oath. Therefore everyone who is honourable amplifies and takes the ordained oath, as one ought to. For thereby, as is proper for the good and loyal citizen, a steady union is made with the government to fight against the King of Spain and his mercenaries. Doing otherwise we would doubtless not escape the wry distress of infamy, and would advocate an unjust matter.

After all, nothing brings more dishonour than when somebody brings or seeks to bring himself into eternal slavery, and his fellow citizens into the hands of the lions and murderers; which would not happen if they were to remain faithful to each other. The Count of Egmont would not have been found guilty, nor would the innocent Count of Hoorne have been put in such disgrace and scornful death, if he had remained faithful to his Excellency and the allies of the country. On the contrary he would have remained victorious, with great honour and to the everlasting glory of his house. He lost the great honour which he had previously obtained on various occasions on the day he lost his head, which (so was said) had frequently made France tremble. The Banneret of Heze[9] would not have been executed by the sword of those he served, if he had not, despite sworn fidelity, defected and sought to damage, against his conscience and mind, those who rendered him but honour and virtue.

Just as an organ or any other instrument, which is improperly tuned, cannot give good resonance, and just as a wagon cannot run straightly if the horses do not pull equally hard, so a country cannot prosper if the community is not in tune with the government.

For Cicero says in *Lelio* 'Dispares mores disparia studia sequuntur, quorum dissimilitudo dissociat amicitias',[10] that is, 'Disparate manners follow disparate desires, and this disparity breaks up all friendships'. Here one sees how greatly he recommends unity, the maintenance of friendship. That is why, he furthermore says, the pious cannot concur with the impious, for there is a distance as great as can be between them, both in manners and desires. We should therefore be united in oath and in cloth, and those who do not desire this should be suspected as impious and unfaithful.

[9] William of Hoorne, Lord of Heze (1553–80) had been commander of a regiment for the States General. He was executed in 1580.

[10] Cicero, 'Lealius De Amicitia', 20. 74 in Cicero, *De Senectute, De Amicitia, De Divinatione* (Cambridge, Mass. (Loeb edition), 1959), p. 183. The translation of this passage gives it a specific twist. The Loeb translation is as follows: 'Difference of character is attended by difference of taste and it is this diversity of taste that severs friendships.'

Indas Machabaeus,[11] a prominent chief among the children of Israel, and an excellent great lover of his fatherland said, trying to encourage his soldiers and citizens to fight the enemy: 'They come against us unjustly with an army, to spoil and to rob us and our wives and children, but we fight for our life and laws, and God will squander them for us.' And the citizens themselves admonished each other, saying: 'Let us take this oppression away from our people, and fight for our people and our religion.'

Joab, that powerful and severe chief of God's people, spoke to his brother, when he was about to fight the Syrians, saying: 'If the Syrians are stronger than me, you shall come to help me, and if the children of Ammon are stronger than thee, then I shall give you help and assistance. Therefore be strong and let us fight strongly for our people and for the towns of our God'.[12]

The Evangelist John, admonishing us to help each other in trial and tribulation, says in the third chapter of his first missive:[13] 'By this we know love, that he laid down his life for us, and we ought to lay down our lives for our brethren.' The soldiers who fight for the sake of money, pursuing injustice and war and risking their lives, will judge the citizens who leave their fatherland; because they risk their lives for a little money, whereas these cowardly and brooding citizens do not want to put their lives in danger for government, wives, children, goods, blood, freedom and fatherland.

In case anyone is not convinced by these wonderful examples and testimonies, let him look at what the pagans thought of this subject. The famous orator Cicero says in the first book of Offices that those who have tried to oppress their own fatherland, are all the more execrable, and that one should fight for the fatherland until death. These are his words: 'But one native land embraces all our love; and who that is true would hesitate to give his life for her, if by his death he could render her a service. So much the more execrable are those monsters who have torn their fatherland to pieces with every form of outrage and who are and have been engaged in compassing her utter destruction'.[14] If Cicero thus condemned Caesar and Anthony for infamy and dishonour, because they did not champion their father-

---

[11] A prominent member of the famous dynasty that governed the Jewish people between 166 and 63 BC, bringing them political and religious independence.

[12] 2 Samuel 10:11–12.

[13] The reference is to 1 John 3:16.

[14] Cicero, *De Officiis* 1. 17. 57 (p. 60).

land but sought to suppress it, how much more should the Malcontents be condemned now, who still wear their masks in some places and in whose bodies, if one were to cut them open, one would find Spanish hearts. Neither can those who oppose the aforesaid oath escape from this distress of infamy and dishonour, for in doing so they declare to credit the King of Spain (who is the sworn mortal enemy of the country) with more advantage than disadvantage, and do not regard him as an enemy.

Marcus Curtius, a brave and noble Roman hero, considering the great honour that lies in championing the fatherland and, by contrast, what blame there is for those who do not do so, did not hold back from throwing himself into a cave (to rescue those of Rome from a stinking death).[15]

Codrus, the laudable King of Athens, having understood from Appollinis's response that the city of Athens could not be saved but by his death, and that the enemies had ordered not to wound the King's body, took off his royal clothes, and put on common dress and, thus approaching the enemy, forced someone to kill him.[16]

The two brothers Philaeni were bent more on not shortening the boundaries of their fatherland than on extending their lives, and so they let themselves be buried alive.[17] Will not these pagans and others, too many to list, disgrace and accuse of infamy, those who pretend, but with a false and double pretence, to be patriots? The evil which they wish their fatherland lies next to their hearts. Some act thus of ignorance, some because of a fierce and evil mind, and some because they would rather have their lives than to swear as the enemy the King of Spain and his slaves, the Malcontents.

However, the latter is God's true counsel, who has induced the government to do so, in order that one may know those who previously kept the joker up their sleeves and so, to the unspeakable damage and disadvantage of the common good, were covertly ambidextrous. This has been found by experience of la Motte, the Count of Lalaing, Montigny, and others, and most recently of the

---

[15] The story of this Roman epic hero is told by Livy in Book 7, chapter 3, nos. 1–6 of his *Ab urbe Conditio*.

[16] The author may have found Codrus' story in Cicero's works, particularly in *De Natura Deorum* 3. 49 and *De Finibus* 5. 62.

[17] The story of the Philaeni brothers who sacrificed themselves for Carthage's fate is told by Sallust in *Bellum Iugurthinum* (The War with Jugurtha) 79. 5–10. See *Sallust* (Cambridge, Mass. (Loeb edition), 1985), p. 301.

Marquis of Bergen,[18] of whom one can only hope that they will no longer let him blind the eyes.

I think I have proven sufficiently with parables, examples, sentences and testimonies how honourable, praiseworthy and laudable the aforesaid oath is, and, by contrast, what dishonour they bring to themselves who refuse to take it, namely, that they should be despised as unfaithful to their fatherland and as rebels against their government. For it is difficult to fight against the soldiers of the King for a man, who does not want to forsake him and declare him his enemy by oath.

In order to pursue my argument properly, it is now my task to prove how profitable it is to solemnize and swear this oath. For this will be an important argument and reason to content those who look for problems (like the button in the piping) in the oath and to move them to swear it frankly.

It is known all over the world what great harm our Countries have suffered as when, in taking up arms against the Spanish tyranny, they did not expressly resolve to seek the King and his men of arms with considered courage and to strike where one could, but instead of an offensive war, merely waged a defensive war. At the quarters in Templou the States of the country had together an enormous amount of people, both on foot and on horseback, well equipped with arms and all sorts of amunition, but what was done with it? Nothing but that the flat country was spoilt, the householder emaciated, and all sort of insolence caused. There the means of the country have been consumed. The Count of Lalaing, la Motte, Gognies, de Frezin, the Vice Count of Ghent, Montigny, Heze, Egmont[19] and similar fine patriots, who mock the States and regard them as fools, filled their pockets. When a hundred thousand guilders arrived at the army quarters, it was necessary that two-thirds of it came into the hands of

[18] All were leaders of the Malcontent forces. La Motte (1530–95) had served as officer in the States' army. Philip of Lalaing (1537–82) had joined the States' side in 1576 and had been one of the commanders of the States' army during the lost battle of Gembloux, together with his half-brother Emmanuel Philibert of Lalaing, Baron of Montigny (1557–90).

[19] Philip of Egmont (1558–90), the son of the beheaded Count Lamoraal of Egmont, had returned to the Netherlands in 1576 to recover his father's property and possessions. In 1579 he took the Spanish side and later became Stadholder of Artois and Knight of the Golden Fleece. For Heze, see p. 172, note 9.

Gognies and de Frezin were officers in the States' army.

the aforesaid great masters. Now that the money is gone they are all Malcontents, because they have not been able to put out of action, or, what is to be feared, to kill his Princely Excellency. Indeed, he who writes this has seen that the Count Vander Marck and the Colonel Balfour (who had the cause at heart) were hardly allowed to enter the Council of War, that the soldiers barely received a third part of the money the States managed to provide and what little effort was made to besiege the city of Namur. Such was not allowed to happen, for it would have offended the King, the natural Lord. It was considered enough to keep our entrenchments, to surprise a miserable castle, or the House of Selles, with a few other small nests. In the army quarters it was better. There was enough of everything there to court, to banquet, to tailor one's beard or to make red bonnets, which perfectly expressed the guise, for they were precisely the caps which those who go to mass usually wear. Had they had a couple of earrings, they would have been like their appearance, in spite of the fact that they pocketed the money and brought this dismal Civil War upon their allies. It was not feasible, with seven or eight regiments of infantry, namely the regiment of Egmont, Bossu,[20] Balfour, Montigny, Heze, vander Marck, a German and a Walloon and the Regiment of the French, not to mention the rest of the infantry, which does not come to my mind, and with such beautiful and well-equipped cavalry, thirteen or fourteen bands or cornets, in addition to 400,000 horsemen under the command of the Lord of Cruyningen to besiege the city of Namur, for neither wood nor ships could be obtained to build a bridge across the Meuse. Also the war would have come to a standstill. Now, just as they have oppressed the fatherland and brought misery and war upon its allies, these men can put Tournai, Cambrai and other towns in peril with fewer soldiers, but when Don Juan and the King were involved, nobody came forward. God save the mark! What else but perjury and betrayal, as was shown sufficiently to our harm, disgrace and education by the defeat at Gembloux[21] has been the cause of all these great troubles? What else is the reason why

---

[20] Maximilian de Hennin, Count of Bossu (1542–78) was appointed Stadholder of Holland, Zeeland and Utrecht after William of Orange's departure in 1567. He was imprisoned by the Sea Beggars in 1573 after a sound naval defeat on the Zuiderzee. Released in 1576, after the Pacification of Ghent, he became one of the commanders of the States' army.

[21] On 31 January 1577 the army of the States General was taken by surprise by the new governor of Philip II, Don Juan, at Gembloux.

we did not strike the enemy in the field at Rijmenam and why we are still under pressure, but that the persons, mentioned above, to whom we entrusted these affairs, have been mummers, double-hearted persons, more inclined to the King of Spain than to their fatherland and its inhabitants, haughty, grand, full of ambition and revenge, seeking more their own good and profit than the prosperity of the country and its poor subjects, and what is worst, they were all folk who did not consider hindering or offending the King of Spain.

I pray you, beloved fellow citizens (but please speak and judge impartially), is the government – having overlooked all these matters and having learnt to its cost and harm – wrong in desiring to secure itself and the country and, in doing so, to commit and bind us all to itself and to each other by means of oath, and, moreover (so that we can go to work with resolved people, whom we do not have to watch closely), in seeking to have us renounce the King of Spain and his adherents by oath? I do think that nobody can have a different judgment, unless he were out of his mind or Spanish-minded, and still hoping for the King's arrival, expecting that he will be in control, when (which God may forbid and we should guard ourselves against) neither they nor we would find mercy; unless one regards, in the last extremity, being an eternal slave as an act of grace, which is the most execrable and detestable matter one can suggest to a free man. Therefore Cicero says in the aforesaid book on duties, 'Mors est servituti turpitudinique anteponenda, & libertatis causa omnis a magnis viris suscipienda contentia'.[22] That is, that for the sake of liberty and in order to maintain it, one should consider nothing too arduous, and that one should rather die than bow to any slavery.

To this end the aforesaid oath is useful and profitable. First of all, once it has been taken, the government will know what it has to do against the King of Spain and his adherents, when the people and subjects are of one mind in confronting public enmity, even though they still differ in religion. This will be the cause of great progress in the common good, for as is said in the Latin language for the same reason, 'Concordia res parve crescunt, discordia maxime dilabuntur'.[23] That is: 'In concord prosperity, in discord deterioration.' And,

---

[22] Cicero, *De Officiis* 1. 23. 81 (p. 82) where it is argued that one should prefer death to slavery and disgrace, and *De Officiis* 1. 20. 68 (p. 70), where Cicero argues that 'in defence of liberty a high-souled man should stake everything'.

[23] This saying, popular in the political literature of the Dutch Revolt, especially during the

as Cicero says in the second book of his *De Officiis*, concord is the foundation of all republics, or states of government.[24]

Secondly, those who previously were suspicious and feared the power of the King (although they should not have) will be the more animated to fight bravely for their fatherland, wife, children, goods, blood and liberty. For through the oath a resolute and considered spirit will be rooted in them, in the place of their previous irresolution which made them want to swim between two waters, always extensively pondering a matter which is honourable and profitable. Against such cowardly people it may be of use to point out what Cicero says in the third book of his *De Officiis*: 'Away, then, with questioners of this sort (for their whole tribe is wicked and ungodly), who stop to consider whether to pursue the course which they see is morally right or to strain their hands with what they know is crime. For there is guilt in their very deliberation, even though they never reach the performance of the deed itself. Those actions, therefore, should not be considered at all, the mere consideration of which is morally wrong'.[25] Which means, in short, that one should neither doubt nor deliberate on matters which one knows to be rightful, for in doing so one commits an evil and ungodly work, which is not without crime.

Thirdly, when the aforesaid oath has been taken, we will be able to distinguish between those whom we trust and those whom we cannot trust, so that in times of need we may employ the trustworthy, be it in affairs of state or other affairs, and keep an eye on those whom we suspect, and not without important reason, because of the refusal of the oath. For if they no longer thought to favour the King more than their fatherland, they would not object to taking the oath.

Therefore Cicero says in the third book of *De Officiis*: 'Our ancestors were of the opinion that no bond was more effective in guaranteeing good faith than an oath'.[26] That is: the oath is the strongest bond with which to tie oneself to somebody, so that it is not requested without reason to forsake the King of Spain by oath and to act in accordance with the contents of this oath, for by this very oath

early 1580s, came from Sallust, *Bellum Iugurthinum* 10. 6. See *Sallust* (Cambridge, Mass. (Loeb edition), 1985), p. 148. Another source was Seneca, *Epistolae Morales* Liber 14, letter 94, section 46. A more literal translation of this proverb is 'concord makes small commonwealths great, discord disrupts the greatest ones'.

[24] Cicero, *De Officiis* 2. 22. 78 (p. 254).
[25] Ibid., 3. 8. 37 (p. 304).
[26] Ibid., 3. 31. 111 (p. 390). This quote also features on the front page of *Political Education*.

those who otherwise might pretend exception or find some excuse, are committed to do so.

It is to be wished that nowadays men were still as conscientious in observing the oath as the Romans and other pagans have been in the past, for then one would not find so many perjurers and traitors. Sabelli, in the ninth book of the *Aenead*, describes the notable example of the conscientious observance of the oath by M. Attilius Regulus, who was taken prisoner by the Carthaginians.[27] He was sent to Rome to the Senate with the possibility of either releasing several prisoners or of returning to Carthage himself. On arrival at Rome, he approved of not releasing the prisoners. Yet, he preferred to return to Carthage, with the danger of being executed and killed, rather than to break a sworn oath.

Aristotle, asked what a liar gained by his lie, responded: that he is not believed when he tells the truth. See how the perjurious Christians, and dissimulators against their fatherland, stand ashamed in the eyes of the pagans. It is to be pitied that they have listened too often to their schoolmaster Dionysius the Tyrant, who said (as Plutarch writes in his book on the prosperity and virtue of Alexander) that one should cheat men with an oath as one cheats children with the game of knuckle-bones.[28]

Taking into account these and other reasons, one hopes that no pious citizens will be moved by these problems from taking the oath. For if it is not taken, the government can never know the humours of its subjects, whether they are united to uphold the fatherland with body and blood in true enmity against the King of Spain and his adherents. Thus the country and towns cannot be secured, nor can the loyal be known from the disloyal.

For it goes with the subjects and their government as it goes with a ship that drifts across the waves by a tempest of winds in the middle of the sea. Although it has a good pilot and steersmen, these differ in temper, one wanting such, the other wanting such, the one thinking the wind is East, the other West. And so, falling into controversies

---

[27] See Marcus Antonius Sabelli, *Rapsodie Historiarum Enneadum Marci Antonij Loccij Sabelli. Ab orbe conditio. Pars prima* (Paris, 1509), Enneadis 4. Lib. 9, fol. CCCCIIIb (originally published in 1504). The story is also told in Cicero, *De Officiis*, 3. 26. 99 (p. 374).

[28] Plutarch, 'On the fortune or the virtue of Alexander', 1. 330F, in Plutarch, *Plutarch's Moralia*, vol. 4 (Cambridge, Mass. (Loeb edition), 1962), p. 407.

and different opinions, the ship, with all that is in it, drifts along, indeed is in danger of running aground and going down.

Here the story of fable suits well, which an expert philosopher put forward to the Athenians when they were under siege and had fallen into discord, having different opinions. He said and admonished them to beware of falling into the same hardship as had befallen the dog and the fox: namely, that after they had fought each other, the wolf came and ate and devoured them both, which would not have happened to them, had they been united. Here one could add a similar fable which Aesop has told about the mouse and the frog.

Titius Livy writes in the fifth book of his fourth decade about the Chalcidians that after the Aetolians asked them to become their allies, propounding with various arguments to that end, for example that they would always be protected from the one side or the other, the council of the community of Chalcis answered that they could not make such an alliance, knowing full well that one cannot at the same time properly serve two masters who are of contrasting opinion.[29] Therefore it is also impossible to please both the government of these Netherlands and the King of Spain. One must hate the one, love the other. For one advocates his fatherland, liberty, wife, children, privileges, goods and blood, while the other seeks to oppress them with force or other malpractice. It is therefore profitable that the subjects are of one oath and cloth, and that the good ones are tested and purged from the evil ones by the oath, as gold is purified by touchstone and fire. Otherwise partisanship is to be feared amongst the citizens, which the government ought to shun (as the plague). Because of partisanship, as Titius Livy writes in the fourth book of his first decade,[30] the town of Ardea fell into great misery and calamity so that on both sides many lost their lives. Because of the factional conflict between the Hannonites and the Barchanians, Carthage was brought to ruin. For sixty years France suffered the hardship of conflict and war because of the factional strife between the Houses of Orleans and Burgundy. The reconciliation of the enmity between Marcus Livy and Claudius (so Titius Livy writes in his second and seventh book of the third decade and in his fourth and fifth book of

---

[29] See Livy, *Ab urbe Conditio*, Book 35. 16, especially no. 7 (Cambridge, Mass. (Loeb edition: vol. 10), 1935), p. 133.

[30] Ibid., Book 4, Chapter 9, nos. 2–4 (Cambridge, Mass. (Loeb edition: vol. 2), 1922), p. 287.

the first)[31] was extremely profitable for the Romans and their republic, for previously the factional conflict between Paulus Aemilius and Terentius Varro, both captains, but the one wise, the other stubborn, was the reason why the Romans were nearly brought to utter ruin and collapse. In order to praise unity, that same Titius Livy tells in his tenth book of the first decade[32] of Fabius Maximus who, after he had-been elected to the consulate for the fifth time, stood up when an attempt was made to establish Lucius Volumnius as his companion, and said: 'My lords, I have shared the consulate twice before with Publius Decius and we always agreed properly and in unity. Therefore I pray to you to give me the same man for this journey. Do me this favour in my old age, as it will now be difficult for me to get used to another companion. You know, my Lords, that nothing more assures the protection of the republic than magistrates who are in accord, for everyone communicates his advice more frankly to one whom he knows, who is like him in manners and condition, than with another.' In another place the same Titius Livy tells of Quinctilus Capitolinus, who, admonishing his people to go to war, said and spoke thus:[33] 'Our enemies do not jump upon us because they put trust in our cowardice or in their own strength, for on various occasions they have experienced both. However, they put trust in our faction and strife, which always exists between patricians and community, for it is faction which poisons and spoils this town with venom.' Here one may learn what loss is to be expected from discord and what advantage from concord. Therefore, for the sake of the profit and utility that comes from it, this oath must be taken. And those who refuse must be put under surveillance. For those who are united to each other by oath are more faithful to each other. This is why, when a new captain is accepted, the soldiers swear a new oath to him. Of course this case is not about swearing to any other lord, it merely serves to argue by comparison and examples.

However, the aforesaid oath should not only be embraced, accepted and sworn for the sake of profit and honour but also because it is founded on justice. For even though (as will be proven later in the

---

[31] Most explicitly Livy makes this point in Book 27, chapter 35 (Cambridge, Mass. (Loeb edition: vol. 7), 1970), pp. 348–52.

[32] Ibid., Book 10, Chapter 22, nos. 2–4 (Cambridge, Mass. (Loeb edition: vol. 4), 1926), p. 440.

[33] Ibid., Book 3, Ch. 67, nos. 5–7 (Cambridge, Mass. (Loeb edition: vol. 2, 1922), p. 227.

appropriate place with biblical passages, written rights and pagan examples) all government stems from God, and being God's servant, should be honoured, obeyed and acknowledged, for which reason one might say that it were illegal to forsake and repudiate the King of Spain (being our natural lord), I nonetheless maintain that if the government, whatever it may be, either Monarchical or Popular, abuses the authority and the right to rule over its subjects, and turns it into force, violence or tyranny, as the King of Spain, as everybody knows, has plainly done, one should no longer acknowledge such a government, including the King of Spain. For he has created and hired one party of subjects, the Malcontents, to persecute, kill and massacre, murder cruelly and execute the other, namely us, who keep ourselves under the protection of his Princely Excellence and the States General of the united Provinces. They are to force honourable women, to rape young girls, to rob, plunder and burn houses, towns and villages, and to do other similar ungodly and terrible unbearable things, especially to bring those who are free into eternal slavery, and after that themselves with us. For they have not studied the fable and moral of the wolf and the sheep. The wolf wanted to make peace with the sheep, but first he wanted to have the dog killed so that, having got rid of the protector, he could destroy and devour the sheep. Not that I regard the Malcontents as sheep and our government as dogs, for it is completely the reverse. This merely serves to show the opinion and ulterior intention of the king, a wolf by nature: namely, to master them too, once these Malcontent dogs have swallowed us. Ah, I wish everybody had understood this as well as his Princely Excellence, well advised and considered, has. The Count of Egmont and the Count of Hoorne would not have lost their heads so ignominiously, nor would they have been, as his Princely Excellence rightly predicted, the bridge which the enemy would cross. For, God save the mark, to our damage and disgrace this prophecy has come true.

In such matters one should not obey such a tyrannical and barbarous government – far from it. For all pious nobles and faithful subjects are permitted, for various causes and reasons, to resist and stem such tyranny and barbarous cruelty, employing body, goods and blood to this end. One should remember the oath, which the Athenians took in accepting offices, dignities or similar matters, as one may take here in confraternities, guilds, crafts and so forth. They swore this: I will fight and struggle, alone and with others, for myself and the holy things, that is to say, the religion, the fatherland, the government, the liberty, wife and children.

In order to explain this matter further, it would be necessary here to deal firstly with the government, what it is and to what purpose it is ordained by God, subsequently with tyrants and tyranny, its origin and end, because (so the philosophers say) one should start all matters with description. However, since I intend to discuss this particular matter briefly hereafter, for the further comfort and assurance of those who are troubled by this oath, I will reserve it for that place, and now pursue my proposed argument and argumentation.

I say and maintain that it is impossible that any state of government, whatever the government may be, can remain, when the government is a tyrant, or when aristocracy changes into oligarchy, that is, when the government of the best among the people changes into usurpation, or when democracy changes into systrema; that is, when the power, which is with the whole people, turns into rebellion and sedition. For the pious and godly citizen or subject can have no common ground with a tyrant, usurper or seditious person. This is why Cicero rightly says: just as for the conservation of the body one has to amputate some rotten limb, so that the whole body is not ruined, so one should also exterminate and destroy such a bloody and vicious beast, which can bring down human concord, making it decay.[34]

However, it is to be noted here that one should scrutinize the matter very closely before taking up arms (as has been said), for there is no man so unreasonable that he can say with right or reason that it is permissible to take up arms against a lawful government. And no man is born such a coward, so weak-minded, or with the character of an insensible animal, nor is anybody of such false judgment, that he would not happily profess with me that it is permissible to resist and to take up arms against the furious cruelty, and barbarous tyranny, usurpation and rebellion of those, who should protect the good and punish the evil in fear of God and with justice.

The principal end for which God ordained government to men was not to convert the good, won and gathered through great labour and industry, into its own property, for each loves and follows what is his. Neither to misuse the power, which is rendered to it, for intemperate and unreasonable desires, for it is the character of men to envy or hate

---

[34] See Cicero, *De Officiis* 3. 6. 32 (p. 298).

the most powerful. Nor to change right into wrong, and to govern at will, as the King of Spain does, when he writes: 'for so it pleases us', after Juvenal's verse: 'This is my will and my command; let my will be the voucher for the deed.'[35] For the government is ordained to protect the subjects against each other and against the foreign enemy from injustice, force and violence. Therefore in the fifteenth chapter of his nineteenth book of the *City of God*, Augustine very rightly says that those who foster and take care of the welfare of another, are rightly called 'Imperatores', that is rulers: so the man orders his wife, the father his child.[36] On the other hand, those whose welfare is fostered and taken care of, such as the wife and the child, are called subjects, even though those who rule in this way in fact serve those whom they are said to rule. For (as he continues) he who takes care of the welfare of another does not act out of lust for dominance, but out of affection for care, not out of the haughtiness to rule but out of concern and compassion.

In his 91st letter Seneca writes that in the time of the golden world, the imperial or supreme power was with the wise.[37] These subdued acts of violence and protected the subjects against usurpers, they counselled and dissuaded, and showed what was profitable and unprofitable. Their prudence nourished them (so that they would not be in want). Fortitude stemmed adversity, and clemency multiplied and glorified the subjects. To rule was an office, not an empire. Thus he shows (as with a finger) that the rule, which lies with the government, is nothing but to counsel divinely and with justice, and that the sole end of the government consists in the welfare and prosperity of its community and subjects. It is the duty and office of emperors, kings and authorities to render assistance to the subjects. Therefore their dignity is actually not glory but rather burden, not liberty but servitude, not dissolution but public service.

In the past, the reason for the people to subject themselves to the King and other authorities was that the latter would protect the good and punish the evil, either by good laws or by arms, that they would

[35] Juvenalis, Satire 6, no. 223; see *Juvenal and Perseus* (Cambridge, Mass. (Loeb edition), 1961), p. 100.
[36] This is probably a reference to the final passages of the fourteenth chapter of Book 19. See St Augustine, *The City of God against the Pagans* (Cambridge, Mass. (Loeb edition, vol. 6), 1960), p. 184.
[37] Seneca, *Epistola Morales* Book 14, Letter 90 (not 91 as mentioned in the text), no. 5, which is quoted at length.

judge the people in time of peace, and lead them in time of war, and, finally, that they would not only resist the enemy but would also expel all anger, violence and injustice from the people. Therefore the praiseworthy Emperor Justinian, in the beginning of his Institutes of Imperial Rights, rightly asks an emperor to be two men, namely a man of arms and a man of laws or learning, when he says: 'Imperial Majesty should be not only embellished with arms but also fortified by laws so that the times of both war and peace can be rightly regulated'.[38] In his Oration *On the Manilian Law* Cicero says that an emperor should be endowed and honoured with four qualities, namely with knowledge of warfare, authority, prosperity and virtue, and these virtues are especially demanded, namely that he is persistent in his duty, strong in peril, shrewd in taking the initiative, rapid in exploiting and prudent in strategy.[39]

In the beginning God's people knew no other King but God, who, being in their midst, counselled and led them. He ordained them field commanders and judges, but stadholders were not necessary since the highest King and Regent was always there. However, when they wanted a King (as it is told in the eighth chapter of the first book of Samuel), they asked for a King who would govern and lead them in battle. For it says: 'that our king may govern us and go out before us and fight our battles'.[40]

Aristotle writes in his book of *Politics* that in the times of heroic men, all Kings had been governors and leaders of the wars.[41]

Cicero says in the second book of *De Officiis* that all well-mannered Kings have been instituted for the sake of justice. As he puts it: 'Now it seems to me, at least, that not only among the Medes, as Herodotus tells us, but also among our own ancestors, men of high moral character were made kings in order that the people might enjoy justice.'[42] Furthermore he points out that the cause and reason for electing kings and for the origin of good laws has been one and the same, namely natural equity.

---

[38] The reference is to the opening sentence of the *Institutes* of Emperor Justinian. See J.A.C. Thomas, *The Institutes of Justinian. Text, Translation and Commentary* (Amsterdam/Oxford, 1975), p. 1.

[39] Cicero, *On the Manilian Law*, 10. 28; 11. 29. See Cicero, *The Speeches* (Cambridge, Mass. (Loeb edition), 1966), pp. 40, 42.

[40] 1 Samuel 8:20.

[41] Aristotle, *Politics*, book 3, chapter 14, section 1285b3–8.

[42] Cicero, *De Officiis* 2. 12. 41 (p. 208).

The Holy Apostle Peter orders in the second chapter of his first letter that men should obey the government, and he points out the reasons why, for he says that it is sent by God for vengeance on the wrongdoers and praise of the good.[43]

Solomon writing about himself in the book of Wisdom, says in the ninth chapter, speaking to the Lord: 'You have elected me King over your people, and Judge over your sons and daughters.' And the same Solomon, praying to the Lord, does not pray for riches, nor for goods, nor for honour, nor for the soul of his enemy, nor for a long life, but (as appears from the first chapter of the second book of Chronicles)[44] for wisdom and knowledge, so that he may go out and come in for his people, that is, champion them and judge them with moderation.

Since, then, kings have been ordained by God for the welfare and benefit of the subjects and have been accepted by the people, and since the welfare and benefit of the people (as said before) consists of two main chapters, namely of justice amongst the citizens and strength against the enemy, it cannot be argued that he is a Prince or lawful government who does not seek the benefit of the subjects but of himself, serving his own unbridled desires, who seeks to suppress what is right with force and violence, who alarms and frightens widows and orphans, in short who exploits his people with more cruelty and tyranny than Nero, Caligula, Caracalla and suchlike tyrants ever did. To him the name of tyrant is to be ascribed.

It is founded in right, reason and equity that the one who has the power of making laws is also subject to the laws. For this we have clear testimony in the Codex under the title 'De legibus & constitutionibus', where the Emperors Theodosius and Valentine write: 'Digna vox est maiestate regnantis legibus alligatum se principem profiteri: adeo de authoritate iuris nostra dependet authoritas.'[45] That is: it is a worthy voice that the one who has been put in majesty, professes to be a Prince and to be bound by the laws, for our authority so strongly depends on the authority of the law. The Emperor Alex-

---

[43] 1 Peter 2:13–14.

[44] 2 Chronicles 1:11–14.

[45] The reference is to the Codex Justinianus, Book 1, Chapter 14, no. 4; see S.P. Scott, *The Civilian Law*, XII (New York, 1973), p. 86. Throughout the medieval period this text, a constitution of Theodosius II in 429, played a major role in the discussion on the limits of princely rule, being primarily used to sustain the idea of limited, 'constitutional' rule.

ander says in the 'lex imperfecto' of the Codex under the title 'De Testamentis': 'Licet enim lex imperii solemnibus iuris Imperatorem solverit, nil tametam proprium imperii est, quam legibus vivere.'[46] That is: 'even though the law discharges the emperor from the solemnity of the laws, nonetheless nothing is so proper for the Imperial Majesty as to live under the laws.' Now it is well known and founded in right that the law is a rule to which all men must be subject for many different reasons, and especially because all laws are an invention and gift of God, a lesson of all wise men, a punishment of all sins and a bond of civic unity, in accordance with which all who live in a town have to regulate their lives. The law is a certain knowledge of all divine and human affairs. It should serve both the bad and good, and must be a guide for a Prince. Therefore the law is a standard for the just and the unjust. Regarding the things which are by nature civil, it prescribes what one ought to do and prohibits what ought not to be done, as appears from the text in the Digest under the title 'De legibus senatusque consultis', paragraph 2.[47] Consequently it follows that the subjects are neither under obligation nor bound to obey a government which seeks to impoverish its subjects with long-lasting wars, tries to wear them out and to oppress them, and seeks to bring those who are free into slavery, to turn right into wrong and to change its lawful government into tyranny.

For Kings and other governments are charged with being guardians, servants and champions of the laws, not to attempt anything against the latter's disposition. Therefore Pausanias of Sparta says that 'the laws ought to have authority over the men, not the men over the laws'.[48] And Agesilaus, the King of the Spartans, says that it befits the Emperors to do what the laws command.[49] Subsequently Cicero says in the third book of *De Officiis* that the laws concern the

---

[46] Codex 6. 23. 3. The translation of Scott, p. 329 is as follows: 'Although the jurisprudence of the Empire exempts the sovereign from complying with the ordinary legal formalities, still no duty is so incumbent upon him as to live in obedience to the laws.'

[47] In fact these sentences are an almost direct quote from the Digest of Justinian, Book 1, title 3, paragraph 2. See Mommsen, Krueger, Watson (eds.), *The Digest of Justinian*, vol. 1 (Philadelphia, 1985), p. 11. The reference is to Digest, Book 2, title 'De legibus senatusque consultis', paragraph 2.

[48] Here Plutarch's *The Sayings of Spartans*, 230F is quoted. See Plutarch, *Moralia*, vol. 3 (172a–263c) (Cambridge, Mass. (Loeb edition), 1968), p. 383. Pausanias was king of Sparta between 408 and 394 BC.

[49] Once again the author dwells upon Plutarch. See Plutarch, *The Sayings of Spartans*, 211A (Loeb edition, p. 261).

prosperity of the citizens[50] and, in the first book, that good lawgivers have been of more advantage to the cities than good Emperors.[51] Socrates always considered the civic government to be blessed, when good laws dominate. Therefore those have been so extolled and exalted who first gave the laws: such as Moses by the Hebrews, Phoroneus, the son of Inachus, by the Argives, Mercurius Trimegistus by the Egyptians, Draco and later Solon by the Athenians, Minos by the Cretans, and Lycurgus by the Lacaedemonians, as is testified by Eusebius in book 10 of *De Evangelica preparatione*,[52] Iosephus in the first book against Appionem,[53] Pausanias and others too many to mention.

Now the King of Spain and his adherents do not act as is laid to their charge, as they, considering no violence or tyranny too great, seek to corrupt the good laws, to suppress the conscience of their subjects, to stir up one inhabitant against the other, to consume the subjects in Civil war, to rule with force and violence, to shed innocent blood, to burn and rob, to degrade honorable women, to dishonour young maids, to bring about all sorts of evil, to steal, murder, rob and sack, to destroy the true religion and to slander and forsake God, to regard no violence or tyranny inordinate, in short, to deprive the country and the inhabitants of their Privileges and justice and, finally, to bring those who have always been free into eternal slavery. Therefore their Government can claim no right to be acknowledged as lawful. Instead, they should be regarded as tyrants. For he is a King who governs an empire, obtained either through succession or election and herein confirmed by the subjects, rightly and lawfully after God's commandments, protecting the good and punishing the evil. A tyrant, on the contrary, is he who governs the empire, either conquered with violence or shrewd practices, or surrendered to him by the inhabitants, or succeeded to him in lawful title, with force and violence against right and fairness, and who treats the inhabitants without regard to all laws, contracts and sworn fidelity; as it is argued

[50] Cicero, *De Officiis* 3. 5. 23 (p. 290).
[51] Ibid. 1. 22. 75–6 (p. 76) where Cicero emphasizes the importance of the work of lawmakers such as Solon and Lycurgus ('legibus et disciplinae') in contrast with the work of warmakers.
[52] Eusebius, *De Evangelica Preparatione* (Hagenau, 1522), pp. 225–49.
[53] See Joseph Flavius, 'Flavii Josephi De Antiquitate Iudaeorum Contra Aponium Alexandrianum, ad Epaphroditem. Liber Primus' in Josephus Flavius, *Flavii Josephi De Antiquitate Iudaeorum* (Basel, 1548), pp. 827–44.

by Bartolus in his treatise on tyranny, and Aristotle in the tenth chapter of the fifth book of his *Politics*.[54] For in his treatise Bartolus sketches two sorts of tyranny, one in title, the other in exercise. He calls a tyrant in title he who incorporates an empire or dominion without any title or under the pretext of a false title. He describes as a tyrant in exercise one who, having a lawful title of dominion, does not rule rightly and faithfully, as a good Prince is bound to do.

In order that one might know how to recognize a tyrant, he [Bartolus] lists ten remarkable acts. First, the tyrant has the most dignified and noblest persons amongst his subjects killed and executed by the sword, preventing them from rising against his tyranny. Second, he torments and persecutes the wise and honourable subjects, as he is afraid that, in writing or otherwise, they would assess his vices and discover his tyranny or persuade the community to arm itself against it. Third, he seeks to abolish studies, so that there should be found few learned men and it should be easier for him to tyrannize. Fourth, he impedes confraternities and honest meetings, preventing people from conspiring against his power. Fifth, he is served by spies, who hear and listen among the people, whether anyone admonishes his evil acts. Sixth, he maintains strife and faction in his community, in order that one party besmirches the other, so that neither the one nor the other should stand up against him. Seventh, he exploits all means to impoverish his subjects so that, being occupied with earning their bread, they should have no means to concoct anything against him. Eighth, he seeks to maintain war and to weaken his subjects, in order to destroy the cities and to make himself strong. Ninth, he trusts strangers more than his own subjects, and lets himself be guarded by foreigners. Tenth, in party strife he favours one party more than the other.

---

[54] The reference is to Bartolus of Sassoferrato's *De Tyranno*. A critical edition of *De Tyranno* was provided by Diego Quaglioni in his *Politico e Diritto nel Trecento Italiano. Il "De Tyranno" di Bartolo da Sassoferrato (1314–1347)* (Florence, 1983), pp. 171–213. References are to Quaglioni's edition.

Bartolus of Sassoferrato's (see 'Biographical Notes') denunciation of tyranny was both radical and innovative. For the author of *Political Education* it was a main source of inspiration. In defining tyranny he basically paraphrases Bartolus' argument. The distinction between tyranny in title and tyranny in exercise is made by Bartolus in *De Tyranno*, chapter 5, pp. 184–5. For the description of the marks of tyranny, see chapter 8, pp. 196–9, where Bartolus actually refers to Aristotle, whose views on tyranny are outlined in *The Politics*, Book 5, chapter 10. Here 'the origins and downfall of monarchy' are discussed, for example in 1311*a*; see also chapter 11, for example 1313*a–b*.

In the aforementioned treatise Bartolus shows with vivid argument, too long to be recounted here, that these are all acts by which one learns to recognize a tyrant, and especially by these three, namely that he maintains faction strife amongst his subjects, that he impoverishes them, and that he has them persecuted and tormented in body and goods.

Finally, he concludes that, neither by right nor reason, does one owe such a government submissiveness, but that one should remove and forsake it.

In his practice of criminal matters Carrerius argues with various reasons recounted by him there, that the subjects have the liberty and permission to kill a tyrannical Prince, who oppresses them unbearably, with right and reason.[55] Indeed, Thomas Aquinas (who is yet regarded as the Calvin of the Roman Church) argues in 'secunda secundae articulo penult.' that there is merit in killing such a Tyrant.[56] And that one may kill a tyrant freely and without objection, and with good reason, is proven at length with firm and almost innumerable authorities and examples by Cataldinus de Boncompagnis de Visso in number 15 of his 55th council,[57] by Alphonsus de Castro in the verse 'Tirannus' of the book of heresies[58] and by the Lord Soto in the third article of the first question of the fifth book on *De Iustitia & Iura*.[59] They argue that insofar as a tyrant is

---

[55] Ludovicus Carrerius, *Practicum causarum criminalum* (Lyon, 1562), fols. 186–7. Carrerius was a contemporary jurist from Reggio di Calabria.

[56] Thomas Aquinas, *Summa Theologiae*, IIa–IIae, Questio 42, 2, article 2, where Aquinas, listing the arguments in favour of the position that rebellion is not by definition mortal sin, points out that 'those who liberate the multitude from the power of a tyrant are praised'. In his comments Aquinas argues that resistance against a tyrannical regime should not be equated with rebellion if it is to the benefit of the suppressed subjects.

[57] This is probably a reference to Cataldinus de Boncompagnis de Visso, 'De Translatione Sacri Consilij Basilae' (1488), in *Tractatuum ex Variis iuris interpretibus collectorum*, vol. 14 (Lyon, 1549), especially fol. 348. Cataldinus (*c.* 1370–*c.* 1455) from Foligno was a distinguished jurist and magistrate.

[58] See Alfonsus de Castro, *Alfonsi à Castro, Zamorensis, Ordininis minorum regularis observantiae, Provinciae sancti Iacobi; Adversus omnes Haereses, Libri XIIII* (Antwerp, 1565), fols. 421b–2b. De Castro, a Spanish cleric, who belonged to the School of Salamanca, had dedicated this work to Philip II.

[59] Domingo de Soto, *Libri decem de Iustitia et Iura* (Lyon, 1569), fols. 138b–9b. De Soto was a highly influential Thomist philosopher, who taught at the University of Salamanca and acted as Imperial theologian and as a representative of the Dominicans at the Council of Trent. For a more comprehensive analysis of De Soto's political thought, see Quentin Skinner, *The Foundations of Modern Political Thought. Volume II: The Reformation* (Cambridge, 1978), pp. 136ff.

a lawful Prince, either by law of succession or election, a private person is not allowed to kill him because of his tyranny. Thereby they give plainly to understand that the States of the country and those who represent the subjects are, as public persons, permitted to do so. Indeed, these are obliged to take up arms against such a tyrant, and are not only allowed to resist him, but also to offend him and if possible to harm his body and goods.

Therefore nothing remains to me but to prove that the States of the country, his Princely Excellence and the subjects (who have always had the matter at heart) acquitted themselves rightly and faithfully with regard to the submissiveness they owed the King of Spain, and that, by contrast, this very King abused his royal dignity against them, and that in the regard of the Netherlands he is not a King, Duke, Count or Lord but a complete and well-made tyrant. Therefore neither the States nor his Excellency nor the subjects are any longer obliged or bound to him, but are allowed to resist him by force and to forsake him by oath.

To achieve this, one should first of all note the reason why the King felt induced to send these Netherlands (against his oath and sworn fidelity) a foreign governor, the Duke of Alva, with so many foreign men of arms. It was because on 5 April 1566 some, namely the most principle nobles of these Netherlands, presented a request to the Duchess of Parma (at the time Governess). In it they asked for moderation of certain, too rigorous and at the time recently published placards dealing with the issue of the religion. For they foresaw that to carry through such a hard and cruel ordinance would entail an unbearable Spanish Inquisition and consequently an eternal slavery, and that those of the Reformed Church, growing in numbers day by day, would start to build temples and to preach the true word of the Lord in public.

That the King published such a Placard wrongly and unjustly, thereby shedding masses of innocent blood and sending a foreign Governor, is easily established. First it has to be noted that one must honour, fear and obey God more than man, for God governs by His own authority, whereas the Kings do not govern but because of God, as is testified by Paul in the thirteenth chapter of the letter to the Romans.[60] God governs by Himself, the Kings because of God. God

---

[60] See Romans 13:1.

uses His own jurisdiction, the Kings have it from God. Therefore it is said in the sixth chapter of the Book of Wisdom and in the fifth chapter of Solomon's proverbs that God's jurisdiction is without limits but that the government of kings is demarcated by certain pales;[61] that God has infinite power, but that Kings have limited rule.

From nothingness God has created heaven and earth, and all that is there, including the Kings. Therefore He rightfully rules heaven, earth, all Kings and powers, as the royal prophet David confesses when he says in the twenty-fourth psalm: 'The earth is the Lord's and the fullness thereof.'[62] So it is no wonder that God is a King of all Kings, and a Lord of all Lords, and that all Kings are servants of His Empire, to protect the good and punish the evil. For the wisdom of the Lord declares through Solomon in the sixth chapter of Wisdom: 'By Me Kings reign and Princes judge the earth.'[63] Thus the throne of Kings is called the throne of God, and for the same reasons the people are called the people of the Lord, as one finds written in the ninth chapter of the first book of Samuel and in the twentieth chapter of the second Book of Kings. Kings are but Stadholders and servants of God, from which it follows conclusively that, serving and not resisting God, maintaining and not diminishing God's law, one should honour, fear and obey the Kings for God's sake, and not against the Lord.

To this some courtiers or toadies might say, as some Machiavellians dare to, to support Kings in their tyranny, that God has rendered all His power to the Kings, retaining heaven for Himself. In this respect one should note what Isaiah says in the forty-eighth chapter of his prophecies: 'I will give My name to no other one, nor will I render My glory to another.'[64] It is as if the Lord wanted to say: 'I will give nobody so much power that I will not keep the supreme right unto eternity'. For when the Kings invest or endow some vassal with some fief, they always retain the supreme Jurisdiction, and let themselves be acknowledged by praise and homage; how much more, then, has God reserved such to himself. A vassal binds himself by oath to his overlord and promises him homage and loyalty. Similarly, Kings are

---

[61] This is probably a reference to Proverbs 8:15 and Proverbs 16:12.
[62] Psalm 24:1, of which the original gave the Latin text: 'Domini est terra & plenitudo eius.'
[63] Proverbs 8:15.
[64] This reference is probably to Isaiah 48:9–11.

bound to God by oath, if they swear by God to govern rightly, lawfully and godly.

Moreover the Kings are bound by oath in two respects, first to God and then to the people.[65] Concerning the first covenant one may read about Ioas, Josiah, Moses, Joshua and other Kings and authorities of the people of Israel in the eleventh chapter of the Second Book of Kings, in the twenty-third chapter of the second book of Chronicles, in the twenty-ninth, thirtieth and thirty-first chapter of Deuteronomy, in the first chapter of Joshua and in other passages of the Biblical scriptures. Here one finds that in the name of God the high priest not only stipulated to the people, but first of all to the government that they should ensure that God be served purely and after his command in the empire of the Jews. This obliges the King or government to govern in such a way that he permits the people to serve God purely and to observe His law, and obliges the people to be obedient to the King or government and, above all, to honour Him, who is a King of Kings, almighty above all.

And in order that no one can escape from here with the idea that the aforesaid concerns the Judges of the Old Testament but not Kings, I here present the example of Samuel the Prophet, who said after Saul had been chosen, anointed and confirmed: 'Behold the King you have chosen and desired. Behold, God has set him as a King over you. Be obedient and serve God, both you and your King, who reigns over you, for otherwise you and your King will perish and come to nothing.'[66]

After Saul had disobeyed God, he was thrown out of the empire and David was established in his majesty on the same conditions; and after him Solomon, David's son, with whom God made a covenant, saying: 'There shall not fail you a man, who will sit on Israel's throne for me, if your children will heed to their way to walk in my law, as you have done'.[67] So it is described in the twelfth chapter of the first book of Samuel, the second and sixth chapter of the first Book of Kings, the sixteenth chapter of the second Book of Chronicles and in other parts of the Old Testament.

From all these wonderful examples and testimonies it is clear and

---

[65] At this point the *Political Education* endorses the idea of the double contractual obligation of kings as formulated in the *Vindiciae contra tyrannos*.
[66] The reference is to 1 Samuel 12:13–16.
[67] The reference is to 1 Kings 2:4.

public that the Kings and other governors, as God's vassals in maintaining the law of God, swear to their overlord and therefore, like their own vassals and subjects who lose their loan when they do not keep their promise and sworn faithfulness, they forfeit in God's eyes their empire and supreme power when they despise and do not observe the covenant concluded with God, as was shown to Saul, after he had become disobedient to God, to Solomon (after he had turned to the idols), and to others.

And what has happened to the Kings, Judges and people in Israel can be expected to happen to the Christian Kings and Governors too, if they turn from the pure Evangelical doctrine to perfidy and superstition, for the Christian governments have come in the place of the Jewish powers; the Gospel has followed the law. Therefore there is a covenant, there are the same conditions, the same punishments and the same avenger, namely God Almighty.

This has been sufficiently recorded concerning the tyrants, who took up arms against Christ and his empire and persecuted the Christians with great cruelty, to their utter disgrace and confusion. Herod drowned and died in great calamity, losing his empire; Pilate was woefully tormented by the devil and finally eaten by lice; Julian the Apostate was persecuted and suppressed by the Galilean.[68] In short, all who persecuted the Christians have found a miserable end, as has been clear enough for some hundred years, both in these Countries and in others, where the Christians have been pitifully persecuted for some time, and have had to bear oppression. This could be proven with examples but since this might be too odious and too long to recount, the reader, looking at the history of the time and especially at the book of martyrs, may find what horrors have been blown over the heads of the Christians and how God has punished those who have employed themselves in such a tyranny.

Applying all these wonderful examples and this evidence to our own case, everybody will be so kind as to note what the nature is of the Spanish Inquisition, which some hoped to plant in this country and put in train of execution under the pretext of the rigorous Placards

---

[68] Julian the Apostate was the nephew of Constantine the Great and Roman Emperor from 361 to 363 AD. Educated as a Christian, he turned away from Christianity and sought to re-establish the old religion, thereby restricting the freedom of the Christians. According to the story, recounted by Ibsen in his play *The Emperor and the Galilean*, Julian was haunted by Christ.

and the election of new bishops. Namely, that whoever might in the least deviate from the human commands of the Pope of Rome and his adherents, would be killed by rope, fire, sword or water; indeed, even if he were not inclined to the Gospel but had come to misbehave out of ignorance or simpleness, he could not escape long imprisonment and misery. Finally, by grace he had to carry a yellow cap or something similar as sign and clothing of an infamous person, and he could never rise to any state or dignity.

I pray to each – and use your proper judgment and common sense – is this not an extraordinary example of violence and tyranny? To try to bind the conscience of a man by force to a certain faith, of which he is nonetheless convinced in his mind that it has nothing to do with God's word. I do think that everyone will agree, unless he is thirsty of innocent blood, as those are who try to do such with weapons, treason and evil practices, and therefore should be called barbarians and tyrants.

For as all religion consists of approving certain articles concerning God and God's worship, so it is certain that such approbation comes · from a persuasion which God has sent to the hearts of men. Therefore the Apostle Paul rightly argues in the second chapter to the Ephesians that faith is a gift of God.[69] However, this persuasion cannot come to pass by means of arms, but by good remonstrances, arguments and reasons taken from God's word.

We do not deal here with Turks, Jews, Saracens, or Atheists, from whom the King of Spain and the Angels who serve him may have sprung, but with Christians who concur with each other in name, and merely have some difference about some articles of faith. Therefore I will not refrain from recounting some examples of the Heathens or Turks, who have rebutted, and with reason, that one should compel a man with force to accept another faith than that which he holds or that for this reason one should start a war without any consideration. In this respect Froissaert writes about a highly memorable case in the 18th and 19th chapter of his fourth book.[70] When a Duke of Bourbon,

---

[69] Ephesians 2:8. Of course the author here endorses one of the basic principles of the Reformation.

[70] See Jean Froissaert, *The thirde and fourthe booke of Sir Johan Froyssart* (1525, repr. Amsterdam/New York, 1970), fols. CCLXX ff. Jean Froissaert (*c.* 1337–*c.* 1405), a protégé of the Dukes of Brabant, was the author of the famous *Chroniques de France, d'Angleterre et de pais voisins*.

Captain General of the French army, went to Africa to wage war against the Turk under the pretext of furthering the empire of Christ, the supreme marshal of the Turkish army sent him a herald to find out the reason for his arrival. He was answered that it was to avenge the death of Christ, the son of God and the true Prophet, whom their generation had crucified and killed. Subsequently, the Turk, replying, told the French lords that they had been badly informed and that the Jews had killed Christ, and not their ancestors. And therefore, if the children had to pay for the crime of the parents, they should take up arms against the Jews, many of whom were in the Christian empire. Thereupon the French lords did not know not what to reply, nor could they do anything against the Turks. They returned, having lost the greater part of their men, due to a terrible infection of the air.

In the 68th chapter of his third book Monstrelet[71] recounts another, no less notable example. Namely that in the year 1453 the Turk, having discovered that the Pope had proclaimed the Crusade against him, to avenge the death of Christ, wrote him a letter, in which he gave to understand, among other things, that the Jews had wrongfully crucified Christ and that he descended not from the Jews but from the Trojans, of whom the Italians also praise themselves to be descended. Therefore they should rather wage war together to restore Troy and to avenge the death of Hector. Although he believed that Christ had been a great Prophet, he had never heard that Christ had ever ordered to force someone by means of arms to accept his law, just as he himself did not want to force someone to accept the law of Mohammed. As can be readily seen, he spoke or wrote rightfully. For truly, Christ says in the last chapter of Matthew: 'Go and teach all people, baptizing them in the name of the Father, the Son, and the Holy Spirit, teaching them to observe all that I have commanded you.'[72] He does not say: 'Go and take up arms, wage war and kill or force to believe those who do not want to believe you.' Instead, he says 'Go and teach', and before that He says 'To me has been given all authority in heaven and on earth'.[73] Giving to understand (as He says more clearly elsewhere) that no one comes to the Father but through Him, that is through the gift, infusion and movement of the Holy

---

[71] See Enguerran de Monstrelet, *Chroniques*, vol. 3 (Paris, 1545), fols. 61b–2b. Monstrelet (*c.* 1400–53) was the fifteenth-century successor to Froissaert.

[72] Matthew 28:19–20.

[73] Matthew 28:18.

Spirit, who uses no weapons, but the mouths of the prophets, ministers and teachers.

Now, it is known that, as Cicero writes, defence is natural, and that, as the Digest and the jurist maintain in the law 'ut vim atque iniuriam' under the title 'De Iustitia & Iure',[74] the Prince does not have the power to take this away from someone. Moreover as Baldus writes in his comment no. 15 on the first law under the title 'vunde vi' of the Codex,[75] there are only two means of defence, the one by means of law, the other by means of war and force of weapons. How then can one argue that the pious Lords, having presented the Request (as said before) to such a good and godly end, deserved to be treated, together with the States of the country and the subjects, in excess of promises and sworn faithfulness, by sending them a tyrant, with so much cruelty and so many plagues.

And again, as they were not able to achieve anything by law, and as no one was willing to pay attention to their Request, but they were detained by clever means and beautiful words or holy water of the Court (as it is said) until the time that all violence and force was ready, then how can one blame them for the fact that some of them have taken up arms to resist such force and violence and have taken on a defensive war.

For it is known to everyone how decently and prudently his Excellency,[76] with good assistance of the Count of Hoochstraten,[77] calmed down the popular commotion in Antwerp on the 14th day of March in the year 1566. Undoubtedly, in doing so he preserved for the King his treasure, saved the country which was greatly endangered and

---

[74] Digest, Book 1, Title 1, paragraph 3 (p. 1). This law by Florentinus deals with the 'right to repel violent injuries' and argues 'that whatever a person does for his bodily security he can be held to have done rightfully'. Together with the rule from Digest 43. 16. 1, (sentence) 27 that it is justifiable to repel unjust force with force (vim vi repellere licere), this law was one of the foundations for late medieval justifications of political resistance, later taken up by Lutheran and Calvinist authors. See Skinner, *Foundations*, vol. 2, pp. 125–6. 204ff.

[75] Baldus de Ubaldis, *Baldi Ubaldi di Perusini ... In vij, hiij, ix, x & xi Codicis Libros Commentaria* (Venice, 1615), fol. 134. The comment is on the Codex 8. 4. 1. For Baldus see 'Biographical Notes'.

[76] 'His Excellency' is of course William of Orange, who, in the following sentences, is praised for the way he handled affairs in 1566.

[77] Anthony of Lalaing (c. 1530–68), Count of Hoogstraten, was Orange's successor as governor of Antwerp. He was convicted by Alva's Blood Council, but had already left the country.

prevented great bloodshed. For this one should credit him with nothing but praise and honour.

It is also known to everyone how the Counts of Hoorne and Egmont were arrested treacherously and in contravention of the privileges of the Country and the Order,[78] and taken to Ghent by the Duke of Alva; how, at the inexpressible expense of the country and in order to curb it, the Castle of Antwerp was set up on the following 27th October and later completed; how immediately thereafter the persecution started of the Christians and of those who had the slightest dealings with the affair; how a Blood Council was set up in contravention of the Privileges of Towns and Countries, where a bloodthirsty Spaniard, named Juan de Vargas[79] presided, in order to complete their affairs and to exercise their tyranny even better (so that nothing would remain unpunished that the ordinary and provincial councils might have condoned); how the latter, in contravention of all laws, were expressly forbidden to examine any affairs concerning the troubles, or anything connected with them. What is more, the members of the sovereign councils could be summoned there – something that was previously unheard of and unthinkable.

Moreover, to continue my discourse by recounting some points and acts of tyranny in more detail, it should be noted firstly that, unheard of and against all disposition of law, indeed against God's word, the Request mentioned above was declared by this very Blood Council to be a conspiracy against his Royal Majesty, so that there would be more ground to proceed with both the confiscation of goods and the privation of dignity and body, so that the children would be bereft of the means to avenge them afterwards.

On 19 January 1568 his Princely Excellency, the courageous, devout and faithful Count Louis, his brother,[80] the Count of Hoochstraten and Culemborg,[81] the Lord of Brederode, and other Lords and nobles were summoned without receiving any assurance of their

---

[78] The Order of the Golden Fleece.

[79] Juan de Vargas was a Spanish jurist, who played a leading role in the Blood Council. He left the Netherlands in 1573.

[80] Louis of Nassau (1538–74), Orange's younger brother, played a leading role in the Compromise of the nobles. Later he assisted his brother as a diplomat and military commander. He died during the famous battle of the Mokerheide.

[81] Floris, Count of Culemborg (1537–98) was a member of the Compromise. He too was judged guilty of treason by the Blood Council. His goods were confiscated; Culemborg himself survived as he had already left the Low Countries.

person to appear before the aforesaid Blood Council, together with a great number of merchants and citizens, who had nothing or everything to do with the affairs of the Request, the Religion and the weapons. On 28 May following (the trial was kept short) they were declared guilty of the crime of lese-majesty, and their goods were to be confiscated. To avenge the death of the Count of Arembergh,[82] various nobles were executed by sword, a thing unheard of, among them the banneret of Batenbourg and the Lord of Andelot, a Burgundian by birth and house. In spite of the Privileges of the Order, which maintain that none of its Lords may be judged but by the Council of the Order itself, the Counts of Egmont and Hoorne were ordered to be scandalously beheaded on the fifth of June in Brussels, and to their further ignominy and to express the tyrannical will, their heads were displayed on gallows and pins, their goods were declared confiscable, the House of Culemborch was demolished and a stake was put up there, stating in four languages substantially these words: 'For the execrable conspiracy committed here against the Roman Catholic religion, his Royal Majesty and his countries, this house was ruined.' If there are no people left, small wonder that a tyrant tyrannizes houses or animals, for otherwise he should have to eat and crucify himself, as it is written about Nero, Caligula and others that they complained because their mind was always terrified and tormented.

And in order to corrupt and destroy the studies, the King did not refrain from kidnapping my Lord the Count of Buren, only son of his Excellency from his first marriage, who was studying at Louvain at the time, taking him to Spain,[83] which directly contravened the Privileges of Brabant, the Joyous Entry, and the freedom of the University of Louvain.

To catch those who had been absent, a false general pardon was proclaimed after a horrible massacre and murder of many thousands of persons of all qualities and sexes, but to little avail, as the small number and quality of the persons who put their trust in it did not import that this would reveal his tyranny.

---

[82] Jean de Ligne, Count of Aremberg (1525–68) was killed in the battle of Heiligerlee, in which the Spanish troops were defeated by Louis of Nassau.

[83] Philip William, Count of Buren (1554–1618), was the son of William of Orange and Anna van Buren, William's first wife. Until 1596 Philip William remained in Spain, only to return later to the Spanish Netherlands, where he became a member of the Council of State. See p. 149, note 21.

However, the people were not sufficiently impoverished by the long war. They [the Spaniards] still tried to impose an eternal tenth penny, and set themselves to introduce this by force in spite of various remonstrances on this issue, which argued that this could not be put into practice and could not take place without the consent of the States General of the country. Nonetheless, he [Alva] did not succeed (because of the courage of those of Brussels, who opposed it assiduously).[84]

The Count of Bossu, passing through Rotterdam with a troop of Spaniards ill-fatedly sacked and murdered a lot of poor citizens.

And as an evident sign of Spanish impudence and tyranny, on 2 October 1572 the citizens of Malines were plundered, some of them were killed, many female persons and young daughters were raped, as is deplored unto the present day. For there are many in Malines who learned to know the Spanish cruelty through bitter experience. Only few think about it now, but it was of little avail that they hailed them with crosses and flags, and conveyed the King of Spain good affection, saying that they did not want to forsake him by oath, but would rather leave their office. O great foolishness, o great blindness, o great insensitivity, read the letter of Escovedo in which he writes to the King of Spain that the issue of the religion will be of great use to subject some to him by means of others. What else does this mean but that he will spare no one, as he says: 'There is no one who wishes you well.'

I would like these people, so blinded and deafened, to tell me what advantage those who are so scrupulous with regard to their natural Lord and the Roman religion, have had in the towns of Zutphen, Naarden, Rotterdam, Haarlem, Maastricht and others. For they sing about it permanently, indeed for this cause they would want to be plundered again, even though many fellow citizens, all those who are differently minded, would suffer.

It would take too much time to recount here what happened in these towns and what followed at the time of the Duke of Alva, the great Commander of Castile, Requesens, Don Juan, who was an

---

[84] Protest against the introduction of the Tenth Penny was widespread. Staunch resistance was especially found in Brussels. When Alva wanted to enforce the collection of the Tenth Penny in his residence, local shopkeepers and beerbrewers responded with a general strike. Eventually the town magistrate made a compromise with the brewers, which again infuriated Alva.

arrant fox as it turned out later, and now under the Prince of Parma and the Malcontents. It will suffice that I have touched on some subjects, from which one may conclude how tyrannically the King of Spain and the Malcontents with their servants have acted in these countries. I will only add that within Tournai too, tyranny and violence has befallen some dead bodies. For this is an execrable matter, which no good government should tolerate, let alone execute.

It is well known to everyone how reasonably his Princely Excellence and the States General, who have remained in the union,[85] have always acted with regard to the submission to the King of Spain and the maintenance of the Roman religion, so that there is no need to deal with the subject. It should be mentioned only that his Excellency, before taking up arms against the King, received many complaints from various great Lords about the tyranny and injustice of the Duke of Alva. On these issues he has demanded right and justice. The States General have done likewise, as appears from their Justifications, but it would take too long to recount them here.

I think this is worth mentioning here, just as it was briefly dealt with by the States General of the united Netherlands in their Placard of 26 July 1581,[86] signed by Jan van Asseliers, in which they explained why the King of Spain was abrogated from the government and rule of the Netherlands and forbidden by them to use his name and seal in the Netherlands from now on. Namely, that he in government cannot be taken for a Prince but has to be considered a tyrant, and as such may, by right and reason, be no longer acknowledged as Prince but abjured, at least by his subjects, especially by deliberation of the States of the country, and to protect themselves, another may be chosen in his place as overlord without abuses: this may happen when he does not protect and save the subjects from all injustice, annoyance and violence, to which task he has been set, as a shepherd for the protection of his flock; or if he, forgetting that a Prince derives his authority and power, after God, from the subjects without whom he cannot be a Prince nor have authority, exploits his subjects as if they were created by God for the benefit of the Prince, to serve as wretched slaves and to be obedient to him in everything he orders, be

---

[85] The 'union' refers to the Union of Utrecht. See 'Introduction', p. xxii.
[86] The 'Act of Abjuration', which forfeited Philip II of his sovereignty over the Low Countries.

it godly or ungodly, just or unjust, reasonable or unreasonable, good or bad. Even more it may happen when the subjects cannot assuage their Prince with humble remonstrances, nor stop him from his tyrannical plans and murderous wilfulness and make him understand that he should maintain and protect the innate freedom of themselves, their wives, children and descendants. Such should principally take place in these Netherlands as these have been governed from all old times, and also had to be governed, after the contents of the oath taken by their Prince at the inauguration, following their Privileges, customs and old habits, especially considering that most of the Netherlands receive their Prince on conditions, by contract and agreements, which lapse when the Prince breaks them even if he has the right to rule the Country. For even though Baldus and some other commentators maintain in their first comment 'De Natura Feudi'[87] that the emperor is not subject to any laws (against the very words of the text *Digna Vox*), they nonetheless feel (as Marianus Socinus Junior does in Consilium 77, number 125 of his first volume)[88] that the emperors, and with more reason all Princes, are subject to the laws they have made, conditions they have sworn to, contracts they have made, and agreements they have concluded.

That they are subject to the laws they have made is shown clearly in the gloss on the law 'Princeps legibus solutus est' of the Digest's title 'De legibus & senatusque consultis'[89] with the words 'Princips legibus ab alio conditis', where it is observed that a Prince is indeed exempted from the laws created by others, while by contrast it is argued that he is subject to the laws made by himself.[90] That they are bound to respect the conditions sworn by them, is wonderfully shown by Guido de Susa, Cynus and all doctors in their comments on the law 'digna

---

[87] Baldus de Ubaldis, *Baldus de Perusio Super Feudis. Opus aureum iuris utriusque luminis domini Baldi de Perusio Super Feudis* (1542), fol. 19.

[88] Marianus Socinus, *Consiliorum sive malis reponsorum Mariani Socini Iunioris, Volumen primum* (Venice, 1571), consilium 77, no. 125, fol. 137. Socinus, a jurist and, as he was labelled on the title page of his works, a 'Sienese patrician', belonged to the generation of later, fifteenth-century commentators on Roman law.

[89] Digest 1. 3. 31. Ulpian's famous law 'The emperor is released from the laws' was the foundation of many medieval pleas for absolute rule.

[90] See, for example, the standard interpretation of Accursius (c. 1191–1263), a teacher of Roman law at the university of Bologna and one of the principal Glossators, in his *Accursii Glossa in Digestum Vetus* (Venice, 1487), fol. 9, reprinted in the series *Corpus Glossatorum Juris* (Turin, 1969).

vox',[91] and by Albericus on the law 'Princeps legibus solutus est',[92] with Panormitano in Comment 10 on the title 'De Iudiciis'.[93] Indeed, a Prince who concludes a contract with a private person, entering with him into some convention or compact, is bound to fulfil it. According to Laurentius Krichonius in the eighty-fifth conclusion of his common opinion 'conturia iii', this is the common opinion both of the canonist and the legist.[94] Thus the prince is even more bound to keep his promises to the States General and the common subjects of the country. Indeed, he is fully obliged, so that there is no way he can be discharged in this respect, not even from the capacity of his full power; as is wonderfully testified by Paulus de Castro in his comment on the text 'digna vox', no. 5,[95] and by Bartolus in his comment number 21 (third Questio) on the law 'omnes' of the Digest.[96] Restaurus Castaldus expresses the same feeling in his treatise *De Imperatore*, Questione 111, vers. 81.[97] In addition to these authors Andreas Alciatus argues (in Responsa 167, at the 'tertium dubium',

---

[91] Guido de Suzaria was professor of law at Padua and Bologna in the second half of the thirteenth century. He was famous for a so-called 'quaestio' on the obligation of the 'princeps' to adhere to his contracts, which however was lost. It is referred to by Cynus de Pistoia (1270–1336/7), who was not only an important Italian poet but also an influential jurist: he introduced the scholastic techniques into Italy. One of his pupils at Perugia was Bartolus of Sassoferrato.

[92] See Albericus de Rosate, *Commentarii in primam Digesti veteris partem* (Venice, 1585) reprinted in the series *Opera iuridica rariora*, vol. 21 (Bologna, 1974), fol. 31. Albericus was a distinguished Commentator (or Postglossator).

[93] Panormitanus, *Commentaria in V decretalum libros* (Venice, 1605), fol. 21. Panormitanus (1386–1445), who was appointed Archbishop of Palermo (and thus got his name) was born as Nicolas de Tudeschis in Catania. He was one of the most important Canon lawyers of his time, teaching at Bologna, Parma, Siena and Florence. He participated in the 1431 Council of Basel and propounded conciliarist ideas. The reference is to a comment on the first title of the second book of Gregorius IX's Decretals, a standard part of Canon law.

[94] A reference to the work of the Rostock law professor Lorenz Kirchhoff, *Receptarum, sententiarum, sive, communium opinionem IV . . . per clarissimum iureconsult. D. Laurentium Kirchovium* (Frankfurt, 1576).

[95] Paulus de Castro, *Prima Super Codice* (1527), fol. 26, where the author refers to Cynus de Pistoia. Paulus de Castro, a pupil of Baldus, was one of the outstanding late fourteenth- and early fifteenth-century commentators.

[96] Bartolus of Sassoferrato, *In primam Digesti vet. partem Commentaria* (Turin, 1589), fol. 12.

[97] Restaurus Castaldus, 'De Imperatore', in *Duodecimum Volumen Tractatuum e variis iuris interpretibus collectorum* (Lyon, 1549), fol. 85. Castaldus was a sixteenth-century jurist (he died in 1564) from Perugia who taught in his home town and in Bologna. *De Imperatore* was a comment on the title 'De Institutionibus' of the Codex Justinianus.

number 10)[98] that when a ruler does not uphold his fidelity, one is no longer obliged in conscience to remain faithful to him. Therefore it is said in the Latin verse 'To whom breaks faith, faith is broken'. The same is straightfowardly founded in the written laws, see under the second law 'cum proponas',[99] also Bartolus in his comment on the title 'De pactis' of the Codex,[100] the gloss, the law 'qui fidem licitiae transactionis' under the title 'De Transactionibus' of the Digest,[101] the paragraph 'offerri' of the law 'Iulianus' and the law 'qui pendentem' under the title 'De Actionibus Empti' of the Digest.[102] Indeed, this rule is so common that it also applies to contracts and conventions between parties, which are solemnized by oath. See paragraphs two and three of the title 'De Iureiurando' in the Digest,[103] and the law 'si quis maior' under the title 'De transactionibus' of the Codex.[104]

This should also be applied to contracts and agreements between the Prince and the States of the country, concluded by the subjects: namely, that they must be fulfilled. For all conventions, contracts and agreements, although they previously consisted in the will and the discretion of the parties, have to be fulfilled, after they have been completely aggregated by mutual consent, in all points; not at will but by necessity, as appears from the Codex under the title 'De obligationibus actionibus', the paragraph 'sicut'[105] and the Digest's rule 'sicut autem voluntatis' of the law 'in commodato hace pactio' under the title 'Commodati vel Contra'.[106]

---

[98] Andrea Alciato, *D. Andreae Alciati Mediolanensis iureconsulti celeberrimi Responsa* (Basel, 1582), column 299 (in this edition this is Liber 3, Consilium 7, no. 28; in the earlier Lyon edition of this work the passage featured under Consilium 167): 'Quod si dominus non servat fidem vasallo, quod vasallus similiter non tenetur ei servare iurementum fidelitatis'.

Andrea Alciato (1492–1550) was a principal exponent of legal humanism, which he exported from Italy to France. Thus he greatly contributed to the introduction of humanist techniques in legal interpretation, abandoning the more traditional scholastic methods. Alciato used these techniques, among other things, to formulate a theory of popular sovereignty, taking traditional views, such as Bartolus had offered, as a starting point. One of his pupils, during his stay at the University of Bourges, was John Calvin.

[99] Codex 2. 3 (De Pactis). 21.

[100] Bartolus of Sassoferrato, *In primam Codicis partem* (Turin, 1589), fol. 59, where Bartolus directly starts his comment with this proverb.

[101] Digest, Book 2, Title 15, paragraph 16.

[102] Digest 19. 1. 13. 8; Digest 19. 1. 25.

[103] Digest, 12, 2, 2–3.

[104] Codex 2. 4. 41.

[105] Codex 4. 10. 14.

[106] Digest 13. 6. 17. 3.

In applying all these wonderful passages of law to our purpose,[107] it should be noted that after the death of the Emperor Charles V of blessed memory, from whom the King of Spain [Philip II] had received these beautiful Netherlands, the King forgot so many loyal services which these Countries and the subjects had rendered both to himself and to his father, thanks to which they had obtained so many praiseworthy victories over their enemies that their name and power were glorified and respected in the whole world. Neither did he pay attention to the opposite admonitions given him in the past by the aforesaid Imperial Majesty. He rather lent his ear to the bloodthirsty Spanish Council beside him than to the pious nobles, landlords and Princes of these Netherlands. The Spanish Counsellors, having an inextinguishable appetite to usurp these Netherlands where they wanted to command and to govern, and replacing the eminent States, as in the Kingdoms of Naples, Sicily, at Milan, in the Indies and in other countries of the King, persuaded the King and drummed it into him – out of the innate envy and hate which they bore against the nobility and inhabitants of these Netherlands and out of hope that their unbridled plan and mischief would be effected – that it was better for the reputation of his Majesty to conquer these Countries afresh, be it with guile or weaponry, to rule and command them thereafter freely and absolutely at his own will and discretion (which is to tyrannize), rather than under the conditions and restrictions by which he had sworn to govern when he took over the government.

Following this blind guide and instead of acquitting himself of his oath, he sought by all means to take away the ancient freedom from these Countries and to bring them into a miserable slavery under the government of the Spanish bloodhounds. To this purpose he used (as mentioned before) as the most convenient means, the pretext of the Roman religion, the Spanish Inquisition and the introduction of new Bishops and Canons, whom he provided with what he took from the abbeys without right. This meant that the Bishops (who also might be strangers – it was well premeditated to exclude all natives so that it would be much easier to proceed with the devious enterprise) would have had (directly contravening the Privileges of the Countries) the first places and voices in the assemblies of the States of these Countries, so that, in following the example of the Pope, the King's

---

[107] The following paragraph paraphrases part of the historical gravamina as laid down in the *Act of Abjuration*. See E.H. Kossmann and A.F. Mellink, *Texts*, pp. 217–18.

plan would not fail. For nobody then would have wanted to contradict him, either in minor or major matters. Rather they would have filled their ears with evil devices and practices, for all of them would have been people standing under his command and devotion as his sworn creatures. All of this to the unspeakable disadvantage of the Countries and their inhabitants, as was understood by the said Imperial Majesty, who warned them and who prevented the effectuation of the Inquisition (which was always resented in these Countries as being the worst form of slavery one could imagine).

It happened in spite of this and of various remonstrances which were submitted at various times both in writing and by word of mouth, both by particular towns and provinces and by some of the most principal nobles of the Countries, namely the Lord of Montigny and the Count of Egmont, with the consent and advice of the Duchess of Parma, the Council of State and the States General. These pointed to the trouble, misery and calamity that were to be expected as a result of these innovations. Moreover, the king pretended to understand them, thereby giving good hope that he would do something to effect them. Nonetheless, in some letters, shortly afterwards, he sharply commanded the opposite, against all promises and faithfulness. On penalty of his indignation the bishops were to be accepted immediately and had to be put in peaceful possession of their dioceses and incorporated abbeys. The Inquisition was to be put into effect and the Ordinations of the Council of Trent (which in many points contradicted the Privileges of the Netherlands) were to be enforced. This gave the community sufficient reason to withdraw its good affection towards the King. For it noticed that it was not only his intention to tyrannize over its goods and persons, but also over its conscience, against all right, reason and fairness. For no Prince is allowed to take from somebody what the Law of God and of nature allows him. So it is discussed in the Digest and in Ecclesiastical Law under the title 'De Constitutionibus' and the law 'si quid contra ius vel util public' of the Codex.[108]

Likewise he could not forbid the subjects to serve God in their conscience following His word and will, for in doing so, he would kill their souls, which is against God and against nature, as we have previously deduced at length. And this is (seen properly) why the

---

[108] Codex, Book 1, last law.

King of Spain was moved to wage war against this country and to persecute its inhabitants so pitifully. Namely, (as mentioned above) that in the year 1566 some of the most principal of the country's nobility, out of sympathy with the subjects, have submitted the remonstrance outlined above.

There may be somebody who still does not understand this matter sufficiently, who is so blinded by his evil passions that he cannot be persuaded by any argument in the world to acknowledge the good right which the faithful and obliging nobility (I mean the righteous ones) and the subjects had and still have, to arm themselves against the tyranny of Spain and to forsake and renounce the King as being no longer a ruler but a tyrant. For these stubborn and deluded fools, I will present another piece of evidence, which centres around the two parts and statures of man, namely the soul and the body, which together constitute the whole man.

It is certain and well known that the whole man, created by God out of nothing, consists of a reasonable soul and an earthly body. Both God and the government have power over this man, on the understanding, however, that the Kings and authorities have only been granted by God the power of using the bodies and goods of the subjects for their protection. In no way may they exploit them for slavery, tyranny, or any other form of irrationality. From this we may infer that it was God's great mercy and liberality, that he set one man above the others, for he could have ruled alone externally over his creature. Therefore it should first be noticed that the government has no command over one part of man, namely the soul. For the Scripture teaches us that the spirit of truth comforted the persecuted Christians by saying that they should not fear those who seek the body, but he who is capable of slaying both body and soul.

However, the government and the Princes on earth take toll and tribute from goods (with the approval of those who represent the country and the subjects) and let the subjects serve them (if necessity requires it). Thus, while God's power over both soul and body is unlimited, the power of the worldly authorities cannot transgress the bounds of the body and goods of the subjects. And, to prove this forcefully, the wisdom of the Father, Christ, says in Matthew, chapter 22, verse 21, 'Render unto Caesar the things that are Caesar's, and unto God the things that are God's.' Tribute and honour to Caesar, fear to God. And Peter, the Apostle, says in the second chapter of his first letter, 'Fear God, honour the King',[109] as if he wanted to say: 'Honour the King in such a way that the fear of God is always in your mind', or, 'Keep the commandments of the King so that you do not break the law of the Lord, your God.'

On this matter, the royal prophet David appointed different gatekeepers for God's and the King's Empire (as is written in the twenty-sixth chapter of the first book of Chronicles).

Likewise Jehosh'aphat appointed different ministers for the judgment of Jehovah and for the court of the King, which means that he appointed some for the exercise of the true religion and others for the maintenance of the King's law.[110]

Daniel writes in the third chapter of his Prophecy that Nebuchadnez'zar raised his voice and said: 'Blessed be the God of Shadrach, Meshach, and Abed'nego, who has sent his angel and delivered his servants, who trusted in him, and set at naught the king's command, and yielded up their body and life rather than honour and worship any god except their own God. Therefore this will be my decree: Any people, folk, or language that slanders the God of Shadrach, Meshach, and Abed'nego shall die, and their houses shall be disgracefully ruined; for there is no other God who is able to deliver such as this one.'[111] Is this not a wonderful and laudable example which proves forcefully that the Kings have no competence to govern or command the souls and consciences of men? Verily, it is an example worthy to be written in golden letters in the courts of Princes and in the places where they converse most, so that, in following the example, they might remember that they are not permitted to usurp the command over the conscience of their subjects and to force them to idolatry or disbelief by use of weapons. For if, from his youth on, this example had been implanted in the King of Spain, like the doctrines of the Machiavellians, Atheists, Libertarians, unbelievers and the like, undoubtedly he would have let himself be persuaded by reason to accept the remonstrances, which were submitted to him with such good manners and reverence. He would not have sent, against all rights, the Duke of Alva (a stranger, not of his blood) with a large bunch of robbers, thieves, murderers, godless, slanderers, cruel crooks, rapers, sodomites, perjurers, and similar scum, to the Low

[109] 1 Peter 2:17.
[110] 2 Chronicles 19:11.
[111] Daniel 4:28–9.

Countries, not only to rule cruelly over goods and bodies, but also to force the consciences, as he has signified himself. For immediately after his arrival he placed garrisons in the most principal towns, built castles and fortresses, executed the most eminent of the nobility by fraudulent means, and modified the judicial order according to the ways of Spain. He set up new councils, extorted unusual tributes and left nothing undone, by which he might hurt or destroy the power and excellent persons of nobility, learning and trade, oust merchandise and manufacture (of which consist most of the riches of these Netherlands), suppress studies, destroy the countryside, impoverish the countryman, injure each and everybody and exterminate the Privileges. All this in order to practice and accomplish his ungodly device to be dismissed of the promises, contracts and oath by which he was bound to the subjects, and, consequently, to usurp from us title of conquest, so that his insatiable tyranny might have some foundation, and he would be able to treat us, our wives, children and their descendants as he has in all cruelty treated the Indians. Of this the Histories testify in such a way that even someone with a permanent heart of stone could not read them, without being moved by compassion and pity. I wish they would reread them often, who act so relentlessly against their fellow citizens that night and day they wish nothing but that the king would come and triumph over these heretics. For if all our wounds were salved, they would doubtlessly turn around and change their mind. For a tyrant tyrannizes his own blood rather than give up his tyrannical intentions. This was clearly shown by Nero, who cut open the belly of his mother when she was alive, saying he wished to see the place where he had lain in his mother's body. Similarly the King of Spain, displaying his tyrannical nature, did not spare his son, indeed he did not shy away from killing his legitimate wife, the Queen. Even though these two persons were closest to him, his cruelty was so great and his thirst for blood so insatiable that he longed to satiate himself with them.[112]

It would be possible for me to adduce many other examples of his murderousness, cruelty and tyranny but the reader might find it too much and too sad that even the burned-down places and the bodies in their graves still mourn and weep for his felony. Therefore I will leave it at that and conclude my argument.

---

[112] Here serious accusations against Philip II are repeated which by 1581 had become commonplace. See also, p. 57, note 62.

In my opinion I have proven sufficiently that, first, one ought not to be submissive to a government, which abuses its authority, and changes the right of rule into force, violence and tyranny. On the contrary, all devout nobles and dedicated subjects are permitted on account of many causes and reasons, to resist such tyranny. They should employ their body, goods and blood to this end. However, it should be clearly seen that one may not rebel against a just government.

Second, that, in accordance with the origins of the laws the office of the government is to protect the good and to punish the evil, to administer justice over the people, and to take the lead in war against its enemies, and that therefore the government too is subjected to the laws, which it is obliged to advocate.

Third, that there is a major difference between a good government and a tyrannical prince, and the characteristics that distinguish them.

Fourth, that the characteristics of a good government cannot be found in the King of Spain but only, on the contrary, all the marks with which a sincere tyrant is branded.

Fifth, that there are only two ways of defending oneself, namely by right and by weapon, and that one may use the weapon where there is no place for right.

Sixth, that no government has power over the conscience, neither may it constrain someone by force to accept the faith it has itself, but that power over the soul is reserved to God.

Finally, that the King of Spain has sought for means to rule over the soul, and to treat the body and goods with tyrannic abuse in order ultimately to dominate his subjects as a people that has been newly conquered, namely with injustice, irrationality, force, violence, murderousness and tyranny.

Consequently it follows that, since the King has refused to listen to reason and has lent his ear to toadies, his Princely Excellence and other Lords of the country together with the good subjects had every right to take up the other means of protection, namely, first a defensive war and, after the King tried to suppress this, an offensive war, in order to keep him out of the country, not as a good Prince but as a tyrant, if only because (leaving aside his gruesome cruelty) he was found to be perjurious. He has not kept his promises to the subjects, as he is obliged to do, being accepted by his subjects on such conditions and promises. Therefore those who say generally that the

Princes are not subjected to the laws, indeed are not obliged to observe their promises and agreements, are sinning against God and are deceiving nature, unless these people want to exclude and except the laws of God and of nature, and the just conventions and contracts that have been agreed upon. This subject is discussed wonderfully by Accursius in his comment 'Princeps' under the Title 'De legibus' of the Digest,[113] and in Plutarch's *Apophtegmatibus graecorum*,[114] that is, in the lovely sayings of the Greeks. They record the striking example of Dionysus, the Tyrant of Sicily, who said to his mother (who had asked him of something against the law of God and of nature and his promises): 'I may dispense with the written laws and customs of the Syracusians, but not with the law of nature', making it clear enough that no Prince, however great he may be, is permitted to act against his oath and promise, for these are founded on natural equity and the law of God.

Likewise contracts or testaments of particular parties cannot limit the ordinations of magistrates, following the law 'ius publicum privatorem pactis mutari non potest' under the Digest's title 'De pactis'[115] and the law 'nemo potest' under the Digest's title 'De legatis'.[116] Neither can the magistrates' edicts obliterate the old customs, nor can the old customs prejudice the written Rights by the fifth sentence of the third law under the title 'De Sepulchro Violatio' of the Digest,[117] and the law 'quae sit longa confuet' under the second title of the Codex.[118] Similarly the laws of Princes and governments can not change God's law and natural justice.

Thus it should follow that Princes too stand under the command and prohibition of the civil laws, when these are equitable and reasonable. The laudable sayings of Pacatus to the Emperor Theodosius are to this end, when he says 'Tantum tibi licet quantum per leges licebit', that is, 'You are allowed to do as much as the laws permit

---

[113] See Accursius, *Glossa in Digestum Vetum*, fol. 9, a comment on the crucial law 'Princeps legibus solutus est' (Digest 1. 3. 31).

[114] This probably refers to Plutarch, *Moralia*, vol. 3, which in the standard 1572 Stephanus edition included texts on 'Sayings of Kings and Commanders', 'Sayings of Romans', 'Sayings of Spartans', 'The Ancient Customs of the Spartans'. 'Sayings of Spartan Women' and the 'Bravery of Women'.

[115] Digest 2. 14. 38: 'Public law cannot be changed by private pacts'.

[116] Digest 30. 55.

[117] Digest 47. 12. 3. 5.

[118] Codex 8. (52) 53. 2.

you'.[119] Elsewhere Seneca says: 'Caesaricum omnia licet propter hoc minus licet'.[120] As if he wanted to say: 'As the Emperor is allowed to do everything, he is not permitted anything.'

Among other beautiful and notable legal decisions, one concerning the obligation of the Prince with regard to his subjects crosses my mind: namely, that if a Prince orders or acts against his promises, the law should be applied to all cases of abuse, and nothing is to be presumed. For the obligation has two sides. On the one hand, natural equity demands that all agreements and promises are kept. On the other hand, as far as his faithfulness is concerned, the Prince is obliged to uphold it unconditionally, to the extent that he guarantees the loyalty which the subjects have amongst each other even if it can be expected that this will cause him damage. There is no crime so detestable for a Prince as perjury, as described powerfully by Alexander in 'Consilium 97, nu 13' of his third volume,[121] Cynus on the law 'rescripta' under the title 'De Praecib. Imperatori offrend',[122] Jacobus Butrigarius on the Codex, Book I, 'si contra Ius',[123] Innocentius' decretal 'ad Apostolicam' under 'De re iudicate',[124] Panormitanus, Imola, and Felinum in c.1. 'De probationibus'.[125]

Therefore Ulpian is right in writing in the first law under the title

---

[119] See Pacatus, 'Latini Pacati Drepanii Panegyricus Theodosio Augusto Dictum' 12. 5, in Edouard Galletier (ed.), *Panégyriques Latins*, vol. 3 (Paris, 1955), p. 80. Pacatus was a fourth-century rhetorician from the area of Bordeaux, who became famous for this panegyric on Theodosius I.

[120] Seneca, 'De Consolatione ad Polybium' 7.2, in Seneca, *Moral Essays*, vol. 3 (Cambridge, Mass. (Loeb edition), 1958), p. 374.

[121] This is probably a reference to Alexander Tartagnus (or Alexander of Imola), *Liber tertius. Consiliorum Alexandri Imolensis* (Lyon, 1547), fol. 70, where the author refers to both Cynus and Butrigarius (however, Consilium 97 only has twelve numbers). Tartagnus was a fifteenth-century commentator, who died in 1477.

[122] Cynus de Pistoia, *In Codicim et aliquot Titulos primi Pandectorum tomi id est Digesti Veteris. Doctissima Commentaria* (Frankfurt, 1578; repr. Turin, 1964), fols. 35a–7, which offers a comment on Codex 1. 19. For Cynus see p. 203, note 91.

[123] Jacobus Butrigarius, *Lectura super codice* (Paris, 1516), fols. 37–40, reprinted in the series *Opera Iuridica rariora*, vol. 8 (Bologna, 1973). Butrigarius (c. 1274–1348) taught law at the University of Bologna. Among his pupils was Bartolus of Sassoferrato.

[124] See 'Liber Sextus Decretalium Domini Bonifacii Papae VIII', Book 2, Title 14, Chapter 2, in Aemilius Friedberg (ed.), *Decretalium Collectiones*, vol. 2 (Leipzig, 1879; repr. Graz, 1959), pp. 1008–10. This is a decretal of pope Innocentius IV (c. 1200–54), who was a highly distinguished canon lawyer.

[125] Imola probably refers to Alexander of Imola who was in fact identical to Alexander Tartagnus. Felinus Sandeus was a canonist. The reference is probably to the comment on the title 'De probationibus' of the second book of Clementius' 'Constitutions', a standard part of canon law. See Friedberg, vol. 2, pp. 1124–99.

'De pactis' of the Digest: 'There is natural equity in this edict. For what so accords with human faith as that which men have decided among themselves to observe?'.[126] That is, the uniformity of the edict or ordination is natural, for what is more proper for human faithfulness than to maintain the things they have contracted amongst each other.

This legal decision deserves to be imprinted with golden letters on the gates of Princes' courts, so that each day they might be warned of what they assail if they treat the subjects contrary to promises and sworn faithfulness.

Peter Lombard, the master of the *Sentences*, regarded as one of the foremost among the doctors of the Roman Church,[127] writes that God himself is bound to fulfil his promises. For, he says, God spoke thus: 'Bring to me all people of the earth so that they may judge between me and my people if there is anything that I was bound to do but have not fulfilled.' Thus there can be no argument about whether or not a Prince is obliged to observe his oath, to keep his promises, and to treat his subjects as contracted. For if the Creator, our Almighty God is not free in this respect, how much less can a Prince, who is His creation, be excused here?

Furthermore it should be noted that if a Prince is called an absolute Lord this should be understood merely in the sense of a just ruler and supreme judge, whereas every individual subject remains in possession of his property and goods, by the law 'in rem actio' under the title 'De rei vindicatione' of the Digest.[128]

Therefore Seneca says in the fourth and fifth chapter of the seventh book on benefits: 'The right of ownership of all things belongs to the king, the actual ownership to individuals', and, a little later, 'Everything belongs to the king by his right of authority, and to the individuals by rights of ownership.'[129]

Thus for these and other reasons, too long to be recounted here, each subject (wishing to be called patriot) should be ashamed to dawdle in taking the oath demanded of him. For if the present

---

[126] Digest 2. 14. 1.

[127] Peter Lombard (*c.* 1100–60) was one of the most distinguished medieval theologians. His *Four Books of Sentences*, written between 1155 and 1188, was accepted as a standard work of theology.

[128] Digest 6. 1. 23.

[129] Seneca, *On Benefits*, Book 7, chapter 4, section 2, and chapter 5, section 1. See Seneca, *Moral Essays*, vol. 3 (Cambridge, Mass. (Loeb edition), 1964), pp. 466 and 468.

government is allowed (as is sufficiently proven to correspond with fairness, utility and justice) to arm itself against the tyranny and mischief of the King of Spain, to defend itself with arms against him, and to keep him out of the country with the power of the people, so it is very well permitted to depose him from the government and rule over these Netherlands, and to forbid the use of his name and seal. Consequently it is not forbidden for the government but permitted, with even more reasons and stronger grounds, to request that all forsake the King of Spain by oath and regard themselves as dismissed from all duties and bonds, likewise that all promise and swear by the same oath to be faithful, obedient and helpful to the united Netherlands and their associates, also to the country's council and authorities established by the States of the provinces, to give them all help and assistance against the said King, his adherents and all other enemies of the country, and, in addition, to do everything that corresponds with the bounden duty to our government and fatherland.

A common rule of law dictates that he who is permitted something higher, can not be refused anything lower, by the clear words of the third sentence in the paragraph 'nec in ea' under the title '(Ad legem Iuliam) De Adulteriis' of the Digest,[130] in the Authentica 'multo magis' under the Title 'De sacr. sant. eccl.' of the Codex[131] and the chapter 'Ex parte tua' of the Title 'De decimis' in the Decretals.[132] Now, as is well known, words are less of a punishment than beatings, and beatings are less of a punishment than death. Also, the sword is less of a punishment than fire or another more terrible and harder death. Therefore, he who may punish with beatings, may even more so punish with words; he who may punish with death is free to punish with beatings and so forth. It follows that if the States of the country are permitted to resist someone and to take up arms against him, they are also free to declare his rule forfeited, and even more so they are allowed the very least, namely to request the subjects to forsake by oath the one who is seeking to oppress them, and to take an oath of loyalty to those who seek to protect them, and to further their cause with goods, blood, counsel and deeds.

---

[130] Digest 48. 5. 23 (22). 3: 'A person who has the power to kill an adulterer is all the more able lawfully to inflict rough treatment on him.'

[131] The Authentica 'Multo Magis' was derived from Novella 7, caput 11 and Novella 120, caput 7, and based on Codex 1. 2. 14.

[132] *Decretalium D. Gregorii*, Book 3, Title 30, Chapter 27 in Friedberg, vol. 2, column 565.

Although, at first sight, this seems to be a tough matter, if one takes into account right, reason, natural equity, indeed, God's word and the examples and teachings of the pagans, it appears clearly that neither the States of the country nor his Princely Excellency can be blamed at all in this affair. The King of Spain should impute himself and remember that he will fare as did those David refers to when he says: 'Incidit in foveam quam fecit'.[133] That is, 'He has tried to entangle others, but has fallen himself into the pit he had dug for others.'

Moreover, it did not happen without the just verdict of the Lord, who is veracious and just, and therefore does not punish without reason and also does as he has promised. In the fifth, eighth and other chapters of the book of Exodus, the Lord speaks to Pharaoh (who was a Tyrant over the children of Israel): 'Let my people go, that they may serve me and bring offerings to me.' However, due to the arrogance of his heart, Pharaoh said that he did not know this God, and immediately his downfall came. Nebuchadnez'zar orders his statue or image to be honoured and himself to be worshipped, but God forthwith constrains the unrestrained recklessness of a miserable man who wanted to appear like God, ceases to be a man and becomes like a donkey, who has left the right path and roams around in the wilderness. Alexander the Great rejoiced when toadies called him the son of Jupiter and therefore asserted that he should be worshipped. But before the triumphing had actually started, he was hit by a hasty death.

Under the pretext of uniting his empire, Antiochus[134] ordered everyone to leave God's law and to follow his. He desecrated the temple of the Jews and profaned the altars. However, after many calamities, miseries and defeats his power was curtailed. Suffocating in the anxiety of his heart, he bemoaned that this had befallen him for trying to force the Jews to impiety.

If I were to tell about the end of Nero, Caligula, Domitianus, Commodus[135] and others who persecuted the Christians and tried to suppress God's word, I could only write about misery and disaster.

---

[133] Psalm 7:15.

[134] Antiochus IV Epiphanes (215–164 BC) was Seleucid King of the Hellenistic Syrian kingdom from 175 until 164 BC. In 168 BC he conquered Jerusalem and tried to hellenize the city, forbidding the Jewish religion. In response Judas Maccabeus raised a successful Jewish rebellion.

[135] Lucius Aelius Aurelius Commodus, Roman emperor between 180 and 192 AD, was famous for his cruelty.

Whereas about Trajan, Hadrian, Antonius[136] and others, although they did not serve the true God but nonetheless allowed the Christians to do so, I could tell nothing but good.

All these reasons and examples have made perfectly clear that the requested oath should be enacted and effectuated for the sake of fairness and utility, and that such a request from those who are qualified to make it, is founded on justice, and exists in the law of God, in the written laws and in the law of nature.

Nonetheless, fearing that somebody may yet raise some objections in this respect, and since it is my intention to rebut these as much as possible, I think it is still necessary briefly to underpin my argument (although sensible people will find it sufficiently validated) with a fourth argument, namely its legality.

The conjunction and kinship between justice and legality is so great that the one cannot exist without the other. For he who abolishes justice, abolishes the laws as well. And where there is no law, justice cannot be found. Likewise there is a connection and similarity between the administration of justice and the law. This does not mean that there are no differences. For the administration of justice consists but in equity, whereas the law brings with it commands and prohibitions, inasmuch as the law is nothing but the command of a government employing its power and authority. Law orders men to do good and to leave off evil, and the administration of justice executes such an order. Everywhere there are laws, but the laws are not the same everywhere. For there are different laws in France, Spain, Germany, the Netherlands,[137] etc. In conformity with the diversity of areas and the diverse humours of the people, the laws are different. Nonetheless, everywhere there is only one justice, namely to live virtuously without hurting the other and to render to everyone what is his. It means to do good, to avoid evil, to champion the good and to punish the evil, to render to God and men what is theirs. This appears from the Institutes, the paragraph 'iuris praescripta' of the Title 'De Iustitia et iure'.[138] Therefore Lactantius Firmianus says in the ninth chapter of the sixth book on *De vero cultu*: 'So one thing is civil law,

---

[136] This is probably a reference to Antoninus Pius, Roman Emperor between 138 and 161, whose reign was celebrated for its tranquillity and prudence.

[137] At this point the author uses the present Dutch name of the united provinces 'Nederlant'; he no longer speaks about the Dutch provinces in plural but in singular.

[138] Institutes, Book 1, Title 1, Paragraph 3.

which customarily is different everywhere, and another thing is justice which was given to man as simple and uniform.'[139] By the law 'legis virtus haec est imperare vetare permittere punire' of the Digest's title 'De Legibus senatusque consultis',[140] the force of law is to order, prohibit, permit and punish: everything that does not concern executive tasks, but certain rules. Amongst the laws there is also diversity. Some are imperial written laws, some edicts of Princes, others customs and matters which the community has taken for laws, and so forth. Nonetheless there is the law of God and of nature which is equal for all Christians, as has been sufficiently deduced previously. It is these laws that I deal with.

Amongst these laws the most common is that each guards and arms himself against force, violence and injustice, and is readily supported in this by the truth. However, often someone is not powerful enough on his own. And if one is, sometimes discord impedes one to use power and thus creates the danger of being surprised, so that it becomes necessary to seek counsel and means in another way. Either one must conclude alliances with others, or choose a powerful Prince as protector, or if one does not want this, discord must be pacified. I do not intend to persuade us to elect some mighty potentate as protector (although I do not mean to say that this would be wrong, considering the tyranny and mischief which the King of Spain would love to bring over us, and noticing the great diversity of humours amongst the subjects), but only want to induce the community to the other remedy, namely the animation and creation of unity. Therefore I think it is advisable to attest with the law of God and of nature that there is nothing which can preserve concord amongst the citizens and subjects more than the oath. They should look to the person who seeks to suppress them, and kill that one with the assistance of the others.

It cannot be doubted that the origin of human concord is matrimony. For God ordained matrimony so that two persons, man and wife, would be faithful to each other, would live in concord and would reproduce united children. In order to uphold such fidelity and concord, two things are necessary, namely to order with moderation and justice, and to obey faithfully. This is not possible if the government acts contrary to the opinions of its subjects. That is why this

---

[139] Lactantius Firmianus, *Lucii Coelli Lactantii Firmiani. Opera. Tomus II. Divinarum Institutionem. Liber Sextus, De Vero Cultu* (Leyden, 1660), p. 573.

[140] Digest I. 3. 7.

calamitous war of the King of Spain and the Malcontents has come over us (leaving apart our stinking sins which are the main cause). It is a good lesson and chastisement for us to guard ourselves against falling into yet more trouble, by willing something different than the States of the country and his Princely Excellency deem advisable for our redemption, which happens if discord arises between them and us, because of the refusal of the oath, which is so godly and so lawful.

Just as the strong promise of faithfulness and eternal friendship which man and wife make to each other in solemnizing matrimony, in the eyes of the Lord and in the presence of the community, causes them greatly to love each other even more, to remain faithful, to live in friendship in all concord and peace, so the oath is a firm and indissoluble bond with which the government and its subjects ally themselves in fidelity and concord against their enemies. What then would move us to refuse it, to make trouble about it? Unless we did not approve of our government, and did not love those who love us so much that they put their body, goods and blood at stake for it. Surely we would deserve to be punished for ingratitude and impudence, if we would not forsake our mortal enemy to ally ourselves with friends, under oath, in fidelity and obedience. Rightly one might say against us, 'Ingratis servire nefas', that is, it is evil to serve the barbarous.

When he made an alliance with King Abimelech, Abraham swore. God's people often swear under the Kings, when they make a covenant with God to uphold their religion in all purity and piety.

Paul writes to the Hebrews, in the sixteenth verse of the sixth chapter, that the people swear by one who is greater than themselves, and that the oath is final confirmation in all disputes.[141] David says: 'The Lord has sworn and He will not regret it.' If God Himself, our father Abraham and others, God's people, Paul and other Christians have not objected to taking an oath and to confirming matters by oath, which they intended to complete and uphold, then why should we be ashamed to take an oath of fidelity and to forsake our enemy with it? Unless in our minds we are convinced that we would rather come to be slaves than fight against the King, our mortal enemy. For it is less to forsake him by oath than to use weapons against him. In this respect it is appropriate what Fulgentius writes in his first book of *Trasimundum*: Not to be willing to profess one's faith is to deny this

---

[141] The text of Hebrews 6:16 is as follows: 'Men indeed swear by a greater than themselves, and in all their disputes an oath is final for confirmation.'

faith.[142] Likewise it should be understood that whoever does not want to forsake the King by oath, is also not thinking of leaving or resisting him in any way either. In his first letter, *De coniugali debito*, the same author writes, 'So faithfulness in matrimony takes away the sin, which is aroused by the weakness of the flesh',[143] to make us understand the power of the bond by oath, which is so great that one could not dissolve it in any way, without falling into a crime, detested by all generous hearts as eternal infamy.

How could somebody say 'I am a good patriot and wish to fight for my fatherland, my liberty, my privileges, wife, children and descendants, and to die against the King of Spain and his allies, but I do not want to forsake nor abjure him by oath, or to set aside the duty I owe to him'? This cannot go together, for it concerns two matters completely opposite and directly contradicting each other. It follows that with such people there is no love for the fatherland or for those who try to uphold the right of the subjects.

For in his book *De Amicitia*, Cicero writes: 'It is on these two charges that most men are convicted of fickleness: they either hold a friend of little value when their own affairs are prosperous, or they abandon him when his are adverse. Whoever, therefore, in either of these contingencies has shown himself steadfast, immovable, and firm in friendship, ought to be considered to belong to that class of men which is exceedingly rare, yet almost divine. Now the support and stay of that unswerving constancy which we look for in friendship is fidelity; for nothing is constant that is unfaithful.'[144] With these words he wants to make clear that fidelity and constancy are required in true love and concord, and that from somebody who has no love, fidelity cannot be expected. 'It is impossible,' he continues, 'for a man to be faithful whose nature is full of twists and twining',[145] thus condemning hypocrisy and all those who like to remain neutral. To further

---

[142] This is probably a reference to one of the works of the great mythographer Fulgentius, who lived in the late fifth and early sixth century, perhaps to his work *On the Ages of the World and of Man*. See Leslie George Whitbread (ed.), *Fulgentius the Mythographer* (Ohio, 1971), pp. 177–231.

[143] Fulgentius, 'Epistola 1: De Coniugali debito et voto continentiae a conjugibus emisso', in Sancti Fulgenti, *Epistolae in unum corpus collectae* (London/Paris, 1884), p. 92. St Fulgentius was a sixth-century bishop of Ruspe (in modern Tunisia). He has often, but perhaps mistakenly, been identified with Fulgentius the mythographer. See Whitbread, pp. 4ff.

[144] Cicero, *De Amicitia* 17. 64/18. 65.

[145] Ibid.

confirm this and to praise those who, in trial and tribulation, declare and resolve themselves, he had recited, shortly before, the poet Ennio: 'When Fortune is fickle the faithful friend is found.'[146] As if to say: the true friend who is willing to prove the friendship in deeds, should declare himself before the clog is worn out. And those who want to see the outcome of troublesome affairs before binding themselves, are wonderfully assessed by him, when he says: 'Passing by material conditions, pray consider how grievous and how hard to most persons association in another's misfortunes appears. Nor is it easy to find men who will go down to calamity's depths for a friend.'[147] As the poet also says: 'Donec eris foelis multos numerabis amicos, Tempora si fuerint nubila solus eris.' Which means: 'As long as things go right, you will surely have friends, but in times of tribulation you will find yourself alone.'

Thus it is found appropriate to get to know those in time, who have a different impetus inside from that expressed by their external look. Assessing such fellows, Cicero says in the third book of *De Officiis*: Ergo et Pythius et omnes aliud agentes, aliud simulantes perfidi, improbi, malitiosi sunt, nullum igitur factum eorum potest utile esse, cum sit tot vitiis inquinatum.'[148] That is: 'Pythius, therefore, and all others who do one thing while they pretend another are perjurious, impious, and malicious scoundrels. No act of theirs can be expedient, as everything they do is tainted with so many vices.'

On the contrary, praising integrity, love and friendship, Cicero says in the said book *De Amicitia* that friendship is neither deceptive nor subject to any hypocrisy. Everything that is part of it is truthful and willing.

This suffices to make clear how concord and truthfulness are recommended, while faction, discord and ambiguity are condemned. Also, by reason of both God's Law and of Pagan and Christian authors, it becomes clear that in order to attain public concord and to stay out of all struggle and diffidence, one should reassure each other by oath.

Nature teaches the same. For in the third book of *De Officiis* Cicero says that to take from somebody what is his or to seek profit by

---

[146] Ibid., 17. 64 where Cicero quotes Ennio, *Scenica*, no. 210.
[147] Cicero, *De Amicitia* 17. 64.
[148] Cicero, *De Officiis* 3. 15. 60 (pp. 328/30).

another's loss, is notoriously against nature.[149] Indeed, it is more unnatural than death, which everybody fears, than poverty, than pain, than anything else that might affect the body or the external goods. Firstly, it breaks the unity which is so natural among men. Secondly, nature cannot bear us filling our pockets by robbing others. Likewise, it is not permitted to obstruct another for the sake of one's own profit. Natural reason (like divine and human law) demands that this be punished. Just as it is not natural that a man hurts himself, so it is also against nature that one subject rises against the other. Just as a man consists of many parts and members, so the community consists of many people and subjects. Nature teaches man to defend himself, as testify the dog against the wolf, the bull against the lion, the chicken against the henharrier. If nature teaches the irrational and senseless animals to arm themselves against force and violence, then so much the more does it teach the sensible man to defend himself against another man, who is a wolf and tries to kill him. And since nature teaches that one man is created for the benefit of the others, so it is also reasonable, by the very same nature, to defend and stand up for each other in trial and tribulation. Finally, in so far as nature demands from everyone what is right and reasonable, it follows conclusively that the request to take the oath (as recounted above) is right, reasonable and founded in natural equity, for by means of the oath many will become one, as Pythagoras requires of true friendship.[150] And in the first book of *De Officiis*, Cicero says that of all societies none is more noble, powerful or more secure than that in which good, pious, upright men, of congenial character, are united in friendship and bound to each other by fidelity.[151]

As the occasion presents itself, I have to ask, especially for those who are looking for the horse on which they are seated, why and for what cause does somebody swear or take an oath? For no other cause but to emphasize with an indubitable external sign that he speaks from the heart and in all earnest, and that he sincerely means what he says. This cannot be claimed by those who refuse the requested oath and (looking for the fifth leg in the pig) make such a big trouble about it, that they prefer to leave their offices and states rather than to

---

[149] Ibid., 3. 5. 21 (p. 288). The analysis which follows is largely based on this section of *De Officiis*.
[150] See Cicero, *De Officiis* 1. 17. 56 (p. 58).
[151] Ibid., 1. 17. 55 (p. 58).

forsake the King of Spain. With their mouths they say 'We want to be faithful to the fatherland', but they cannot be believed. As Paul says, one cannot truly serve two Lords, but must hate one and love the other. For this reason too, to make known those who previously were and appeared different, the request of oath is founded in God's law and the law of nature. Thus the oath is honest, useful, just and legal, particularly as nothing is so much in agreement with the laws as when the States and government of the country stand up for their laws, rights and Privileges, and disgrace those who seek to destroy them. However, if my argument contradicted God's law and the law of nature, I would deserve to be caught and rebuked for founding the oath on the very same laws.

Just as the father of a family works for nothing so hard as for the maintenance of love, friendship and union amongst his children, servants and family, and the steersman for keeping his tools in order so that they serve him under all circumstances, so a government should take care that there arises no discord in the community and that nothing gets out of hand.

In the Old Testament, God orders the King to accept the Book of Law from the Priest, to read and to study it properly so that he may judge rightly. Likewise the government of the Netherlands requests the subjects to reassure both the government and each other by oath, so that it can tell the sheep from the goats and may know who it can employ at its service, when necessity and circumstance require it.

If the oath is taken by the subjects and if it is observed, there will be a lovely resonance in the common good. With all misunderstanding taken away and all pettiness averted, each will serve his office and duty properly. The government will order godly, rightly and lawfully, and the subjects will obey what is honest, profitable and agreeable, to the inexpressible delight of all inhabitants, insofar as after a good war a constant and permanent peace can be expected. Everybody will praise the Dutch courage, and our leaders the States General, his Princely Excellency and all those who are in government will be raised to heaven. The wonderful deeds and the lovely union, which makes them faithfully resist tyranny, will be material for historians to leave a memoir of this time, as an eternal jewel of Dutch valour. The courageous deeds of each will come to the ears of all potentates of the world, to the regret of tyrants and to the pleasure and joy of pious governments.

If, on the contrary, we haggle and quarrel about the oath, we can only expect that it will later be said of us that we were a bunch of rabble-rousers and rebels against our fatherland, who by our mutiny and discord brought this country into the claws of roaring lions and vicious dogs, who seek to violate us and our souls. And we will bring our descendants into eternal slavery with more of such lamentable and ridiculous propositions, to the joy of all tyrants and to the sadness of those who rule their people with justice and moderation, to the disgrace of us all, to the disadvantage of the pious Princes, and to the eternal ruin of the country.

The heroes of past times, to their immortal praise, live on in eternal memory by their courageous deeds in invading and conquering many countries and towns, because they were decisive. Likewise we will earn ourselves a treasure of eternal praise for saving our country and towns, for protecting our wives and children, for standing up for our Privileges, laws, religion and liberty, and for dispelling our enemies from the fields, if we keep our arrows together and do not fall into the prophecy of Escovedo, who wrote to the King that our faction and discord could be of great assistance and use to beat one party by means of the other. However, as the shadows follow the body, so honour will never again be separated from the Netherlands.

The Monarchy of the Romans would still be in full glory and power, Athens would not have been brought down, no city would have fallen into desolation, had the subjects and government remained pious and faithful to each other.

Cicero says: 'Summa igitur et perfecta gloria constat ex tribus his: si diligit multitudo, si fidem habet, si cum admiratione quidam nos honores dignos putat.'[152] That is: 'The highest, truest glory depends upon the following three things: Does the community love us, does she trust us, does she, in admiration, deem us honourable?' Who will not love us? Who will not trust us? Who will not consider us worthy of all glory, if we dispel the enemy with decided and united courage, save our town and countries, be an enemy only to tyrants, and stand up for liberty?

We can achieve this very well, if we only follow my advice: that is, to

---

[152] Ibid., 2. 9. 31. The subsequent translation is rather liberal. The translation in the Loeb edition (pp. 199/201) is as follows: 'The highest, truest glory depends upon the following three things: the affection, the confidence and the mingled admiration and esteem of the people.'

set aside all particular passions for one or the other religion, and, each staying by his religion in his conscience, to resolve ourselves and to join each other by means of the requested oath. Each should put the thought out of his head: 'How can I do this? The King might still assert himself. I, my body and goods, my wife and children could be in want, we could become vagabonds.' These and similar thoughts are all distractions and means to turn you away from what is honourable, just, lawful, glorious, and possible. They are dreams and persuasions of those who seek your ruination. They are suggestions of Spanish ministers and instruments of our mortal enemies. Only think of and consider the final outcome, which will be so generous.

Just as no young man should be defeated by a bit of labour, or a young student by the devouring of masses of words, so Dutch courage is not permitted to tremble for the power of the enemy, and to prefer one's life over one's fatherland, liberty, Privileges, wife, children, etc.

Those who still cannot understand this matter, should consider what Cicero says in the fourth book of *De Officiis*:[153] 'Well then, are not the claims of fatherland paramount to all other duties? Aye, verily; but it is to our fatherland's interest to have citizens who are loyal to their parents. But once more – if the father attempts to make himself king, or to betray his fatherland, shall the son hold his peace? Nay, verily; he will plead with his father not to do so. If that accomplishes nothing, he will take him to task; he will even threaten; and in the end, if things point to destruction of the fatherland, he will sacrifice his father to the safety of his fatherland.'

In short, this means that one is not bound to anything so much as to the fatherland, and that one should prefer (if necessity requires it) the welfare of the fatherland to the welfare of the father. Cicero says in the first book of *De Officiis*, that for the sake of the fatherland one should not fear death.[154]

And if someone would urge me, arguing that the oath does not only entail forsaking the King, but also that I would swear enmity against all adherents of the King, possibly including the Pope, the Cardinals and the heads of my Roman and Catholic religion, I will answer him briefly, and give him as much contentment as I can. The person of the

---

[153] The reference is to Cicero, *De Officiis* 3. 23. 90 (pp. 364–6).
[154] The reference is probably to *De Officiis* 1. 17. 57 (p. 60), where Cicero asks rhetorically, 'and who that is true would hesitate to give his life for her [the fatherland], if by his death he could render her a service?'

Pope and his associates should be seen as containing two persons. One person is he who is the head of the Christian Roman Catholic Church, as some holds him to be, and as such he is understood not to bear arms. For, as previously has been deduced in full, Christ has never said to Peter, nor to any other of his disciples: 'Go, take up arms, and force them to believe (who do not want to listen to you) by means of force and suchlike things.' Instead, he told Peter to put his sword back into its sheath, teaching him that what God has ordered in his wisdom, must happen, and that in championing the church one should act and work with the sword of the godly word rather than with a weapon. If, on the other hand, the Pope bears arms as an adherent of the King of Spain, he should be regarded as a worldly Potentate. As such he may ally himself with other potentates and form a league, as some Popes have made an alliance and league with the Turk, although he has been called the hereditary enemy of the Christians.

Making this distinction in the person of the Pope and his adherents, seeing him as consisting of two persons, a good Catholic man may, without straining his religion, swear fidelity to a government, which is against the Pope, not against the person who is head of the Church but against the potentate who is in alliance and league with the King of Spain. Therefore he is an enemy not only of heretics (as those are called who belong to the Religion),[155] but also of those who call themselves Catholics, whom he should support by right. As we have sufficiently deduced already, the sake of religion has never brought either of these groups much advantage. Therefore, discarding such idle dreams, each should assume a manly heart, and can keep a clear conscience, in the good hope that a general council, after the fighting has come to an end, will make a good basis and firm resolution regarding the question of religion, following the concept of the Pacification of Ghent, by which neither the one nor the other will be a loser.

So it has been proven sufficiently, that it is honourable, profitable, rightful, lawful and desirable that each good subject should take the prescribed oath, that each can and may do so by right, reason and fairness, and, finally, that it is necessary to take it. For it is written, 'Omne regnum se divisum desolabitur', that is, 'an empire divided within itself, will fall into desolation'. We may expect this to happen to

---

[155] That is, the Reformed Protestant religion.

us if we are not and do not stay united in our enmity to the King of Spain, the Malcontents, and all his other adherents. As David praises concord highly in his Psalm 133, singing: 'See, how good and pleasant it is that brothers live with each other in peace',[156] and considering that union is the strength of all towns, so I want to have it prayed to all good subjects that they embrace the oath, casting off all irresolution, passion and faction. So that, being united, we may dislodge the enemy and be released from this murderous and bloody war. So give us, God Almighty, who rules it all after His Will, and who has so often delivered His people when they thought they had been forsaken.

FINIS

Proverb:
An empire divided within itself,
will fall into desolation.

Psalm 133:
Behold how good and pleasant it is
for brethren to dwell together in unity!

[156] Psalm 133:1.

SHORT EXPOSITION

of the right exercised from all old times
by the knighthood, nobles and towns of Holland
and Westvriesland for the maintenance of the
liberties, rights, privileges and laudable customs
of the country.

*

1587

The Nobles and Deputies of the towns of Holland and Westvriesland, representing the States of this country, have seen and seriously considered a certain treatise addressed to the States General of the united Netherlands and the States of Holland and presented in the Council of States of the said united Netherlands by Sir Thomas Wilkes, Councillor on behalf of Her Royal Majesty of England.[1] It concerns certain points and articles, by which his Excellency understands the authority of his Excellency[2] and of the Council of State to be reduced and curtailed. He requests this to be repaired and improved by us, as we are bound to do by virtue of our office and as the honour of his Excellency deserves. The Nobles and Deputies of the towns of Holland and Westvriesland, representing the States of this country, declare that, after their deputies have given them full report of what has come to pass in this matter, they have, reluctantly and with great sadness, concluded two things from this treatise, which in their judgment concern the state of these countries more than anything else.

First, that the legal state of these countries (which for more than five, six, seven hundred and more years has never been contested by anybody but our sworn enemies) has now been put in dispute by those, whom we consider our special friends, who are obliged and bound by oath to maintain and protect the justice and state of these countries.

---

[1] That is, Queen Elizabeth I of England.
[2] This time, 'His Excellency' refers to Leicester, the English Governor-General of the Netherlands.

Second, that we are accused of having curtailed, reduced and violated the honour of her Majesty and the authority of his Excellency.

Verily, at present nothing weighs more heavily upon us (who are prepared for the violence of the enemy and all the ways God Almighty pleases to use us without complaining) than these matters. Therefore we feel obliged to defend (as much as we can) the lawful state and the honour of the country of Holland, in accordance with our oath and duty, by declaring what follows hereafter. We earnestly beseech the said Sir Wilkes and all others who will see this to judge it as impartially and peacefully as the sad state of these countries demands.

As Sir Wilkes, and many others who have no full experience with the affairs of these Countries, feel very uncertain about the first point, not being sufficiently instructed as to the foundation of the state of these countries, we think it necessary to discuss this at some length and to give full information.

The country of Holland and Zeeland has been governed and directed for a period of 800 years by Counts and Countesses, who were lawfully charged and commissioned with the rule and sovereignty of these Countries by the nobles and towns, representing the States of the aforesaid country. They conducted their government with such prudence and moderation, that they have never disposed of waging war or making peace, levying tributes and contributions on the Countries, or of any other matter concerning the state of the country (although they were usually provided with good counsel from the nobles and natives of the country), without the advice and consent of the nobles and towns of the country, each being then convened and assembled. And, in addition to the aforesaid council, in all affairs and at all times, they have given the nobles and towns of the country favourable audience, perfect faith and good resolution in all matters they ever put forward concerning the state and welfare of the country.

This, being an entirely lawful government, as free from tyranny as any government has ever been found to be, has produced results which have remarkably and especially furthered the honour and reputation of the aforesaid Counts, as well as the welfare of the aforesaid countries and their inhabitants. Above all, the Counts of Holland, Zeeland and Friesland have, for the rule of such a small territory, been held in extraordinary respect, honour and reputation by all Princes and potentates of Christendom, as is shown by the high alliances of marriage which they have made with nearly all of the most powerful Kings and potentates of Christendom, and by the election of King William II to Roman Emperor in 1247.[3] Moreover, they have almost always been victorious over their enemies: they have securely protected, and also greatly expanded, the frontiers of the country against all its enemies, however powerful they were, because of which they were greatly esteemed and left in peace by their neighbours. For with truth we may say that the state of the countries of Holland and Zeeland has never been conquered nor subjugated by sword for a period of 800 years, neither by foreign nor by internal wars. We do not know whether at present the same can be said of any other empire (unless it be the republic of Venice). No other reason can be provided for this than that there has always been good concord, love and understanding between the Princes and States of the country, as the Princes (who had no power in their own right) could do nothing without the nobles and towns, having no ordinary means but the revenue from the domains to meet the costs of their court and the payment of the ordinary officers.

One also finds what authority the States of this country have had to bring their Princes to right and reason (if, misled by evil counsel, they acted to the disadvantage of the country), not only with remonstrances and requests, but also, if these found no proper response, with deeds. They also severely punished those who unsuitably exploited or improperly abused the authority of the Prince, as is shown by many and multiple examples.

It also becomes clear that it has been the office of the States of the country to provide a child Prince with legal guardians, momboirs or gardenobles. This also happened when Count William V went insane.[4]

Finally, there can be no doubt that the administration of the sovereignty of the country has always been legally assured by its States when, due to absence, infancy, insanity, misunderstanding or any other inconvenience, the countries were without the legal service of

---

[3] William II (1227–56), Count of Holland between 1234 and 1256, was elected King of the Romans in 1247 and crowned a year later in Aachen. The Count, who had supported the Pope against the Emperor Frederick II of Hohenstaufen, was supposed to be crowned Roman Emperor in 1256. However, before he could undertake the journey to Rome, William was killed when he fell through the ice in a fight in Westvriesland.

[4] In 1358 Count William V of Holland (1329–89) was deprived of his factual governmental powers and locked in a castle. His brother Albrecht was appointed regent.

the Prince. In such situations they often chose a ruler, who was called 'Guardian' or 'Regent'.[5]

This was even observed at the time of the house of Burgundy, when, after the death of Duke Charles and his daughter Duchess Mary, the Duke Maximilian, opposing the authority of the States with force, brought the entire state of the country into extreme danger and peril.[6] And by the authority of the States, the Emperor Charles himself was provided with guardians, and the country with proper governors, during the period of his minority, and he himself (although in many respects liberty was greatly reduced during the rule of the House of Burgundy) always deeply respected the States of the country, as he easily noticed that his state could be assured by no other means. Then he tried, with various admonitions, to bring his son, the King of Spain, to the same consideration and discretion, expressly declaring that Philip would see his state in peril as soon as he came to deprecate the States in these countries. He has indeed experienced this, to the great disadvantage of himself and of the country. For, however one argues, the only cause of these wars was that, with the violence of Spanish and other foreign soldiers, he forced these countries to act in matters concerning the state of the country in a way that they, as represented by the States, could not endorse.

Although we think that all this is beyond dispute, we have considered it necessary to relate it here, as we find that not only Sir Wilkes, but also many other persons feel very unsure and have different opinions about it. They only respect the assembly of the States in correspondence with how they judge the quality of the persons of the deputies, who appear at the assembly, and of all matters discussed over there. Apparently they think that the persons who are sent to the assembly of the States by the nobles and towns act as if they are the States themselves, and hence have the sovereignty and highest power of the country to dispose of all matters concerning the state of the country at their own discretion. Therefore, in return, they personally receive the trouble, hate and envy caused by their actions.

[5] In Dutch this sort of officer was often called 'Ruwaard', the term also used by Vranck.

[6] After the death of Charles the Bold, who died during the battle of Nancy in 1477, and of his heiress Mary of Burgundy in 1482, Mary's husband Maximilian of Habsburg was recognized as regent, to govern during the infancy of his son Philip. Maximilian was continuously involved in severe conflicts with the States. See p. 63, note 69.

However, those who take a closer look at what has just been told, at other great things accomplished by the Princes of the country with the help of the States, and especially at what has happened in the country of Holland and Zeeland during the past fifteen years, can observe easily that the authority of the States does not consist in the policy, authority or power of about thirty or forty persons who appear at its meetings. The agents of the King of Spain himself, who have always tried to undermine and to discredit our affairs with such arguments, have now learned by experience how greatly they were mistaken and misled in this opinion.

To ascertain the origin of the authority of the States, it should be realized that the Princes who have ever legally governed, not only started their government at the pleasure and with the approval and consent of the inhabitants, but have also continued to govern in such a way that all members of the body, at whose head they were established, remained inviolate, unreduced and uncurtailed. As the Princes are easily deluded by guileful and ambitious folks, this could only be warded off because the inhabitants had the means at all times to oppose such practices with good order and policy, because they could not only always admonish the Prince to maintain their liberty and welfare in the name of all the members, but could also offer opposition with the means of the country, should the Princes be lured into tyranny. To this end the inhabitants of the aforesaid countries are divided into two estates, namely the nobles and towns. The nobles are considered a member, because of the dignity of their birth (which is, without boasting, comparable to and as old as might be found in any other country) and the seigniories they possess in the said countries. On every occasion they deliberate the state of the country with each other and appear in the assembly to give advice on all matters, alongside the deputies of the towns.

Most of the towns have the same form of government, to wit a college of councillors,[7] which consists of the most distinguished persons, from the midst of the entire community. In some towns these number forty or thirty-six persons, in others thirty-two, twenty-eight or twenty-four. These colleges are as old as the towns, for there is no memory of their origins, although some were greatly enlarged, following the growth of the towns, and were approved of by the Prince of the

[7] The Dutch term 'Vroedschap', also used by Vranck, has no proper English translation.

233

country.[8] The members are only on oath to the town, not to the Prince. Once chosen they serve as long as they live or have citizenship. In the place of those who die or give up their citizenship, other persons are chosen from among the citizens by the college at its own discretion, to make up its numbers and they are sworn in by the burgomasters. The power to resolve upon the matters concerning the state of the town lies with these colleges alone. What is ordained by such a college has to be followed by the entire citizenry. There has never been any infringement or opposition from the citizens.

Every year the ordinary magistrates, to wit, four, three or two burgomasters and seven or more aldermen, are chosen by these colleges to serve for one year. In some towns these elections are conclusive, in others they happen (in order to eschew the dissensions which previously arose from direct elections) on the basis of nomination or double numbers, from which the election of the ordinary number is then made by the Princes or stadholders. The office of burgomaster is entrusted with the ordinary policy and command in all political affairs, including both the administration of the town's goods and revenue and its welfare and security; to this end they also hear the advice of the college of aldermen in important affairs, and of the town council in matters concerning the state of the country and town.

Normally the college of aldermen meets to administrate justice, in criminal as well as civil cases. Their oath is to promise to administer right and justice in accordance with their conscience, to which they are admonished by the Officer of the Lord.

The governments of the towns of Holland and Zeeland are, most on equal terms, ruled absolutely by these colleges of magistrates, without the Princes of the country interfering in the town governments in any way, but for appointing the officer who demands justice in their name,[9] be it that some misunderstandings or commotions arose which were settled or smoothed down by their authority. This, in short, is the true condition of the government of the towns of Holland and Zeeland, of each in particular.

From this it can be easily understood that the College of Magistrates and town councils, together with the corporation of the

---

[8] This assertion is historically somewhat beside the point, as most of the town councils in Holland were created during the fifteenth century, when the country was governed by the Dukes of Burgundy.

[9] This officer was the so-called 'schout', the Bailiff.

nobles, undoubtedly represent the whole state and the entire body of the inhabitants. One cannot think of any other form of government which could resolve upon the affairs of the country with better knowledge, or could execute its resolutions with more concord, authority or effect. Therefore it is not surprising that the state of these countries has been invincible, immutable and as constant as any state in the world can be. Add to this the invincible bravery, which this people has had since ancient times, and who shall be surprised that it was never broken or brought to faint-heartedness by any violence, tribulation or trouble?

Now it is not possible to bring together the colleges of nobles and towns in one assembly but by means of their deputies. Thus, when it is necessary to assemble them to deliberate on some notable affairs, they are convened by outlining the principal points which are then put for deliberation to the colleges. Having resolved upon them, trusted delegates are dispatched with such instruction and resolution as the colleges judge proper for the benefit of the country.

The nobles appear in requisite numbers, and the towns send a Burgomaster with some Councillors, as many as they think is required by the importance of the affairs. Moreover, in times of war the delegates have always, as occurrences abound, received a general charge to advise and resolve upon all matters concerning the welfare and preservation of the state of the country, as they find most conducive to the benefit of the country, in particular to maintain the rights, freedoms and privileges of the country and to avert and resist all infraction. Thus united with each other these delegates represent the States of the country. They are not the States in person or on their own authority; they represent their principals only by virtue of their commission. One should not presume that anybody promotes himself to obtain such a commission. For apart from the fact that the nature of this people is to dislike all ambition and to oppose all the ambitious, it cannot be suspected in such a free election. It is even more unlikely that, in the hardship that it has pleased God Almighty to send over this country, anybody would desire to deal with the affairs of the country. Nothing but trouble is to be encountered, nothing but enmity and envy from the enemies of our affairs (who slander even the most qualified and loyal persons falsely, often arousing evil opinions about many good servants of the country), and no profit whatsoever. Therefore the acceptance of such commissions had to be classified as 'inter munera necessaria' (that is, among the obligatory offices). Everyone who has had experience with policy in these countries can testify what troubles have arisen and what constraints have been used to make persons, who have been invited or who have served already, accept the burden of the commission with which they are charged. This has often damaged the affairs of the country to no small extent.

When they meet, the delegates are obliged to conduct a good daily correspondence with their principals, and when they return, they are to report properly and faithfully to their principals on all matters.

This is the foundation of the government of Holland and Zeeland, on which their state has rested for the period of five, six, seven hundred years, as far back as the oldest records go. It is this which, in addition to the help of God Almighty, has kept Holland and Zeeland in good courage and concord during this dangerous war against such a powerful enemy, to such an extent that during this war no member has ever been torn from us except by the most extreme violence. And no citizenry has ever been found rebellious or any soldiers mutinous in the country of Holland and Zeeland. In addition to God's almighty hand, this, we think, is due only to the fact that everything has been done, sincerely, frankly and with open doors. To this end many of the small towns (in fact, all who desired so), who in old times were not convened to the assembly of the States,[10] have been granted free session and vote, so that each, knowing the common affairs of the country, would willingly carry the burden (which would otherwise seem unbearable), with unity remaining unbreakable. To this end the nobles and deputies of the towns were also free to appear with as many persons, from the corps of town councils, as they thought proper, provided that these persons were not excluded from the tenure of office by the privileges of the country.

Now if it could be proved that amongst the nobles, or amongst those who appeared at the assembly of the States as deputy of the towns, anyone might have acted in contravention of the manners just described (of which we are not aware), and not in conformity with his instruction and commission, we would think such a person bound to

---

[10] During the 'old times' only six towns were represented in the States of Holland, namely, in the order of seniority, Dordrecht, Haarlem, Delft, Leiden, Amsterdam and Gouda. During the Revolt twelve other towns entered the States assembly, namely Enkhuizen, Hoorn, Medemblik, Edam, Monnikendam, Purmerend, Alkmaar, Rotterdam, Schiedam, Brill, Schoonhoven and Gorinchem.

render account of this to his principals at any time, being under the penalty of law in case of default. For by reason and fairness everybody is bound to render account of his accepted assignment to his principals. And those who, in good faith, labour to reveal such a case, we regard as good lovers of the fatherland.

However, those who despise and mock the States of the country, and calumniate their actions, are greatly mistaken if they think they are dealing with the delegates of the nobles and towns as particular persons, unless they prove straightforwardly that one of them has done something without instruction or has exceeded his commission. And although many persons do so out of ignorance or naivety, which should not be judged too severely, it is nonetheless sure that those who do so with full knowledge and awareness are certainly enemies of the state and republic of these countries. They can only intend to undermine the foundations of the house, to make it crumble and fall, which pertains both to the Prince and to the community. For what is the power of the Prince (if he is no violent tyrant) if there is no good harmony with his subjects? How will he correspond with them? What support will he obtain from them if he lets himself be persuaded to create a factional conflict with the States, who represent the community, or, properly speaking, against his very people? On the other hand, how can the state of the country exist if the community lets itself be persuaded to take up factional conflict with the States, that is, against the nobles, magistrates and town councillors, who are their advocates and lawful magistrates, who, for the benefit of the community, often have to incur the ingratitude of the Princes and governors as individuals? Therefore all reasonable human beings will understand clearly that the common state of the country could have no harder nor more harmful or mortal enemies than those who would oppose the States of the country in general. Here we do not mean those who can prove that a particular person, appearing at the assembly of the States, should have exceeded his commissions, as described above.

For these reasons then, Sir Wilkes and everybody else should kindly understand that if our delegates declare that the sovereignty is with the States of the country, they do not mean to speak of themselves, but of their principals whom they represent by virtue of their commission. This has also been understood by her Majesty, when negotiating with the States General, and by his Excellency,[11] when receiving his commission as Governor from them, and it may not be contravened by anyone in the world. We cannot believe that Sir Wilkes, in saying that the sovereignty is with the people and not with the States, means anything different from what has been outlined above. For otherwise it should follow that, at present, the nobles, magistrates and town councillors do not have the same power with regard to the exercise of sovereignty, as they had in previous times (which we have proved above) and as they had in negotiating with her Majesty and in constituting the government of his Excellency. For otherwise not only the validity of the treaties with her Majesty and of the commission and government of his Excellency should be called into question, but everything the States have done for their defence over the past fifteen years. Such assertions could only be the work of our public enemies, and we do not in the least expect them from those who approve of our case, and have intervened to help us.

Therefore we consider to have proven clearly and sufficiently [first] how necessary it is to preserve the authority of the States, being the foundation on which the common state of the country rests, and which cannot be damaged without ruining the common good, and [second] that in all matters the sovereignty of the country is with the States.[12]

[11] This reference is to the 1585 Treaty of Nonesuch with England and to the subsequent entrance and inauguration of Leicester in the Netherlands.

[12] This is where the *Short Exposition* stops. In the original declaration the States went on to justify their behaviour in the conflict with Leicester, trying to show that their actions neither contravened the 1585 treaty with England, nor undermined the authority of the Earl of Leicester as Governor-General in any respect.

Index

Names marked with an asterisk refer to entries in the Biographical notes

Index

Calvinism, 77n, 122n, 168n, 197n; see Reformed Protestantism
Cambrai, town of, 25, 30–1, 69, 73, 176
Cambridge, town of, xvi
Canning, J.P., xxxviii
canon law, canonists, 21, 31, 203, 212, 214
Capitolinus, Quinctilus, 181
Caracalla, Marcus Surelius, Roman Emperor, 4, 186
Cardinalists, alleged followers of Cardinal Granvelle, 30, 35–43
Carrerius, Ludovicus, Italian jurist, 190
Carter, Charles H., xliv
Carthage, town of, 179–80
Cassianus, 66
Castaldus, Restaurus, Italian jurist, *De imperatore*, 203
Castro, Alfonsus de, Spanish theologian, 190
Catholicism, Catholics (Roman), x, xxi–xxiii, 1–5, 9, 31, 43, 57–8, 60, 65, 68, 82–3, 120–2, 128, 131–2, 137, 139–42, 148, 153, 156, 199–201, 205, 224–5
Catiline, Lucius Sergius, 169; conspiracy of, 169–70
centre groups, in Dutch Revolt, xi, xix
Chalcis, town of, 180
Champagney, Frederic Perrenot, Lord of, 112
Charles the Bold, Duke of Burgundy, xiv, 63n, 232
Charles the Good, Count of Flanders, 97n
Charles V, ix, xxi, xxiv, xxxvii–xxxviii, xl, 7, 18–23, 36, 55, 65, 74, 76, 98, 100n, 121, 150, 205–6, 232
Charter of Kortenberg (1312), 87–8, 90, 91n, 94–5
Chronicles, biblical books of, 186, 193, 208
church and state, vii, xliv
Cicero, Marcus Tullius, xxv, 173, 174n, 197, 223; *De Officiis*, xxv, 71n, 165, 167, 173, 177–8, 179n, 183, 185, 187–8, 220–1, 224; *Lealius De Amicitia*, 172, 219–20; *On the Manilian Law*, 185

citizen, citizenship, xxv–xxvi, 22, 24, 28–9, 31, 37, 41–3, 46, 48–9, 51, 59–61, 63, 65, 69, 71, 87, 102, 144–5, 172–3, 177, 179–80, 183, 186, 188, 199–200, 217, 224, 234, 236; see also civic duty and virtue(s), civic
civic duty, 125, 145, 167–8, 170, 172–4, 214, 224; to resistance, 182–3 see also virtue(s), civic
Claudius, 180
Claudius, Roman Emperor, 106
clemency, 6, 38, 44–5, 184
Codex Justinianus, see Corpus Iuris Civilis
Codrus, King of Athens, 174
Collateral Councils, 30, 149
Cologne, town of, 69; peace negotiations at (1579), xxii, xxiv, xxxv, xxxvii, 126–7, 130–1, 134, 159
Commodus, Lucius Aelius Aurelius, Roman emperor, 215
common good, concept of the, xx, xxv, xxxiii, 51, 86–7, 92, 96, 102, 104, 126, 146, 152, 174, 177, 222, 238
Compromise, confederacy of nobles, 34, 36, 41–2, 47–51, 101, 198n
concord, xxvi, 88–90, 95, 108, 121, 132, 150, 177–8, 181, 183, 217–20, 226, 231, 235–6
conscience, 4, 6, 8, 10, 21, 53–5, 64, 66, 68, 74–5, 83, 85, 102, 104, 109, 113–14, 119, 121, 128, 137–8, 146, 168, 172, 204, 206, 208, 224–5, 234; oppression of, 16, 23, 33, 44–5, 50, 145, 188, 195–6, 206–10; see also liberty of conscience
consent, x, xxviii, xxx, 23, 34–5, 52, 54–5, 93, 98–9, 101, 135, 204, 233
constancy, 102, 113, 219
constitution(s), ancient, 69, 136, 140
constitutionalism, xiii–xv, xviii, xxiv, xxxii–xxxiii, xliii–xliv, 87n, 91n, 95n, 136, 186n
contract(s), contractarian ideas, xvi–xvii, xxv, 20, 41–2, 46–7, 51–3, 82, 84–6, 188, 192–4, 202–4, 209–13, 233

Index

League of the Great, xxxiv, xxxviii–xxxix, 36
Leerdam, town of, 117
Leeuwen, town of, 87
*Leicester, Robert Dudley, Earl of, xxvii, xxxii, xxxvi, xxxix, 229–30, 238
Leiden, town of, xviii, xxxv, 236n
lese-majesty, 99–101, 199
Libellus Supplex Imperatoriae Maiestati (1580), see Marnix, Philip, Lord of St Aldegonde
liberties (ancient), xvi, xix, xxii–xxiii, xxviii, 8–9, 19, 22, 24, 27, 51, 59, 67–71, 85–7, 90, 93, 235
liberty, x, xiii, xvi–xvii, xx, xxiii, xxviii, xxxii, 7, 17, 19–20, 25, 29, 34, 51, 53, 57, 65, 87, 93, 122, 135, 142, 145, 151, 157, 162, 164, 173, 177–8, 180, 183–4, 188, 190, 202, 205, 219, 223–4, 232–3; and prosperity, xiii, xxxii; see also liberty of conscience and personal liberty
liberty of conscience, xviii, 74–5, 119–22, 130, 135, 138, 141–2, 160, 206–10, 225; see also freedom of religion
liberty of religion, see freedom of religion
Liège, principality of, 25, 160
Lier, town of, 42, 90
Lilles, town of, 60, 157, 162–3
Limburg, province of, 37, 90, 99
Lipsius, Justus, xliv
Livy, Marcus, Roman politician, 180
Livy, Titius, 174n, 180–1
Louvain, town of, 24, 87, 89–90, 94, 96, 149n, 159, 199
Louvigny, Lord, 158
Lübeck, town of, 146
Luther, Martin, 21, 98n, 99–100
Lutheranism (Confession of Augsburg) and Lutherans, 21, 31, 46n, 62, 76–7, 121, 122n; on resistance, 77n, 197n
Luxemburg, province of, 99
Lycurgus, ruler of Sparta (Lacaedemon), 188

Maastricht, town of, 25, 59, 89n, 129, 153, 200

Machabaeus, Indas, Jewish leader, 173
Machiavelli, 112; *The Prince*, 112n
Mack Crew, Phyllis, xlvi
Madrid, town of, 56
Magdeburg, town of, 74
magistrates, town, xxix, xxxi, 6–8, 15, 20–1, 24–5, 32, 40–1, 46, 54–5, 57–8, 65, 86–7, 90, 112, 131, 134–5, 148, 150, 154, 181, 233–8
Malcontents, 168, 171, 174, 176, 182, 201, 218, 226
Malines, town of, xxiv, xxxix, 25, 27, 42, 49, 99, 142, 158, 161, 167–8, 200
Maltby, William S., xlvi
Mansart, Lord of, 158
Mansfelt, Earl of, 41
Marck, Count vander, 176
Marcus Curtius, Roman hero, 174
*Margaret, Duchess of Parma, Governess, xi, xxxiv, xxxviii, xl, 8, 26–7, 29, 32, 34–8, 40–4, 46–9, 53, 58, 63, 140, 161, 191, 206
*Marnix, Philip, lord of St Aldegonde, xv, xxiv, xxxix, 160n; *Defence* (1571) (translation of *Libellus Supplex*, 1570), xv–xviii, xxxiv, xlvii, 1–77; *Oration* (1578), 160n
Marsilius of Padua, xxxi
Mary of Austria, Dowager Queen of Hungary 22, 98
Mary of Burgundy, Duchess of Burgundy, 63n, 74n, 108n, 232
Matte, Sebastien, Dutch minister, 41n
Matthew, gospel of, 196, 207
Matthias, Archduke of Austria, 143, 149, 151
*Maurice, count of Nassau, xxxii, xxxvi, xxxviii–xl
Maximilian of Habsburg, 63–4, 74, 91, 92n, 108n, 232
Maximilian II, German Emperor, 74n, 121
Medemblik, town of, 236n
Medici, Catarina de', xxxvii, 158
Mellink, A.F., xlv, 151n, 205n
Mercurius Trimegistus (Hermes the Thrice-great, Egyptian God Thot), 188

Index

Vrankrijker, A. C. J. de, xlii, xlv

Walloon Charter, 90–1, 95
Wattrelos, village of, xxxiv
Wedgwood, Dame Veronica, xl, xlvi
Wells, Guy, xlvi
Wenclesas, Duke of Brabant,
  Limburg and Luxembourg, 88, 95
*Wesembeeke, Jacob van, xiii, xv, xli
Wilkes, Thomas, English councillor,
  xxvii–xxx, 229, 232, 237–8;
  Remonstrance (1587), xxvii, xxxvi,
  229
William II, Count of Holland, 231
William V, Count of Holland, 231
William of Normandy, 97

wisdom, 15, 22, 57, 68–9, 73, 81,
  83, 87, 132, 186; Book of, 186,
  192, 225
Wissenberge, 90
Worms, 160; Edict of (1521), 21, 98,
  100

Ypres, town of, xxxvi, 59

Zeeland, province of, xviii–xix, xxii,
  xxxv–xxxvi, xxxix–xl, 23, 37, 41,
  49, 73, 82, 84, 99, 112n, 114–17,
  119–20, 131, 138–9, 154, 164,
  170, 230–1, 233–4, 236
Zierikzee, town of, xix n, 116
Zutphen, town of, xxxv, 200

Cambridge Texts in the History of Political Thought

Titles published in the series thus far

Printed in the United States
65148LVS00002B/136-330

9 780521 398091